100 DAYS

How Four Events in 1969 Shaped America

HARLAN LEBO

ROWMAN & LITTLEFIELD
Lanham • Boulder • New York • London

Map of the area around the Woodstock concert site by Monica Dunahee

The words "Oscar" and "Academy Awards" are trademarks and service marks of the Academy of Motion Picture Arts and Sciences, copyright © A.M.P.A.S.®

Published by Rowman & Littlefield
An imprint of The Rowman & Littlefield Publishing Group, Inc.
4501 Forbes Boulevard, Suite 200, Lanham, Maryland 20706
www.rowman.com

6 Tinworth Street, London SE11 5AL, United Kingdom

Distributed by NATIONAL BOOK NETWORK

British Library Cataloguing in Publication Information Available

Library of Congress Cataloging-in-Publication Data Available
Names: Lebo, Harlan, author.
Title: 100 days : how four events in 1969 shaped America / by Harlan Lebo.
Other titles: One hundred days, how four events in 1969 shaped America |
    How four events in 1969 shaped America
Description: Lanham, MD : Rowman & Littlefield, [2019] | Includes
    bibliographical references and index.
Identifiers: LCCN 2019013711 | ISBN 9781538125915 (cloth : alk. paper) |
    ISBN 9781538125922 (electronic)
Subjects: LCSH: United States—History—1961–1969. | Nineteen sixty-nine,
    A.D. | United States—Civilization—1945– | United States—Social
    conditions—1960–1980.
Classification: LCC E855 .L43 2019 | DDC 973.92—dc23
LC record available at https://lccn.loc.gov/2019013711

♾™ The paper used in this publication meets the minimum requirements of American National Standard for Information Sciences—Permanence of Paper for Printed Library Materials, ANSI/NISO Z39.48-1992.

Printed in the United States of America

To Jae and Cory
It's a privilege

CONTENTS

PROLOGUE

Four Events that Shaped America,
With Only 100 Days From First to Last

There are moments in history that are frozen in time—those nation-changing, life-shifting milestones that have transformed the American experience.

These moments are forever etched across the span of our country's collective memory: Pearl Harbor, the signing of the Declaration of Independence, the assassination of Abraham Lincoln, September 11. Such milestones, each in their own way, created deep and lasting effects on our culture. Events of this significance are few and usually far between.

But *one time*, four of the most profound events in American history occurred with only 100 days between the first and the last . . .

AUTHOR'S NOTE

I think it might be helpful to say a word about what I have tried to accomplish here.

The four events that are the focus of this book are linked by a coincidental proximity in time in 1969: they all occurred with 100 days between them. The events could not be more varied if they were chosen deliberately: a magnificent national achievement, a bloody crime spree on a horrific scale, a celebration of youth and music that defined a generation, and a seemingly routine technical experiment that would be generally unknown for almost 20 years but would then have deep and permanent effects across the globe.

My goal is to explain the journey that led to these milestones and how each in its own way has shaped the American experience. With that goal in mind, I have focused on the points that seem particularly compelling in hopes that they will spur your interest in digging deeper. (See the Resources section for some fascinating opportunities.) If this book encourages you to explore these subjects in more detail, I have done my job.

I invite your comments.

H. L.
Los Angeles, California
February 2019
leboprojects@gmail.com

I

MOON

July 16–24, 1969: Astronauts land on the moon

The Saturn V, with its destination overhead. A matchless achievement of American technology in the late 1960s, the Saturn V would send seven crews on their journey to the moon. BOEING IMAGES.

1

CHALLENGING THE IMPOSSIBLE

"No nation which expects to be the leader of other nations
can expect to stay behind in this race for space."

—President John F. Kennedy, September 12, 1962

Titusville, Florida
July 16, 1969
3:32 a.m. EDT

For Mitch Evans, the ritual of the launch day began hours before dawn as
he walked in the darkness along the shore of the Indian River, looking
out to the horizon over the wetlands between the lagoon and the sea.

Evans was not due for his shift at the Kennedy Space Center for another eight hours—long after the scheduled launch time. But as usual on
launch day, he was wide awake early. Evans had worked at Kennedy for only
eight years, however, at 30, he had a much longer and more personal investment in the space program than most of his colleagues: Evans was born and
raised in Titusville, the modest community of 30,000 on U.S. Route 1 in
central Florida that was the closest town to the home of America's space
program. Evans was a child of the early space age, only 10 when the rockets
began to rise from across the wetlands.

"I grew up," said Evans, "with the space program in my backyard."

Twenty years before this launch day, during the economic lull after World
War II that stunted local employment, Titusville had received the welcome
news that the Cape Canaveral Air Force Station on Merritt Island would be
expanding with a new mission: it would become a testing center to launch
missiles. For the aviation-minded youngster, already fascinated by the constant
buzz of military planes at the air station nearby—first the navy during World

3

War II and later the air force—the idea of rockets fired only a few miles from home was especially thrilling. The first launches began in 1950, and the rockets were small—the Matadors and Larks and Snarks and other missiles fired to test their ability to carry nuclear weapons to an enemy a continent away.

In a few years, the missiles got taller; at first, the teachers at Evans's middle school told the students to cover their eyes so they would not be blinded by the flash of the launch. But the children knew better, and soon the warnings stopped. Evans and his space-crazed friends kept track of the mission schedules in the *Titusville Star-Advocate*, and they watched across the wetlands almost every time a rocket was launched, training themselves as amateur experts in measuring distance and speed as the vehicles flew down range—the best science projects they could imagine. On some evenings, Evans could hear the distant rumble of a night flight as the sound of the engines echoed across the lagoon and through his neighborhood.

"Every launch was amazing," Evans said. "I never, *ever* got tired of it."

In the late 1950s, the rockets started to carry small satellites, and then larger satellites. Evans would miss the first of these missions when he was an engineering student at the University of Michigan—a chilly Midwestern excursion that was a brief but welcome change from tropical Florida. He returned to join the space program in 1961 as a project manager for construction at the center during the massive, multibillion-dollar buildup of staff and resources that would be needed for the nation's greatest adventure: to send astronauts to land on the moon.

The first phase of America's race to the moon was Project Mercury in the early 1960s, the solo missions carrying the early legends of the space program like Alan Shepard and John Glenn. Then came Gemini with two astronauts on board—a flurry of 10 missions in 20 months that tested the endurance of humans and machines that were required for the next phase. On the night before many launches, Evans would walk the shoreline near his home, just as he had as a child.

"I was just too amped up to sleep," he remembered. "There was always too much at stake."

In late 1967, the next series of rockets was prepared for the final steps of the lunar program: the massive Saturn V, at 363 feet tall, the largest and most powerful rocket ever built. In the previous two years, Evans had seen eight of the Saturn Vs as they were assembled, and like everyone else who saw the towering rocket up close, he was in awe at the sight. In the hours before liftoff, each Saturn V stood on Launch Pad 39A like an alabaster monument, lit blindingly white by spotlights—a visual tribute to American science and engineering (see page 1).

On nights before satellite launches, Evans was often alone along the shoreline or joined by a handful of colleagues and a scattering of space junkies. But the crowds grew as manned launches progressed, and on this night, for the pinnacle of the program, more than 1 million spectators lined the beaches and streets and parks for 10 miles in every direction, some arriving days early as they waited to share a brief moment in history. Among the guests due to arrive for a closer view would be Lyndon Johnson, who as a senator had been one of the first to recognize the benefits of an American program in space. But John Kennedy had risen quicker in the political arena and had offered the moon as the challenge to the nation; it was a project he would not live to see fully realized.

Like all his colleagues, Evans knew the schedule to come for Apollo 11: soon astronauts Michael Collins, Edwin "Buzz" Aldrin, and crew commander Neil Armstrong would be awakened, and after the traditional launch-day breakfast of orange juice, steak, scrambled eggs, toast, and coffee, they would squeeze into their spacesuits at 5:35 a.m. Less than an hour later, they would be taken by van to Launch Pad 39A eight miles away and by elevator up more than 300 feet to the command module at the top of the Saturn V. By 7:00 a.m., they would be strapped in, ready for their journey.

And then, if all went according to plan—if the countdown proceeded on schedule, if there were no delays, if all the thousands of preflight checks produced a "go"—then at 9:32 a.m., the Saturn V would launch, sending the three astronauts on their extraordinary journey: leaving Earth's orbit, traveling hundreds of thousands of miles through the void of space, and for the first time landing on the moon, in the process traveling farther, with more risk, and with more to gain than anyone before them.

Even before Apollo, space flight was an achievement without precedent, the peak in the evolution of technology that had progressed, in only 58 years, from crude gliders without engines to craft traveling thousands of miles per hour as they orbited Earth. Years before, Evans's grandparents, both lawyers then in their late seventies, had told him about their own memories of the days before airplanes had existed at all.

As a single undertaking, Apollo 11 was the most complex and technically demanding venture ever attempted, engaging the labors of more than 400,000 Americans—contractors, planners, engineers, scientists, technicians, vendors—from every state in the nation. The program that had produced a mission to the moon was also the largest peacetime expense in U.S. history—an outlay so vast in a troubled age that even the president who had proposed it would privately express doubts about its value.

But the money involved was only one of the issues; the scientific groundwork that had led up to Apollo could be recounted as a study in contrasts—the product of noble vision and political brinkmanship, of crushing deadlines and masterly successes, of great personal achievement and broken careers. And Apollo had exacted a dreadful price almost before the program began, when three astronauts, trapped in a spacecraft they knew was flawed, would die.

"In spite of everything, we all believed in the program," said Evans, declaring the view shared by thousands of others. "We believed we could reach the moon—no matter how impossible it seemed for all those years. We knew it could be done."

Apollo 11 was an engineering achievement and a bold adventure that would—if only briefly—unite the world in celebration. The events in America that led to the goal of reaching the moon would have effects far beyond the space program, as they shaped a new direction for the nation that would continue long after the moon missions were completed.

Evans, along with 1 million others, watched the horizon. Six hours to go.

2

MORE THAN BOLD PREDICTIONS

"We shall have rapid or slow advance on any scientific frontier depending on the number of highly qualified and trained scientists exploring it."

—Vannevar Bush, "Science: The Endless Frontier" (1945)

July 25, 1945
Washington, D.C.

America's journey to the moon had many roads; one of those paths began in the 1940s with the foresight of a wiry college professor with an improbable first name.

His name was Vannevar Bush—a singular moniker that was bestowed to honor the family of his father's closest friend in college. But among the academic colleagues with whom he collaborated and the nation's leaders who shared his vision for America's future, he was known simply as "Van."

From the time Bush was a young professor in the 1920s, until decades later when he was a leader of the American scientific elite planning the nation's future, he looked very much the same; at any point in his life, Bush could have been cast in a Hollywood movie of the era as the lanky clerk in a country hardware store or that adored but absent-minded uncle who puttered endlessly on the family jalopy in the garage.

The idea of Bush as an incurable mechanic was not far from reality; even as a university dean, and later a presidential adviser, he remained the eternal inventor whose work would influence fields from computing to the atomic bomb.

When Bush appeared on the cover of *Time* magazine in April 1944, he was called one of the vital scientists of World War II. Yet Bush is forgotten today—except by those who lead dozens of American research universities that thrive because of his vision or who are in the government programs he proposed that now provide billions to support research and discovery, affecting every aspect of American science, technology, engineering, and—in spite of his own lack of interest in the subjects—the humanities and arts as well.

In the mid-20th century, Bush was America's visionary, the oracle of his era who understood that even in the depths of global war, America had the opportunity to shape itself into a new force in the creation of knowledge and education that would guide the future of the country. Today, everyone who attends a major American university owes much about the depth and quality of their education to Bush.

"No American," said Jerome Wiesner, science adviser to President Kennedy, "has had a greater influence in the growth of science and technology than Vannevar Bush."

Despite his many enthusiastic prophecies about the country's future in science and technology, Bush had little faith in the potential for flights into space. Before the war, Bush had said, "I don't understand how a serious scientist or engineer can play around with rockets." In 1949, while U.S. missile programs were rapidly expanding in part because of a framework he had established, Bush wrote that long-range rocketry would not be technically feasible "for a long time to come . . . if ever."

Yet Bush lived to see American astronauts land on the moon six times, journeys that were possible because of the engineers, scientists, and technicians who were trained in programs that thrived in part because of him.

❧

By 1944, when Bush was directing the U.S. Office of Scientific Research and Development—the office responsible for most of the research and development carried out during World War II—he already had nearly a quarter-century of experience to appreciate what did and did not work about progress in American industry and education and how money and support could ensure the success or failure of both.

In 1939, after years in academic and research positions, Bush became president of the Carnegie Institution for Science, an organization created by steel magnate Andrew Carnegie to fund and conduct scientific research. In that role, Bush served as an advocate for science on a national level.

"What Bush did best was to look ahead and think about things that were one step ahead of everyone else," said University of Southern

California historian Peter Westwick. "He understood that bringing together talented people to work on focused objectives was usually the key to getting the job done—especially jobs with the complexity of the needs during World War II."

But Bush's role was much broader than that—even before the United States entered the conflict. At a time when America was underprepared for war, Bush's brand of collaboration and nudging was just what the country needed.

"Of the men whose death in the summer of 1940 would have been the greatest calamity for America," said scientist and inventor Alfred Loomis, "the president is first, and Dr. Bush would be second or third."

When Roosevelt created the Office of Scientific Research and Development in June 1941, Bush became its director, assuming leadership for the organization that would coordinate scientific research for more than 2,500 projects with military application during the war.

The portfolio of the office under Bush included work to improve or refine all sorts of military technology: accuracy for bombs, efficiency for detonators, improvements for radar—projects in all worth more than $500 million, a formidable sum in 1940s dollars, and involving scientists and university researchers across the country.

By the fall of 1944—many months before the final surrender of the Axis powers—Roosevelt was already looking ahead to a postwar world. In a November 1944 letter to Bush, the president proposed a series of questions that he hoped would set the tone for America's next era.

The experience gained by Bush's office, Roosevelt said, "should be used in the days of peace ahead for the improvement of the national health, the creation of new enterprises bringing new jobs, and the betterment of the national standard of living."

To meet those goals, Roosevelt asked Bush to recommend how the government could aid research in science and medicine within both the public and private sectors.

And, Roosevelt asked, "can an effective program be proposed for discovering and developing scientific talent in American youth so that the continuing future of scientific research in this country may be assured on a level comparable to what has been done during the war?"

The president closed his letter with typical Rooseveltian enthusiasm, telling Bush, "New frontiers of the mind are before us, and if they are pioneered with the same vision, boldness, and drive with which we have waged this war, we can create a fuller and more fruitful employment and a fuller and more fruitful life."

Why was Roosevelt concerned about America's future? Was the nation really unprepared for a postwar world? As the conflict wound down and the Allies were anticipating victory, for most Americans such potential problems were difficult to see.

There seemed to be plenty of evidence that the nation was more than ready to continue its role as the world's dominant power. For more than 100 years, the United States had led the world as an industrial giant; in the years leading up to World War II, America produced more food, more cars, and more manufactured goods than any other country in the Western world.

Even more impressive was the country's conversion from a peacetime to wartime economy; after the United States entered the conflict in December 1941, entire industries shifted from peacetime manufacturing to full-scale military production in only a few months.

But while the nation had industrial might, in the early years of the 20th century, its ability to create new knowledge in programs of basic research was not as impressive.

"Today we take it for granted that the United States was always a world leader in scientific research, but that's actually a fairly recent development," said Westwick. "America developed as an industrial power starting in the 1800s, but in science the country only began to flourish in the 20th century. Bush could see that the United States was becoming a global power in science and technology."

What was lacking, Bush believed, was ensuring the United States was also an *intellectual* power—a country with a thoughtful, coordinated, well-funded base of scientists and scholars who could conduct original research and discovery. Bush knew that America, with its focus on growth and not national scientific or industrial policies, would not be able to develop a formal agenda for building its technological base; Bush would need to find an alternative.

⌁

Lack of support for scholars studying new fields was an old problem in every country. Hundreds of years ago, scientific giants such as Galileo, da Vinci, and Copernicus were either wealthy amateurs or were forced to find support through the Catholic Church or wealthy individuals. Some scientists supported their own work; William Gilbert, for instance, who developed the first detailed research in magnetism in the 17th century and who was one of the originators of the word "electricity," was able to conduct his experiments only because he could support his studies through his work as a doctor.

Even Benjamin Franklin, who in the early days of the United States was better known as a scientist than as a politician, supported his explorations of the physical world through his printing business.

Bush saw much of the problem as lack of support for research in America's colleges and universities, which he believed should be the primary breeding ground for progress in research, leading to catalysts for progress in private industry.

In his writings, Bush emphasized the differences between *applied research*, which was conducted primarily by industry, government, and colleges and used existing knowledge to solve practical problems (such as wartime development of new weapons), and *basic research*—the creation of new knowledge in core fields of study.

Research universities—where basic research is conducted in core fields such as chemistry, physics, biology, and other sciences (in addition to the humanities and social sciences)—are a relatively recent innovation. Research universities first emerged in Europe, especially Prussia, in the early 19th century.

Progress would come to America, but slowly. Johns Hopkins University, founded in 1876, was the first American university to be established as a research institution; soon after Hopkins came Clark University (1889), Stanford University (1891), and the University of Chicago (1892). Harvard created the Jefferson Physical Laboratory in 1884 as the first facility at an American university devoted exclusively to studies in physics; it opened 248 years after the school was founded.

By the beginning of the 20th century, several publicly funded universities had begun to establish themselves as leading research institutions, among them the universities of Michigan, Wisconsin, Minnesota, and Illinois.

The idea that research universities would be *the* primary home for knowledge formation—and thus support the country's abilities as an intellectual power—was years away. Much of the scientific research in the United States was conducted in government organizations—many of which were in military bureaus, such as Coast and Geodetic Survey, which produced maps and studies of American geography.

"The federal government had supported science on a limited scale since its founding—the Lewis and Clark expedition from 1804 to 1806 was commissioned by President Thomas Jefferson—as well as many more recent efforts, such as agricultural stations, and the Naval Observatory," said Harvard science historian Matthew H. Hersch. "However, much of the support was piecemeal or limited in duration."

Private giving established and maintained some scientific organizations—such as the Smithsonian Institution, "but without a broad political consensus on the importance of public funding of science," said Hersch, "these entities were perpetually in need of funds."

"Toward the end of the 19th century," continued Hersch, "private corporations filled the void by conducting industrial research that produced a number of key innovations, particularly in chemistry and electronics."

By 1915, some research universities had begun to collaborate with federal government organizations to pursue basic scientific questions—especially medical issues that affected the military, such as malaria, yellow fever, and bacterial infections. Beginning in the late 1800s, industrial research laboratories such as General Electric, Kodak, Bell Telephone Laboratories (now Bell Labs), and Thomas Edison's New Jersey facilities led the field in applied research into the 1930s.

However, in spite of this progress, only limited financial support was available for the universities, such as funding from a few enlightened nonprofit organizations including Bush's Carnegie Institution, which accounted for much of the country's support for basic research.

While many four-year colleges across the United States conducted applied studies and granted degrees and teaching credentials, by the 1930s, fewer than 20 universities could be regarded as first-class research institutions that rivaled the great campuses in Germany, Austria, Italy, and Great Britain. And the American institutions still received little support from the federal government.

That limited funding began to change before the United States entered World War II. By 1940, total funding for research universities had reached $345 million—not much at all when the pie was divided among the dozens of hungry institutions—and the private sector was responsible for more than two-thirds of it; that year, federal funding for university research totaled $67 million—less than the cost of single aircraft carrier during the war. Most of the money from both industry and government was directed to studies with specific application to actual products and not to core research.

A scorecard of the Nobel Prizes, the world's premier awards for scientific achievement, is perhaps an oversimplified tally, but it nevertheless says much about the status of basic research in the United States. Between 1901 and 1945, 111 Nobel Prizes were awarded in physics, chemistry, and medicine; the United States, with more universities and institutes than many of the other leading countries combined, won a total of only 18 of the prizes in those fields.

❧

Bush's concerns were compounded by some bitter lessons learned in America decades earlier about how technological progress did—or did not—move quickly forward in several fields, with aviation being a prime example. In 1903, Orville and Wilbur Wright had achieved a feat that better-trained and better-funded scientists had failed to do: they built an aircraft that was powered, heavier than air, controllable, piloted, and could sustain flight. (For many aspiring flyers who reached the air for a fleeting moment only to crash, achieving four of the five goals did not define success if the missing goal was *sustained* flight.)

Although the Wrights had built the first successful airplane, after their initial achievement, their lack of progress was frustrating. The brothers—who grew more concerned about defending their patents than creating improvements in aviation—made some limited progress in refining their planes in the years that followed, but most of their aircraft were flimsy and dangerous.

Other aviation entrepreneurs, such as Glenn Curtiss, did much better, developing reliable and stable airplanes while the Wrights spent most of their time focused on suing their competitors (including Curtiss).

Wilbur Wright died in 1912, but legal action continued and produced a victory for the Wrights' case in 1914. As appeals mounted, the patent wars became a prime factor in the delays in the development of the airplane in America as a practical, reliable machine—especially for its possible use in the military during World War I.

Eventually, national priorities intervened. In 1915, the government moved to bring some common sense into research that supported all aviation—regardless of what individual entrepreneurs had produced. In part because of the patent fiasco, Congress approved the establishment of the National Advisory Committee for Aeronautics (NACA) "to supervise and direct the scientific study of the problems of flight."

Then in 1917, as America entered the war, the federal government encouraged—demanded—a compromise: in simplest terms, manufacturers agreed to join a national association and pay a fee to use aviation patents.

Through the NACA, the government could encourage industry and academic involvement in defense-related projects; the NACA also conducted work through its own facilities, the first of which was the Langley Memorial Aeronautical Laboratory (now Langley Research Center) in Hampton, Virginia, which opened in 1920.

The agreement opened opportunities for aviation manufacturers, but the patent controversies had already contributed to a disaster for national security and the development of American military aircraft: the ongoing legal battles, combined with a lack of enthusiasm in the military about aviation for the previous 10 years, resulted in the United States entering the war completely unprepared for battle in the air. When the United States declared war on Germany on April 6, 1917, the entire American aviation force scattered across the country consisted of 1,218 men and 280 outdated airplanes.

When American pilots arrived in Europe—in an era when planes were constructed primarily of cloth and sticks and aviation development was a relatively simple affair for countries that had the will to do the work—*not one* U.S. combat aircraft was ready for broad deployment; U.S. combat flyers flew French and British planes, engaging in dogfights against German pilots in well-designed, highly effective aircraft refined through constant development during the conflict.

The U.S. Army had entered the war convinced that airplanes served a role only for observation; they were easy targets for German troops on the ground. Desperate American reconnaissance pilots were soon fitting their scout planes with makeshift racks for rifles and machine guns.

In 1918, Congress allocated $600 million to produce 5,000 planes and train 4,500 pilots, but it was too little too late. Many of the planes and the men to fly them did not arrive in time for the fight; World War I ended in November 1918.

Looking at the American experience in World War I, among many examples, Bush wanted to ensure that the United States would never again be caught without the tools and the talent needed to support the country—either in war or in peace.

"Bush argued for federal support of basic research after the war as the foundation for future military and industrial strength," said Westwick. "Building a broad and strong intellectual base would enable the country to be a leader in scientific and technological progress."

Roosevelt's questions for Bush about America's next steps would require far-sighted solutions. In responding to the president, Bush demonstrated how to create the nation's future.

Bush's reply came in the form of two documents, but Roosevelt would not live to see either of them; he died in April 1945. The first part of Bush's views about the possibilities for a postwar world appeared in an article in the July issue of *The Atlantic* magazine titled "As We May Think."

"As We May Think" served as a free-form platform for Bush's personal views about progress in science and technology. He described a future filled with technological achievements that he predicted and described, many of which would actually emerge decades later, including the precursors to the

Internet, speech recognition, automatic cameras, and electronic storage of information. (For the full text, see page 278.)

Much of Bush's thinking was focused on how to store the vast trove of knowledge that had been produced during the war and how that knowledge could be shared by everyone. In a discussion that eerily foreshadowed the development of personal computers, Bush described a "device for individual use" called a memex, "in which an individual stores all his books, records, and communications, and which is mechanized so that it may be consulted with exceeding speed and flexibility. It is an enlarged intimate supplement to his memory."

The memex, Bush said, "consists of a desk . . . on the top are slanting translucent screens, on which material can be projected for convenient reading. There is a keyboard, and sets of buttons and levers."

In a statement that could have described hypertext several decades later, Bush predicted that "new forms of encyclopedias will appear, ready-made with a mesh of associative trails running through them, ready to be dropped into the memex and there amplified.

"The lawyer has at his touch the associated opinions and decisions of his whole experience," Bush wrote. "The physician, puzzled by a patient's reactions, strikes the trail established in studying an earlier similar case, and runs through case histories, with side references to the classics for anatomy The historian, with a vast chronological account of a people, can follow at any time contemporary trails which lead him all over civilization."

"As We May Think" was an immensely influential article and inspired many young scholars who 20 years later would be part of creating technology that in 1945 did not yet exist: personal computers and the Internet.

But "As We May Think" did not respond specifically to Roosevelt's list of questions; for that, Bush needed to produce more than bold predictions. In the article, Bush asked the question that would serve as the prelude to a report to come soon after.

"This has not been a scientist's war; it has been a war in which all have had a part," Bush wrote. "The scientists . . . have shared greatly and learned much. Now this appears to be approaching an end. What are the scientists to do next?"

For Bush, forming his reply represented much more than creating a list of jobs for scientists about to be left unemployed by the end of global conflict. Bush realized that the devastating losses to institutions in Europe, combined with still-limited capabilities of American research universities, would cause severe gaps in the nation's ability to produce new knowledge—problems that would surely become critical after the war.

Bush's goal was to build a case for strengthening education in America, as an opportunity to ensure the United States' place at the pinnacle of the postwar world. Even for the most powerful and productive nation on earth, looking toward its future and how it could thrive was a daunting challenge.

Applied research certainly has a place in academia and industry, especially in time of war, but Bush's mission was to build a foundation for creating new discoveries and expanded fields of science—work that would become the province of research universities.

To Bush, the issues were clear: When war comes, why should a country be forced to gear up a vast scientific enterprise, wasting months or years in the process, when constant preparedness would not only maintain the nation's security in war but also open doors to new progress in peace?

The answer would be delivered to President Harry Truman in a report dated July 25, 1945, titled "Science: The Endless Frontier."

"Science: The Endless Frontier" described Bush's vision for a commitment to intellectual progress, national security, and public welfare. Bush outlined a long-range plan for America's future based on the broad idea that "scientific progress is essential." He outlined plans for the ongoing fight against disease, support for national security, and increased prosperity, based largely on massive increases in federal funding for these programs. (For the full text, see page 278.)

For many, especially those at America's universities and colleges, the statement that resonated loudest in Bush's report described what he called "scientific capital"—the ongoing training and refreshing of America's technical talent—and not relying on immigrant scientists who come to the United States either voluntarily or because they are driven out of their homelands by oppressive regimes.

"We cannot any longer depend upon Europe as a major source of this scientific capital," Bush wrote. "The future of science in this country will be determined by our basic educational policy."

How could America increase its "scientific capital"? "First, we must have plenty of men and women trained in science," Bush wrote, "for upon them depends both the creation of new knowledge and its application to practical purposes."

Bush made special note of the vital importance of research. "We must strengthen the centers of basic research, which are principally the colleges, universities, and research institutes," he said. "These institutions provide the environment which is most conducive to the creation of new scientific knowledge and least under pressure for immediate, tangible results."

And—most important to Bush—the government should write the check but not constrain the work.

"Bush argued for permanent mobilization of science and technology with government funding—but not with government control—at least that's what he hoped he would get," said Stuart W. Leslie, historian of science and technology at Johns Hopkins University. "World War II brought big science to America. Bush's argument was 'let's extend that level of science into the postwar period.'"

By arguing for basic research to be conducted at universities—and not expecting private companies or government labs to take on such a massive responsibility—Bush created the starting point for the evolution of a de facto science policy for the United States.

"Prior to World War II, the nation's research universities were usually thought of as being on the periphery of the U.S. scientific enterprise," wrote Richard C. Atkinson and William A. Blanpied six decades later. "'Science: The Endless Frontier' suggested that universities should be the principal sites for basic research and the exclusive sites for graduate and post-graduate education. It literally defined whatever national research system could be said to exist in the United States."

None of what Bush recommended was possible through presidential directive; for the commitment of hundreds of millions—soon to be billions—in annual spending, Congress would need to provide oversight and the votes to approve the money.

"Legislation is necessary," Bush said in his conclusion of the report. "It should be drafted with great care. Early action is imperative, however, if this nation is to meet the challenge of science. On the wisdom with which we bring science to bear against the problems of the coming years depends in large measure our future as a nation."

And in a statement that would resonate during a different kind of confrontation—this one the dominance of space 12 years later—Bush warned, "We cannot again rely on our allies to hold off the enemy while we struggle to catch up."

"Science: The Endless Frontier" was—and still is—viewed by many within higher education as the pivotal event in the evolution of American research universities into what they have become today: more than 200 universities and colleges that house basic research and PhD-granting programs that receive billions in annual support—federal, state, and private.

Bush's report is still quoted as gospel in meetings for new administrators at many research universities. It is a text that describes not only the reasons why research universities exist but also the rationale for cultivating federal funding as a major component to ensure the success of the institutions. Bush's report would become the key to unlocking federal funding for research and advanced education.

"The Endless Frontier" would also have spillover effects for increasing federal support in the humanities, social sciences, and the arts—subjects that Bush deliberately excluded from his plans.

"Bush is responsible for the whole architecture of government support for science," said Paul Ceruzzi, curator of Aerospace Electronics and Computing at the Smithsonian's National Air and Space Museum. "Today, everyone thinks terrific innovations come from the minds of bright kids, but they don't realize that these kids needed an environment to be in. It came from Bush."

Bush was not the only one pushing for increased support for universities and basic research, but he pushed the hardest—and he was heard. Within months of the release of "Science: The Endless Frontier," new funding initiatives were presented in Congress that would start to substantially beef up programs for basic research and university projects.

Primarily because of Bush, as World War II ended, the United States had a fundamental plan for the future of science and technology, a mandate to train a new generation of scholars, and some of the money to do it— whether in war or peace. Financial backing would continue to grow, but sparks would be needed to ignite broad, lasting support across the nation. Twelve years later, one of those sparks would light a fire.

3

THAT IRRESISTIBLE CHARISMA

"For von Braun, the implicit bargain he made with the Nazi regime had come due. If he wished to have money for rocketry, if he wished to have a career, he had to participate in stoking the fires of hell. And he did."

—Michael Neufeld, von Braun biographer

German Alps
May 2, 1945

Haus Ingeburg was a mountain resort in southern Germany, a pastoral Alpine setting near the Austrian border 50 miles west of Munich. The resort had the classic gingerbread-house appeal of a cozy Bavarian enclave surrounded by snow-capped peaks—an incongruously peaceful setting while full-scale battle raged only a few hours away. In the late spring of 1945, as Allied forces swept across Germany in the final days of the war in Europe, Haus Ingeburg was the perfect location for a mountain getaway, a pleasant lunch, and some high-altitude dozing.

Or a good place to plan a surrender.

At Haus Ingeburg was one of the most sought-after prizes of the war—at the top of a "black list" kept by American intelligence as objectives for acquisition to develop in a postwar world. But neither Hitler's inner circle nor treasure hoards were at the resort; at Haus Ingeburg was an even more important asset: the scientific talent behind the production of the Nazi regime's most notorious weapon—the V-2 rocket.

For Wernher von Braun, technical director of the German army's rocket center, and his team of engineers comfortably ensconced at Haus

Ingeburg, their surrender marked the end of their careers creating weapons for the Germans and the start of their work with their former enemies.

It was also the beginning of one of the most morally disturbing episodes of the war and its aftermath—a period that would illuminate as much about the engineers who created the V-2 and the slave labor and crimes against humanity used to produce those weapons as it said about America's decisions concerning national security in a postwar world. For with von Braun's surrender and acceptance by the United States, it could be asked, who is more culpable—the men who commit inhuman acts or the country that then embraces them?

⚭

Von Braun had been dreaming of space travel since he was 12 years old—dreams that would be postponed for nearly three decades while he was working on rockets for war. Not long after, von Braun received a book that started him on a lifetime path: *By Rocket into Planetary Space* (*Die Rakete zu den Planetenräumen*), written by Hermann Oberth, one of the pioneers of rocketry in Germany. Inspired by Oberth, von Braun joined an amateur rocket association.

Twenty-five years later, von Braun recalled a magazine story about an imaginary trip to the moon that also spurred his interest. "The article . . . filled me with a romantic urge," he told a reporter. "Interplanetary travel—here was a task worth dedicating one's life to, not just to stare through a telescope at the moon and the planets, but to soar through the heavens and actually explore the mysterious universe. I knew how Columbus must have felt."

But an advanced rocket program required vast resources, and in cash-strapped Germany in the 1920s, there was no civilian effort to support such ideas. Even so, for a young man with an interest in rocketry, the setting and the political mood were ideal: the Versailles Treaty after World War I attempted to hamstring Germany's ability to rebuild its war machine, but the restrictions placed on the country made no mention of advanced potential weapons, such as rockets.

When the German army came looking for prospective rocket scientists to produce missiles that would supplant conventional artillery, von Braun was recruited with enticements of financial support and facilities to carry out his work.

To build a career in rocket research, von Braun saw no other option: he could continue building toy rockets as a hobbyist, or he could develop his interests on a grand scale by working with the military. In 1932, at age

20, von Braun went to work for the German army. It seemed like simply an opportunity to support his country's military, but it was the first of many slippery steps: three months after von Braun joined the government's missile program, Adolf Hitler was appointed chancellor of Germany.

At Peenemünde, on an island in the Baltic Sea, von Braun worked for the most advanced research center for missile development on earth—far outstripping the minimal resources being devoted to such work in the United States. But it was work with a dreadful caveat: von Braun was now building weapons of mass annihilation.

Clever, handsome, and charming, with a gift for organization and inspiration, von Braun quickly moved through the program's ranks; by age 25, he had 400 people working for him. He joined the Nazi Party in 1938—a step he would recall as a requirement to keep his job. Not long after that, he was named technical director of the missile program.

Von Braun had already designed several successful rockets when, in 1937, he began developing the design for the weapon that Hitler hoped would win the war. In the lexicon of the German missile program, it was called the A-4. But in the political realm, it was renamed to become one of the Nazis' *Vergeltungswaffe* (retribution) weapons: it was named the V-2.

The V-2 was the most sophisticated flying machine of its age—the world's first long-range guided missile and the only manmade object to reach outer space. With its graceful curved lines, exaggerated fins, and a pointed nosecone, the V-2 looked like a fantasy vision of an advanced rocket for exploring other worlds. The V-2 would be remembered as the forerunner of rocketry for all space travel after 1945, but in war it was deadly, carrying a 2,200-pound payload of explosives more than 50 miles into the upper atmosphere and then landing more than 200 miles away.

The first A-4 flew in March 1942. Von Braun did not remember the day as an occasion to celebrate German military strategy; 20 years later, he recalled, "This day would be remembered as the day that space flight was born."

Regardless of von Braun's hopes for the future, late in the war the V-2 became a new instrument of destruction. Von Braun's rocket was a killer—not just for its intended victims but also for the thousands who built it.

The V-2 was ready for production in mid-1944, billed to the German people as Hitler's "wonder weapon"—the ultimate armament that would turn the tide of the war back to the Nazis. The first V-2 strike—this one against Paris—was launched on September 8. The launches escalated and in early 1945 reached as many as 20 a day. In all, more than 3,100 V-2s were launched at London, Antwerp, and other targets in England and Europe, killing at least 6,000 people.

To avoid Allied attacks, the primary V-2 assembly work was moved to a facility 350 miles to the southwest of Peenemünde near the town of Nordhausen. The underground construction center had the seemingly quaint name of Mittelwerk (central works), but it would become the site of some of the most appalling horrors of the Nazi regime.

Prisoners from the Nordhausen-Dora concentration camp were forced to serve in the underground factory to assemble V-2s under the most apalling conditions imaginable. Starved and ill-fed, prisoners worked until they dropped, often too weak to survive the beatings by the SS guards. For those caught bravely attempting to sabotage the manufacturing, the punishment was horrifying: execution by hanging from a crane, staged in front of other workers as lessons for obedience. The bodies were left swinging for days; more than once, the German technical staff complained to the SS about the hangings—not because of the inhumanity but because they needed the crane for work.

Eventually some 10,000 prisoners who worked on the V-2 and other Mittelwerk projects would die from disease, starvation, or execution. More people died building the V-2 than would be killed by the missiles' attacks.

How could von Braun have tolerated the viciousness that occurred in the organization under his direction? Was it possible that he was unaware of the heinous tactics employed to accomplish his work?

Unlikely. As head of the Nazi missile program, von Braun knew that slave labor by concentration camp prisoners was producing his rockets. He had seen the plight of the workers at Mittelwerk. And in August 1944, von Braun visited the Buchenwald concentration camp to identify technically educated prisoners who could work in a new laboratory.

For years, von Braun avoided discussing his involvement with the V-2 program and evaded the issue of slave labor entirely. Not until the mid-1960s, when the facts of Mittelwerk began to surface and survivors of the Nordhausen-Dora concentration camp accused him of complicity, did von Braun respond directly to the issue.

Without taking responsibility, in 1966 von Braun wrote in a letter to *Paris Match* magazine, "I readily agree that the entire environment at Mittelwerk was repulsive, and that the treatment of the prisoners was humiliating. I felt ashamed that things like this were possible in Germany, even under a war situation where national survival was at stake."

Three years later, when von Braun described the conditions in Mittelwerk, his comments were astonishingly self-centered.

"It naturally left on me an extraordinarily depressing impression each time that I went into the underground plant and had to see the prisoners at work," he said. "It is repulsive to be suddenly surrounded by prisoners. The whole atmosphere was unbearable."

Von Braun's dream had become the worst possible nightmare: the rocket he claimed was created to foster advances in space travel was killing thousands of victims on both sides of the conflict. But later, critics would admit that nothing von Braun could have done would have saved the prisoners; at that point, any intervention or dissention would likely have resulted in von Braun being executed by a firing squad—a not-unlikely possibility after he was arrested in March 1944 and held for two weeks for his "defeatist" attitude about the war effort.

"For von Braun, the implicit bargain he had made with the Nazi regime had come due," said Michael Neufeld, von Braun's biographer. "If he wished to have money for rocketry, if he wished to have a career, if he wished to keep himself out of danger from the apparatus of repression, he had to participate in stoking the fires of hell. And he did."

But only a few months later, the Americans would help wash it all away.

⸎

By February 1945, von Braun could hear the Russian guns in the distance; the Allies would overrun Mittelwerk in only two months.

Fearful of being executed by his own SS colleagues to prevent his capture—a not-unreasonable assumption—von Braun and a few trusted allies developed a systematic plan for escape. While their terror weapon was still being launched against civilian targets, von Braun's scientists were preparing to turn themselves over to the Americans.

Their choice of which Allied force to surrender to had been an easy one. Said one German rocket engineer, "We despise the French, we are mortally afraid of the Soviets, we do not believe the British can afford us. So that leaves the Americans."

Von Braun and many in the team moved in a roundabout journey more than 300 miles across war-ravaged Germany, eventually arriving at the Haus Ingeburg resort, near the approaching American forces. There they settled in to wait for the opportunity to find potential captors.

⸎

The Americans were already looking for von Braun and wanted him badly. The Allies were on the hunt for Nazi military expertise. The Joint Intelligence Objectives Agency, an office set up by the American Joint Chiefs of Staff under Admiral William D. Leahy, had been created to find and recruit Nazi scientists to work on top-priority weapons projects and scientific intelligence programs.

The desire to grab von Braun grew out of the Americans' grudging recognition of their lack of progress in developing their own rocket technology. Although the U.S. military had a wide assortment of small, unguided missiles that could be launched from ground or air, there had been only modest progress in guided rocketry, and nothing on the scale of the V-2.

While during the war von Braun was directing swift progress in rocket development at Peenemünde, the Americans were attempting to create their own guided delivery of explosives, with one project based on remote-control bombers. Operation Aphrodite (army) and Anvil (navy) were two unsuccessful programs that refit "Weary Willies"—worn-out bombers past their useful service—and crammed them with 30,000 pounds of Torpex high explosive. The planes would be taken airborne to 2,000 feet by a two-man crew that would activate the radio control and then parachute to safety.

Several pilots were killed in the operations, including Joseph P. Kennedy Jr., the eldest son of the Kennedy family and heir to the dynasty's prestige and political power; that mantle then fell to the next eldest son: John Fitzgerald Kennedy.

The Americans needed von Braun—or at the very least, they needed to ensure that the Soviets did not get him first. Even with von Braun's Nazi affiliation and probable complicity with using slave labor, for the Americans, leaving von Braun behind for the Soviets to recruit would have been a disaster.

Working closely on this objective was the Combined Intelligence Objectives Subcommittee (CIOS), which spread experts across Europe to identify men and matériel that would be valuable for postwar military planning. CIOS maintained registries—the black lists—of priority people to identify and retain. In Washington, Special Mission V-2 was established to recover every scrap of the V-2 program it could find. The mission team would move quickly.

On April 11, 1945, the first American army units reached Nordhausen and discovered the atrocities at the Dora concentration camp. A few days behind the American forces, Special Mission V-2, commanded by Major Robert Staver, arrived to sack the factory. Weeks before the German surrender, the Americans were already crating up perhaps the most valuable treasure of the war.

c✂⌾ɔ

On May 1, Adolf Hitler shot himself. Soviet troops had reached the outskirts of Berlin, but the war in Europe was not yet over; the end would not come until May 7. For von Braun, this was the time for surrender. He heard through local sources that the Americans had taken the region, settling nearby on the Austrian side of the border. The surrender was orchestrated by von Braun's brother Magnus, who spoke better English than the other scientists; von Braun and six other senior scientists descended the mountain to U.S. field operations in Reutte, Austria, to surrender.

After a cordial meeting and an overnight stay, the next morning the senior missile team met with reporters, who were eager to inspect the creators of the dreaded V-2. But this was no display of the vanquished; the scientists were happy, talkative, and free to mingle with writers and photographers.

"Von Braun posed for pictures with individual GIs, in which he beamed, shook hands, pointed inquiringly at medals and otherwise conducted himself as a celebrity rather than a prisoner," said one observer, who also noted that the ever-charming von Braun treated our soldiers "with the affable condescension of a visiting congressman."

Von Braun cooperated with the Americans but expressed no regret for his deeds.

"There is recognition of Germany's defeat," said Lieutenant Walter Jessel, the intelligence officer who ran the first debrief of von Braun, "but none whatsoever of Germany's guilt and responsibility." It was an assessment that would echo throughout von Braun's career.

c✂⌾ɔ

By the time the war ended, the concept of "allies" among the invading forces was already deteriorating—especially where Nazi technology was concerned. The competition between the Americans and the Soviets that would soon escalate into full-scale international confrontation had already begun. Special Mission V-2 moved fast; in a few weeks, the American team recovered more than 400 tons of parts and equipment, including 100 partially assembled or complete V-2s. Also found nearby, hidden in an abandoned mine, were 14 tons of plans and documents.

On May 22, a formidable chunk of the Nazi rocket program began its journey to the United States, transported across Germany in more than 300 train cars. The Americans left plenty behind as a concession to the

Russians, but the U.S. forces had all the ingredients needed to jump-start their young rocketry program.

Everything, that is, except the men to run it. Staver wanted to confirm that the Germans would be brought to America as part of the package.

"The thinking of the directors of this group is 25 years ahead of U.S.," cabled Staver, who was also a mechanical engineer, to his commanders in Washington. "Immediate action recommended to prevent loss of whole or part of this group to other interested parties. Urgently request reply as early as possible."

Approval came quickly; the von Braun team would be brought to America. In a stroke, the United States had the core of the world's premier missile program—both men and equipment—to substantially boost the nascent American space efforts. By June 1945, von Braun and more than 100 scientists, who only three months before had been launching V-2s against Allied targets, were on their way across the Atlantic to build missiles for the Americans.

After interrogations and negotiations, in October 1945, von Braun and the first group of his Peenemünde colleagues arrived at their primary destination in America: the army's base of operations for rocket research in Fort Bliss, Texas.

Technically, von Braun and his scientists were prisoners of war—they called themselves "prisoners of peace"—but life at Fort Bliss was hardly prison. At first they were housed in secure areas, but they were free to move around and could leave the compound as needed.

The Germans worked for the army, but they were under the auspices of Operation Paperclip, a secret program managed by the Joint Intelligence Objectives Agency that was operated on behalf of the Joint Chiefs of Staff.

The Soviets and the Americans each had their own programs—and distinct methods—to harvest German scientists. But while the Soviet program recruited scientists with assurances of money, resources, and the ability to stay in Germany—promises that were rescinded a year after the war when they were all abruptly deported to the Soviet Union—Operation Paperclip offered sanctuary and employment contracts.

Through Operation Paperclip's work in Europe, former Nazis were recruited, debriefed, and exported to the United States to work on rocket systems, medical programs, and even chemical and biological weapons—all under the sponsorship of the U.S. government. It was through Operation Paperclip—named because a paperclip was placed on the folders of approved scientists—that von Braun and his team came to America.

Publicly, Operation Paperclip was considered America's answer to Soviet scientific oppression. Even years after the war, when much more was known about Hitler's atrocities, the program was viewed as a benign effort to employ talented Nazis; in 1951, the *New Yorker* described Paperclip as an American program "to recruit as many of these gifted enemy specialists as possible."

But even if viewed in the most positive possible light, Paperclip was engaging former enemies who only months before had been responsible for some of humanity's greatest evils.

"The age of weapons of mass destruction had begun," wrote historian Annie Jacobsen. "Hiring dedicated Nazis was without precedent, entirely unprincipled, and inherently dangerous, not just because, as Undersecretary of War Robert Patterson stated when debating if he should approve Paperclip, 'These men are enemies,' but because it was counter to democratic ideals."

And Operation Paperclip was managed with cold-blooded, ruthless cunning, purpose: Jacobsen found that to ensure that the former Nazis it recruited would be acceptable for employment in the United States, Paperclip manipulated personnel records. Evidence of complicity in Nazi programs evaporated. Immigration rules were bypassed; for example, as part of the plan to help "disappear" their past, the Germans at Fort Bliss were taken three miles to the Mexican border, where they crossed over and were issued visas to reenter the United States. Later, when they applied for U.S. citizenship, they would say their official entry point was El Paso, with no reference to their capture.

The involvement of Germans working in the United States was no secret in Washington. And for many, the idea of the Germans taking the lead in the budding U.S. rocket program was, at the very least, questionable, and to many reprehensible.

In February 1947, the Federation of American Scientists (FAS) issued a call to President Truman to stop the German involvement in the American missile program.

"Certainly not wishing to jeopardize the legitimate needs of the national defense, and not advocating the policy of hatred and vengeance toward our former enemies, we nevertheless believe that a large-scale importation of German scientists . . . is not in keeping with the best objectives of American domestic and foreign policy," the FAS wrote to Truman.

Some in Congress also protested.

"I have never thought we were so poor mentally in this country, that we have to import these Nazi killers to help us prepare for the defense of our country," said representative John Dingell, a senior Democratic congressman.

On the other side of the argument, Truman was pressured to retain the Germans by some surprising sources. Ultra-liberals like former vice-president Henry Wallace, who had been fiercely outspoken about Hitler's rule, lobbied Truman for the Germans to stay, suggesting that the contribution of the German scientists to the peacetime work would stimulate the economy. To Wallace, opposition to Nazis was outweighed by the vision of millions of jobs.

And, many asked, what would have been the point of not using the German expertise? The Allies could have jailed the von Braun team as war criminals, losing out on their vast experience at the expense of America's future security. Also, the Americans had to admit that had they chosen to prosecute von Braun, they had no direct proof of his involvement in slave labor. Or even worse, had the scientists remained in Germany, they could have been "recruited" to work for the Soviets.

President Truman had maintained a low profile throughout the protest. He would not learn the extent of Operation Paperclip until 1946. Before that, Truman had approved the use of the von Braun team for "temporary, limited, military custody." In September 1946, Truman agreed that Operation Paperclip should continue, expanding the program to include more than 1,000 German scientists and technicians in a variety of fields who would be allowed—former Nazis or not—to permanently emigrate to the United States.

Truman had previously banned the entrance of former Nazis into the United States, but years later he recalled that he had not been at all reluctant to approve Paperclip. Truman told a biographer that because of collapsing relations with Russia, "this had to be done and was done."

For the United States, the issue of German scientists boiled down to choosing between two troubling options: complicity with former Nazis who had been responsible either directly or indirectly for the deaths of thousands in forced labor, or lag behind the Russians—possibly for years—in creating advanced weapons. With the United States' missile program just beginning to gear up, and the Soviets forging ahead, the choice was clear, even if the decision clashed with the values and morality that the country supposedly stood for.

The U.S. government did ultimately refuse to recruit some former Nazis. Hundreds of fervent Nazis with proven records of complicity in crimes against humanity were forever banned from the United States, and particularly notorious Nazi scientists and doctors who were directly associated with the concentration camps or other weapons programs—such as chemical warfare—were tried and jailed. But those had been easy black-and-white decisions; embracing the missile team represented many shades of gray.

Operation Paperclip continued to manage foreign-born scientists until 1959, its existence saying much about American ethical flexibility in the aftermath of the war. Paperclip also spotlights a question that has been asked again and again throughout human history: Since both sides in war do unspeakable things to their fellow humans, why is it only the winners who can point to the losers as villains?

By the end of 1946, von Braun's team was already immersed in work for the army's missile program. Von Braun would become thoroughly American; he married a distant cousin and raised a family. When he moved to the army's missile facilities in Huntsville, Alabama, as head of rocket development, he took out a Federal Housing Administration loan to buy a house and became a respected civic leader.

Von Braun's interest in peacetime rocketry and space remained constant. In the early 1950s, his national prominence would grow with the publication of a series of articles cowritten with colleagues for *Collier's* magazine about the excitement and challenges of space travel. Von Braun wrote about adventures in space as a possibility—"not just a ridiculous Buck Rogers thing," said Neufeld of von Braun's articles. "It could actually be real."

Von Braun would connect with Walt Disney and guide him on a tour of the Huntsville operations. Ten years after leading Nazi rocket development, von Braun was on Walt Disney's television series, telling American families about the space projects to come—some real and some only the fondest creations of von Braun's imagination—that would demonstrate the wonders of space travel. He would also lobby long and hard for a space station—a rotating wheel in orbit that would serve as a staging area for ambitious missions to the moon and Mars.

But in the early 1950s, von Braun was again making missiles whose primary function would be as weapons; his dream of space travel would have to wait.

4

THE SIGHT OF WHIZZING FLASHES

"It was work on the frontiers—on the edge."
—Tom Snyder, Ames Research Center

Moffett Field, California
August 21, 1950

On a balmy Monday morning, Sam Kraus drove his new Chevrolet sedan from his apartment in Palo Alto down Bayshore Highway for the 15-minute commute to his office in a building near San Francisco Bay. The building, constructed in the stark post-Depression style that marked government projects from the late 1930s, was part of a complex of offices, sheds, and laboratories at the edge of Moffett Field, which since 1931 had been a naval air station.

The military purpose of the airfield was prominently recognizable then, and now, by massive tube-shaped aircraft hangars—the largest more than 1,100 feet long and 300 feet wide—that had once housed the U.S. Navy's Pacific blimp and airship fleet.

Kraus, a genial transplanted New Yorker who that day was celebrating his first anniversary on the job (thus the new car), did not work at Moffett Field itself. In the complex adjacent to the northwest side of the airfield was the Ames Aeronautical Laboratory (now the Ames Research Center), the second of the units created by the National Advisory Committee for Aeronautics (NACA) to house its programs of research in aeronautics.

The Langley Flight Center had been the first of the NACA field laboratories, but in the days before World War II, concerns about a single center on the East Coast—in theory vulnerable to attack from a European

31

enemy—convinced the NACA to open Ames as a more secure West Coast alternative.

"Ames is actually located on Moffett Field, which is near Mountain View," said historian Layne Karafantis. "But the location was sold as being in neighboring Sunnyvale, because 'Mountain View' didn't sound like a place with particularly good flying weather."

Ames opened in 1939, primarily to conduct research on propeller-driven aircraft. But after World War II, with jet-powered aircraft quickly emerging, Ames shifted much of its work to the issues of speed and aeronautical performance.

Kraus, at age 25, was one of thousands in a new generation of engineers that was beginning to work on answers to new problems in aviation. Like many of his young colleagues born in the 1920s, Kraus was fascinated by airplanes; as a treat when he was 12, his father took him for a ride in a small plane at an airport in suburban New Jersey.

"I told myself," Kraus remembered, "my world is going to be part of the age of aviation."

Kraus's career took the same meandering path that many students in the 1940s would have to follow: education stalled temporarily by military service. In 1941, Kraus started engineering courses at NYU, but World War II intervened. He graduated from Rensselaer Polytechnic Institute with a degree in aeronautical engineering while in the navy. After service in the Pacific, at war's end he returned to Rensselaer for a master's degree.

Kraus worked for two years on propeller research for Curtiss-Wright Aviation; then the West Coast and its milder weather beckoned. In August 1949, Kraus accepted an offer at Ames, joining a team led by Al Eggers, to study airflow in flight while traveling faster than the speed of sound.

In those postwar days, many engineers looked beyond industry for the excitement of research programs at the NACA. For example, across the country and five years before Kraus joined Ames, a Virginia Tech graduate named Christopher Kraft would turn down an offer from Chance Vought Aircraft Company to work at Langley instead. Kraft would later become flight director for many of the spacecraft missions and ultimately director of the Johnson Space Center.

The United States did not need Wernher von Braun to initiate its programs in space—just to jump-start them. In 1946, when von Braun and his team came to America, the United States had already started programs in guided rocketry development. That work had occurred late in the war, as the country's projects that created small unguided missiles and planes converted into bombs had morphed into plans for more advanced efforts that preceded the arrival of the Germans.

Two milestones in 1945 became the springboards for major progress: the NACA opened the Wallops Flight Facility—known first as the Pilotless Aircraft Research Station and later as Wallops Station—a rocket launch site on the Virginia coastline northeast of Norfolk. Much of this work was under the direction of Robert Gilruth, who would go on to be the first director of the Johnson Space Center in Houston. Wallops was then—and continues to be—one of the world's busiest launch facilities: more than 16,000 suborbital launches have been fired from Wallops' rocket testing range.

"By the time the American space program began in the late 1950s, the work at the Wallops Flight Facility had built an invaluable base of knowledge about rockets and missiles," said NASA historian Roger Launius.

In February, Secretary of War Henry Stimson approved the creation of the White Sands Missile Range in the desert of southern New Mexico as a test facility for missile development. In July, train cars loaded with V-2 parts began arriving. Von Braun and his team were not far behind.

By then, several American rocket programs were already active. For example, the Private rocket series developed in Pasadena at the California Institute of Technology (better known as Caltech) had already been launched 24 times in December 1944 from a site near Camp Irwin (later Fort Irwin) in the Mojave Desert of California. The WAC Corporal, built by Douglas Aircraft in cooperation with Caltech, was launched from White Sands on September 16—the first U.S. rocket to carry scientific instruments.

"New Mexicans who live near the Proving Ground," wrote Paul Lang in a 1948 *New Yorker* article, "have become pleasantly accustomed to the sight of whizzing flashes over the desert waste."

It was said by grumbling enlisted men in the missile program that the naming scheme of rockets based on army enlisted ranks—first the Private, then the Corporal—would end with the Sergeant, because that was the last level of the army that did any work.

When von Braun and his team arrived, progress within the army program accelerated quickly; the Germans were soon teaching Americans how to assemble and launch V-2s.

For the American scientists, individual fields within rocketry were their forte—until the Germans got involved, remembered Lee B. James, who would become manager of the Saturn Program.

"What we did was specialize," recalled James. "Some people knew trajectory, some knew propulsion, but not everybody knew it all together.

"Von Braun—you talked to him and you realize you're talking all facets of the subject, because he knew trajectory, he knew guidance, he knew propulsion—he knew everything there was."

In 1949, as American (and German) rockets were refined, the NACA engineers were asking more complex questions about flight, especially the performance of vehicles at speeds faster than the speed of sound.

"It was interesting work. It was important, and we wanted to be part of it," said Kraus.

Only two years earlier, Chuck Yeager had flown the first airplane at supersonic speed. In an age when advanced research on aerodynamics was being conducted at only a handful of research universities, the NACA centers were catalysts for change and discovery in the world of flight. The field known for most of the century as "aviation" was evolving into "aero-space"—work on conventional flying in Earth's atmosphere as well as the issues involving travel in space.

"Our concern had been to get a vehicle that could go faster than the speed of sound efficiently," said Jack Boyd, senior adviser to the director of Ames, who joined the center in 1947. "At that point, we were focused on efficient flight within Earth's atmosphere. But that work evolved into the study of the much faster speeds that we needed to go outside the atmosphere and survive."

Each of the NACA centers dealt with unique and difficult problems and also produced independent breakthroughs. For example, in the late 1940s, Langley would take a lead role in rocket research in conjunction with Wallops Island; Ames had primary programs in exploring the issues of advanced studies for aircraft.

"Our mission at Ames was to further the country's work in aeronautics—especially with the continuing demand for airplanes with higher and higher speeds," said Victor Peterson, an engineer who joined Ames in 1956 and would become deputy director in 1990.

Ames's giant wind tunnel facility—the largest in the world—would be used to test almost every military jet built in the United States. All American spacecraft would eventually be tested there as well.

"We were working on major advancements in aircraft," said Tom Snyder, who would join Ames in 1962. "Our projects would later shift over into the space program. It was work on the frontiers—on the edge."

The research into increasing speed in flight would have profound effects on aviation and later on travel in space. For example, Ames researchers were exploring a problem so fundamental that it would affect the design of every vehicle that has orbited the planet and returned safely to earth ever since. But at the time of its discovery, the solution seemed so counterintuitive that it could not possibly work.

"A crucial major difference between aviation and aerospace is heat," said Peterson, who worked with Harvey Allen, an engineer who explored a broad range of problems involving high-speed flight. "As aircraft fly farther, higher, and faster, the question becomes how to protect the vehicle from heat—whether it's an airplane or a missile or a manned spacecraft."

Dealing with the problems of heat when vehicles fly beyond the speed of sound becomes critical. Even before orbital spaceflight, the question was looming: What would happen to a vehicle flying thousands of miles an hour when it reentered Earth's atmosphere?

The logical answer would seem to be right out of science fiction: use an arrow-shaped rocket flying point-first—the idea being that the small point would experience little heat.

"It turned out that a pointed craft was the worst thing to do," said Peterson. "The shock wave attaches to the point of the vehicle, producing massive amounts of heat."

Allen developed the solution; he found that a rounded body—and not a sharp point—would transfer much less heat to a vehicle. A blunt body, Allen learned, effectively disperses hot gases, allowing the spacecraft (with proper shielding) to survive the inferno.

"Without Harvey's work we would have been stuck in the mud, trying to figure out how to get our spacecraft back to Earth," said Peterson.

Allen's concept continues to guide spacecraft design today; all American spacecraft from Mercury to the space shuttle have a blunt end for reentry.

Many NACA engineers and technicians would use their experience at the centers to move on to the specific challenges of building spacecraft. Kraus, for example, would work on both the Apollo program and the space shuttle. Most involved in the NACA centers in the late 1940s and early 1950s would never see the launch of one of the spacecraft their work would one day help build. But the engineers who joined the NACA centers in those early days would, without realizing it, become pioneers in America's space program.

c⟨∞⟩ɔ

White Sands, with its vast uninhabited desert, was 40 miles wide and 90 miles long—more than adequate for early missile testing. But with a future based on longer-range flights that would go into orbit, a coastal site would be better. White Sands would continue to operate, but in 1950, much of the launch program moved east to the air force facility on the central coast of Florida known then as the Joint Long Range Proving

Ground at Cape Canaveral. Over the next decade, Cape Canaveral would become synonymous with the American space programs, with launches set for "The Cape."

Other service branches were also making steady progress with missile development. The navy's program launched Viking missions—12 of them between September 1949 and February 1955—rockets that explored the atmosphere above 100,000 feet. The Viking rockets did not circle the Earth—no rocket had orbited by 1955—but they did achieve several records, including the highest altitude reached by an American single-stage rocket—158 miles.

But what would eventually prod the United States into a massive effort in space was an event that should have been expected but was a complete surprise to most: when it came, it arrived in the form of a solitary beeping sound and a tiny flash of light across the sky.

5

BEEP

"It's up."

—Scientist Richard Porter informing a colleague
that the Soviet Union had launched Sputnik I,
the first manmade object to orbit Earth

Clayton, Missouri
October 7, 1957

Clayton, Missouri, is a comfortable suburban neighborhood 15 minutes from downtown St. Louis, a home to the families of midlevel executives from local industry and beer production. With 11 parks and the St. Louis Zoo just across town, in the 1950s Clayton was a snug locale for growing up in the Midwest.

Bill Jeffries, a stocky, smart 17-year-old, lived with his family on a wooded cul-de-sac three blocks from his high school. Bill's bedroom, on the second floor with windows that faced the apple trees in the backyard, had all the trappings of a midcentury boy in his teens. His hockey gear was stashed in the corner, ready for the upcoming season. On the bedpost hung a coonskin hat, a modestly embarrassing but fondly treasured legacy of the Walt Disney *Davy Crockett* TV show craze of two years before—"back when I was just a kid," he would explain. On a shelf was a spring training portrait of Stan Musial—"Stan the Man" to generations of worshiping fans of the St. Louis Cardinals.

But for Bill, as for many teenagers of the time, it was airplanes that dominated his world: models of World War II fighters hung from threads in carefully positioned simulations of dogfights over Europe. The walls—in spite of his mother's protests—were covered with taped-up pictures: F-86 Saberjets flying sorties over Korea and a squadron of B-52s, the mighty strategic bomber that became the stable platform for the air force for decades beginning in 1952. And in the corner was a drawing of a private indulgence: at a time when most boys his age were fascinated by speed, Bill's favorite plane was the DC-3, the elegant, rugged two-engine passenger plane—looking as much in flight while sitting on the tarmac as it did in the air—that had transformed commercial aviation in the 1930s.

In the transition from boy to young man, Bill's interests had grown more technical; he tinkered with a crystal radio kit and had a brief but smelly debacle with a chemistry set. His parents noted the change in his interests; the previous Christmas brought a surprise: a ham radio. For Bill, it opened a door to the world as he listened to transmissions from enthusiasts around the globe, unknown voices speaking from far away.

But tonight's listening would be something very different—a voice of a very different kind.

Bill checked the *St. Louis Post-Dispatch* for the time and frequency; the opportunity would be short—only a few minutes. He turned on the radio. The vacuum tubes glowed bright for a moment and then settled into their routine glow. Bill tuned to 20.005 megacycles, hearing only the soft monotony of static, and waited.

At 10:18, right on schedule, Bill heard a faint sound. It was not much, but it was something new and very special—a sound that symbolized a milestone for the world that even the young listener knew would change everything. Bill's eyes widened as he listened with a sense of wonder about what he had been told he would hear but had not quite believed would happen.

It was the solitary "beep beep beep" transmitted from a round, silvery object flying in orbit around Earth 180 miles overhead.

Bill heard Sputnik I, a satellite launched by the Soviet Union on October 4 that was the first manmade object in orbit. The "beep beep beep" was just a modest transmitter, but it was a deliberate signal from the Soviets of the beginning of a new age—an age in which, as one newspaper headline put it, "the world has a new moon."

The world was listening.

⚬⚬⚬

The first few days of October had been busy for President Dwight Eisenhower. Then in his second term in office, Eisenhower was juggling issues at home and abroad: a nagging recession and modest inflation were chipping away at the comfortable midcentury economy, delighting Democrats who were already angling for success in the upcoming midterm and presidential elections. Overseas, French control over Algeria was deteriorating, and American diplomats were meeting with Saudis to discuss the ongoing tensions in the Middle East.

At the moment, perhaps the most volatile problem was on the domestic front: in the American South, the desegregation of schools that resulted from the Supreme Court decision in *Brown v. Board of Education* in 1954 had become increasingly complicated and confrontive. In Little Rock, Arkansas, the issue had evolved into a public showdown involving attendance at local high schools that required federal intervention. Eisenhower had ordered U.S. troops into Little Rock on September 24 to escort nine black students to Central High School.

A less critical problem, but still important, was space—what we would do in it and how we should exploit it. With the involvement of the Germans and steady progress by the Americans, missile research continued with dozens of successful launches for both military testing and civilian scientific research.

And then there were the Russians. The Soviet Union, since shortly after the 1953 death of Josef Stalin under the leadership of Nikita Khrushchev, continued to be a noisy combination of political irritation, potential expansionist adversary, competitor for alliances, and an endless problem in the quest to maintain the safety of free nations in a Cold War world.

There were some momentary thaws in the United States–Soviet relationship. The International Geophysical Year marked a new opportunity for scientific cooperation between East and West. First proposed in 1952, the International Geophysical Year was scheduled for July 1, 1957, to December 31, 1958, engaging 67 countries in projects involving earth sciences, gravity, geography, and other related fields. The United States and the Soviet Union both agreed to participate.

The International Geophysical Year was truly a broad commitment to international scientific cooperation, but it was also a showcase for national achievement and political one-upmanship. On July 29, 1955, the United States announced that part of its contribution to the upcoming International Geophysical Year would be the launch of small Earth-circling satellites. On August 2, a spokesman for Khrushchev revealed that the Soviet Union would also launch a satellite. The timing was described as "the near future" but apparently planned for the fall of 1957.

The Soviet announcement was received in the West with public compliments but private smirks. The Soviets' space efforts were aided by an infusion of mostly unhappy German scientists who were "recruited" during the Soviet's version of Operation Paperclip. Yet many observers scoffed at the Soviet announcement, either out of outright competitiveness or in recognition of the long-held belief that the Soviets, with massive losses in World War II, their seemingly unsophisticated scientific program, and crushed by Stalin's internal purges, were simply incapable of producing a vehicle that could orbit Earth in space.

"The Russians had taken a horrible beating in the war, and 10 years later it seemed to America that the Soviets would be forever catching up with the west technologically," said historian Robert Dallek. "It was impossible to take the Soviets seriously as a competitor in space. Americans viewed them as a bunch of tractor drivers."

The "tractor driver" perception prevailed even after the Soviets announced their intentions to launch a satellite for the International Geophysical Year. Before Sputnik was launched, von Braun tried without success to convince a congressional hearing—especially Senator Allen Ellender of Louisiana—that the Soviets were in fact skilled enough to launch a satellite.

Recalled General James "Jumpin' Jim" Gavin, commander of the 82nd Airborne Division during World War II and in 1957 the army's chief of research and development, "Dr. von Braun began to talk about the Soviet capabilities for satellite launching. After listening for a while, Senator Ellender said that we must be out of our minds—the Soviets could never develop a satellite."

Ellender, an entrenched segregationist who had opposed antilynching laws in 1938, had a simple explanation for his view, remembered Gavin.

"Ellender had just returned from the Soviet Union, and after seeing the ancient automobiles, and very few of them, on the streets, he was convinced that we were entirely wrong."

With the "tractor driver" view of the Soviets prevailing in American political circles, the U.S. space program—in a decision endorsed by Eisenhower—opted for quality over early launch and began preparing a sophisticated (for its day) spacecraft that would produce a host of scientific findings. The question of being first in space was not a priority.

As a result of this slow and steady approach, America would spend years trying to catch up, both technologically and politically.

In June 1957, the Soviets announced their plans for space, including an approximate launch date in the fall. But in the United States, the announcement was considered red-tinged hogwash, viewed as another failure in the making for the Soviets' track record that included everything from unmet goals for steel production to missed targets for wheat crops. But in a Cold War world, the question of who would be first in space was already bubbling: a headline on the cover of the March 4, 1957, issue of *Newsweek* asked the question, "Race into Space: Can We Win?"

In September, von Braun knew that something was up.

"I am convinced," he stated, "that, should the Russians beat us to the satellite punch, this would have all kinds of severe psychological repercussions not only among the American public, but also among our allies."

A month later, the Soviet Union would confirm the prediction.

⌘

On Friday, October 4, Eisenhower looked back on the last two weeks and liked what he saw. His plan to support school desegregation was a major victory for the president that received strong support from most in the North and even some in the South.

Eisenhower, taking a break at his private home in Gettysburg, Pennsylvania, which overlooked the historic battlefield, could afford to relax, if only momentarily. On Friday, the nine students had attended school without major incident; everyone in Little Rock could take a breather for the next two days. The president decided to stay in Gettysburg for the weekend.

And then the bells started to ring.

In newsrooms across the United States, the teletype machines that carried the wire service stories of the world's press rang frantically with a 10-bell message—the highest priority alert, usually reserved for the death of a king or the outbreak of war—that a "flash" news story was arriving.

This flash message brought the news from the East that the world had changed forever. At the Cosmodrome on the plains of southern Kazakhstan, the Soviet Union had launched a satellite into space that was orbiting Earth: Sputnik I, a silver, beach-ball-size, 184-pound orb with four trailing antennae.

For the first time, the Earth had an artificial moon—a manmade object was darting across the sky at 18,000 miles per hour, circling the globe every 96 minutes.

For the Soviet government under Khrushchev, the launch was a technological and political triumph—a slap to the face of the Western capitalist world. The news reached Washington with ironic timing: 50 scientists, in the capital for a conference about the International Geophysical Year, were gathered at a reception at the Soviet embassy. They were informed by the *New York Times* of Sputnik's launch and orbit. American physicist Lloyd Berkner made the announcement, no doubt gulping when he said, "I wish to congratulate our Soviet colleagues for the achievement."

For some in the Soviet space program, the launch was an elegant, almost romantic venture—and a prediction of things to come.

"It is small, this first satellite," wrote Valentin Vassilev from the Soviet Academy of Science, "but after it, we will launch others.

"In the olden days, explorers like Vasco De Gama and Columbus had the good fortune to open up the terrestrial globe," wrote Vassilev. "Now we have the good fortune to open up space, and it is for those in the future to envy us our joy."

In Texas, on hearing the news, U.S. Senate majority leader Lyndon Johnson and his wife, Lady Bird, left the house on their ranch in Stonewall, Texas, near Austin to look up into the heavens. In the days that followed would come the flood of political reaction, with Johnson leading the charge. But at the moment, Johnson was reacting as a stunned American, worried about his country's greatest global adversary.

"We did not speak," Johnson recalled. "I felt uneasy. In Texas, we live close to the sky. But now in some way, the sky seemed alien. I said to myself that another nation had achieved superiority over this great country of ours. That thought shocked me."

The next morning, in full-width headlines reserved for only the most profound human events, the *New York Times* announced, "Soviet Fires Earth Satellite into Space; It Is Circling at 18,000 MPH; Sphere Tracked in Four Crossings over U.S." The *Los Angeles Times* reported, "Russ Satellite Circling Earth." The *Arizona Daily Star* said, "Russians Launch Baby Moon."

NBC Radio News reported, "Ladies and gentlemen, we are bringing you the most important story of this century"—quite a statement in an era that included the birth of flight, the development of penicillin, and World War II. "For the first time, mankind has reached for the stars, and found them within his grasp."

On the CBS *Evening News*, Walter Cronkite, often called "the most trusted man in America," put the issue into perspective: "Sputnik is a serious threat—if not to our immediate security, then to our sense of security."

Life magazine—often the great interpreter of the American character—declared that Sputnik was "a devastating blow to the prestige of the United States."

Two weeks after Sputnik, Chalmers Roberts wrote in the *Washington Post*, "Not even the most dim-witted State Department Official needed more than a second glance at those news bulletins on Sputnik to realize that the United States had suffered the worst psychological licking in the history of its relations and struggle with the Soviets and the Communist world."

Three months later, Soviet leader Nikita Khrushchev would be named *Time* magazine's Man of the Year, featured on the cover wearing the Kremlin as a crown and smiling at Sputnik as a orb balanced on his fingertips (see plate 2).

The news had come to the American people in many forms, but Sputnik itself spoke with one voice, and anyone with a ham radio could listen as the satellite flew overhead to the steady "beep, beep, beep" that marked its path.

"The Eisenhower administration has underestimated the American people's interest in space exploration," said author Ken Hollings. "The Soviet Union's Sputnik program has created a public spectacle that even Disney and von Braun might envy."

Around the world, in the days after the launch, listeners tuned in—in homes like Jeffries's in Missouri, on naval ships at sea, in radio clubs across the country—the radios receiving the "beep, beep, beep."

The Soviets conveniently reported a schedule of where Sputnik would fly over American cities so listeners could tune in. The Russians took special care to note when Sputnik would fly over Little Rock—a blatant reminder to unaligned countries that "the land of the free" was still struggling to not oppress its own people.

And when the Russians announced that Sputnik could actually be seen on its journey over the United States, nightly viewing parties spontaneously sprang up everywhere, looking for a tiny dot of light floating across the sky.

"I was almost five years old when Dad took us out to a park in Chicago to see it," said Jane Lindsey. "There were a lot of people there, and then someone yelled 'There it is!' and the park got as quiet as a church in about two seconds.

"It was weird to see a tiny light gliding across the sky, not making any noise or even blinking," Lindsey said, "just silently scooting along, oblivious to the throngs of people watching it."

On a crisp autumn night in New England, graduate student Chris Anderson was watching in Ludlow, Massachusetts. "It was cold and clear," said Anderson. "We could see the Milky Way shimmering across the sky. I stood in my front yard, my family with me. The entire neighborhood, the entire city—the entire nation, it seemed, was standing outside, watching what the Russians had done."

In Oklahoma, teacher Frank O'Rourke could see it, too. "Just at the time the Russians had said," O'Rourke remembered, "a tiny light appeared in the western horizon and glided over our heads. Some of us cried. I stood in awe."

Of course, it was not actually Sputnik that observers could see; no amount of 1950s miracle Soviet technology could make a flying object the size of a basketball visible 150 miles up in the sky (although many astronomers later claimed that Sputnik itself was visible, even more admitted it was not possible). What *could* be seen was a reflection off the Soviets' 98-foot rocket that launched Sputnik I, trailing not far behind the satellite.

But were Americans feeling awe, amazement, or outright fear of what the Soviets had done? In the decades that followed, the launch of Sputnik would be recalled as a terrifying, defining event for Americans, who were shocked and paralyzed at the mere idea that a potential enemy could endlessly travel unchallenged overhead only a few hundred miles away.

Johnson aide George Reedy recalled, somewhat floridly, that Sputnik's launch hit Americans "like a brick through a plate-glass window, shattering into tiny slivers the American illusion of technical superiority over the Soviet Union." Von Braun, in his eagerness to push forward the now-lagging American space agenda, proved to be something of an alarmist, stating that by falling behind, Americans might be "surrounded by several planets flying the hammer and sickle flag."

"I am quite sure," von Braun predicted, "that when our young astronauts blast off into space, they will meet Russian customs officers."

However, at the time no one seemed overly terrified. Even fear of the unknown did not increase concerns about Sputnik; earlier in 1957, a national survey showed that only half of Americans had even heard of a satellite. Later a similar survey found that only about 17 percent of Americans had a realistic idea of what a manmade satellite was or had any idea of what kept it in orbit.

But another poll released a month after the launch showed that when Americans were asked what they considered "the most important problem facing this country today," only 6 percent said Sputnik. Even after an American launch failure and a second successful Soviet launch, that number increased to only 11 percent and then declined throughout 1958.

Anthropologist Margaret Mead and colleagues had already created a project to study images of the scientist as perceived by American students. After Sputnik, they studied children's images of the satellite; the drawing revealed a sense of wonder and curiosity in Earth's new moon.

If there was any shock among Americans, it came from the genuine surprise that the "tractor drivers" had been able to pull off the stunt.

At the White House, the reaction to Sputnik was portrayed as calm and measured, but many Americans perceived the response as naïve and oblivious. Charles Wilson, the secretary of defense, described Sputnik as "a nice scientific trick." When asked how the United States would catch up, Sherman Adams, chief assistant to Eisenhower, brushed away the idea, saying the U.S. program would not take part in "an outer space basketball game." Later a White House statement congratulated the Soviets for their achievement.

Incredibly, Eisenhower stayed in Gettysburg for three days after Sputnik. In the months after his 1955 heart attack, Eisenhower had relied on golf to relieve stress; after Sputnik, he hit balls for several hours. But presidential golf playing in moments of crisis was—and is—perceived as evidence not of calm but of disconnection from the issues.

Years later, Eisenhower would say, "There was no point in trying to minimize the accomplishment or the warning it gave that we must take added efforts to ensure maximum progress in missile and other scientific programs."

Adams would recall that "although Eisenhower maintained an official air of serenity, he was privately as concerned as everybody else in the country by the jump ahead that the Russians had made in scientific enterprise."

But the president of the United States cannot be "privately concerned." And it was the "official air of serenity" that worried everyone outside of the White House.

Even though by 1957 the United States already had an active rocket program that was producing strong military applications and beneficial scientific findings—in many ways far ahead of the Soviets—by downplaying the problem of Sputnik, Eisenhower allowed the United States to be depicted as unprepared and lagging behind its primary global adversary in their most important competition to date. To many Americans, Eisenhower's response was puzzling, frustrating, and counterproductive.

"Sputnik reinforced for many people the idea that Eisenhower was a smiling incompetent," said NASA historian Roger Launius. "It was another instance of a do-nothing, golf-playing president mismanaging events."

But even worse than the idea that the Soviets were in space was that they had accomplished the task *first*. In directing the American satellite program mounted for the International Geophysical Year, Eisenhower had listened to scientists who urged for a mission that would have significant scientific importance, even if that goal meant not being first in reaching orbit.

"The United States had a viable satellite program underway," said historian Layne Karafantis, "but we were focusing on a more sophisticated satellite, while the Soviets understood the prestige factor and how it would devastate American morale just to get a little satellite up there first. As we learned the hard way, the 'first' business was important, and it would stay that way throughout the development of the U.S. space program."

Choosing the scientific high road was a mistake that would plague Eisenhower for the rest of his administration, as the pressure to develop any kind of viable orbital space program was compounded by the problem of trying to stay close to the Soviets.

Of the post-Sputnik criticism, the theme that may have resonated loudest came from those at home who pointed out that the United States had not used its scientific talents to the fullest.

"We believe," said *Aviation Week* editor Robert Hotz, "that the people of this country . . . have the right to find out why a nation with our vastly superior scientific, economic, and military potential is being at the very least equaled and perhaps surpassed by a country that less than two decades ago couldn't even play in the same scientific ball park."

An American reporter was asked by a British editor, only half-jokingly, "How does it feel to be a citizen of a second-rate power?"

It hurt, and it cut right to the core of the American experience of the 1950s. The nation that was supposed to be the richest, most powerful, and most successful had been undermined with a single stroke by an adversary that in the popular consciousness could not even feed its own people.

On the world stage, Sputnik was a disaster for the United States. A study conducted in multiple countries showed large percentages of locals said that Sputnik eroded American stature—with friends and potential foes alike.

"In the eyes of the world, first in space means first, period," said Johnson in the days after the launch, now speaking as a politician. "Second in space is second in everything."

In September, the Little Rock situation had positioned Eisenhower as a decisive leader; now after Sputnik, he seemed feeble and out of touch.

The Sputnik issue was raw meat for the hounds in Congress.

Senator Henry M. Jackson of Washington described Sputnik as "a devastating blow to the prestige of the United States as the leader in the scientific and technical world" and brazenly demanded a "National Week of Shame and Danger." Clare Booth Luce, representative from Connecticut, called the beeping of Sputnik's transponder "an intercontinental outer-space raspberry to a decade of American pretensions that the American way of life was a gilt-edged guarantee of our national superiority." Johnson called Sputnik "one of the best publicized and most humiliating failures in our history."

It was all political posturing at its most colorful, but it was also the truth. Even the Republicans had to admit something had to be done; said Senator Alexander Wylie of Minnesota, "We had better get on our toes."

In Johnson's office, there were both strong feelings of genuine concern for national security as well as recognition that the Sputnik issue was too good a political issue to pass up.

"It is unpleasant to feel that there is something floating around in the air which the Russians can put up and we can't," wrote Reedy to Johnson. "It really doesn't matter whether the satellite has any military value. The important thing is that the Russians have left the earth, and the race for control of the universe has started. The American people do not like to be 'second best.'"

To Reedy, Sputnik was a "wedge issue" in the presidential election.

"If properly handled," Reedy said of Sputnik, "it would blast the Republicans out of the water, unify the Democratic Party, and elect you president."

For the politically ambitious Johnson, Sputnik could not have been more perfectly timed. The Senate majority leader was preparing to mount a campaign for president in two years, and with Sputnik he could now step into a brighter spotlight.

Anxiety about Sputnik would be remembered, perhaps too simply, as political fodder spread by Democrats to undermine Eisenhower. But the nation's leadership had concerns that were more than justified about the satellite as an unprecedented scientific achievement that also had potentially catastrophic implications for national security.

"Johnson certainly used Sputnik as a stick to beat up Eisenhower and the Republicans," said Dallek, "but he also had legitimate concerns about how Sputnik reflected on America."

Johnson announced that the Senate Preparedness Subcommittee that he chaired would soon hold hearings to "take a long careful look" at why the U.S. space program was trailing that of the Soviet Union.

The strategic issue for the Americans and the political problem for Eisenhower would be further compounded a month later, when on November 3, the Soviets launched Sputnik II, this time carrying a live animal—a dog named Laika.

The canine passenger was not the issue; the new concern came from the weight of Sputnik II—more than 1,000 pounds—which confirmed that the Soviets could actually launch an object with the mass of a nuclear weapon into orbit.

The inevitable question was loud and clear: If yesterday's Sputnik is a silver ball, and today's holds a dog, could the next Sputnik be a bomb in the sky?

There was no question that the Soviet satellites could be platforms for very real threats; the Associated Press reported that Sputnik had orbited over the United States twice before it was detected by the Americans.

On October 9, Eisenhower was grilled by reporters at his regular press conference—personifying in front of reporters the lack of decisiveness exhibited by his administration about Sputnik.

Reporters received a statement that described the background of the American satellite project called Vanguard, which confirmed that the original intention of the American program was to not launch until March 1958. The statement also tried to explain that the nation was taking a high road by cooperating with global partners.

"Our satellite program," read the statement, "has never been conducted as a race with other nations. Rather, it has been carefully scheduled as part of the scientific work of the International Geophysical Year."

The White House also tried to explain away the lack of a launch by falling back on national security concerns.

"Vanguard has not had equal priority with that accorded our ballistic missile work," read the statement. "Speed of progress in the satellite project cannot be taken as an index of our progress in ballistic missile work.

"I consider our country's satellite program well designed and properly scheduled to achieve the scientific purposes for which it was initiated," Eisenhower's statement concluded. "We are, therefore, carrying the program forward in keeping with our arrangements with the international scientific community."

When Eisenhower took questions from reporters, he waffled about the purpose of U.S. space efforts, complained about the costs, and reiterated the reason Americans had been beaten into orbit was because the U.S. effort had scientific benefits that outweighed the need to be first in space.

"We are still going ahead on this program to make certain that before the end of the calendar year 1958," Eisenhower told reporters, "we have put a vehicle in the air with the maximum ability that we can devise for obtaining the kind of scientific information that I have stated."

Reporters gave Eisenhower several opportunities to soothe the country and lay out the progress in the American program, but with no success.

Asked Kenneth Scheibel from Gannett Newspapers, "Mr. President, could you give the public any assurance that our own satellite program will be brought up to par with Russia, or possibly improve on it?"

Replied Eisenhower, "Now, quite naturally, you will say, 'Well, the Soviets gained a great psychological advantage throughout the world,' and I think in the political sense that is possibly true."

And the more Eisenhower tried to downplay the Soviet achievement, the less convincing he sounded.

"Are you satisfied with our own progress in that field," said Laurence Burd from the *Chicago Tribune*, "or do you feel there have been unnecessary delays in our development of missiles?"

"I can say this," Eisenhower admitted. "I wish we were further ahead . . . I wish we knew more about it at this moment."

The media bloodbath concluded with a straightforward question from Hazel Markel of NBC, eliciting an answer that played right into the Democratic plans.

"Mr. President, in light of the great faith which the American people have in your military knowledge and leadership," asked Markel, "are you saying at this time that with the Russian satellite whirling about the world, you are not more concerned nor overly concerned about our nation's security?"

"So far as the satellite itself is concerned, that does not raise my apprehensions, not one iota," concluded Eisenhower. "I see nothing at this moment, at this stage of development, that is significant in that development as far as security is concerned, except, as I pointed out, it does definitely prove the possession by the Russian scientists of a very powerful thrust in their rocketry, and that is important."

Johnson's subcommittee would hold hearings on November 25.

⚬⚬⚬

In public, Eisenhower did not seem on top of the Sputnik problem, but in the Oval Office, he was building a plan to move ahead.

The administration regrouped, but with difficulty, in part because of cautious tip-toeing around the Russians, which Eisenhower believed was necessary in the Cold War world. The president worried about Soviet hypersensitivity over American technology in any form flying over their country—even though Sputnik, which was busily orbiting over the United States every 96 minutes, seemed to be negating the issue. (Unknown to the Soviets, the United States had been conducting ultrasecret overflights of Communist territory with the U-2 spy plane since 1956.)

Of equal importance, in Eisenhower's view, were his worries about how the Soviets would perceive a civilian scientific satellite if it was launched by the military.

It seemed a strange consideration, even with Eisenhower's concerns about tender feelings in Moscow, given that the rocket used to fly Sputnik I was derived from the R-7 Semyorka intercontinental ballistic missile. Nevertheless, Eisenhower was convinced that an American satellite should fly aboard a civilian rocket.

The United States, with its space programs split between three military service branches, mounted two space efforts for the International Geophysical Year. The army's program was based on the Juno 1—a rocket derived from the Jupiter C and a proven vehicle that had been launched several times. Juno had been developed by the team led by von Braun—now at the army's Ordinance Rocket Center in Huntsville, Alabama (in 1959 to be renamed the George C. Marshall Space Flight Center)—using the vast open spaces and a former arsenal as the primary design and technology centers for the American missile program.

The navy's "civilian" project was based on the Vanguard rocket; the Vanguard project was civilian by definition because it was managed by Naval Research Laboratory, a scientific operation perceived, at least by Eisenhower, as a nonmilitary project. (The air force missile program at the time did not involve satellites.)

Eisenhower chose the nonmilitary route: the Vanguard project managed by the Naval Research Laboratory would be America's first satellite in orbit.

"It was simply a decision made by President Eisenhower that the military carrier was inappropriate for a civilian-type satellite," said Walter Wiesman, who came to America at age 25 as the youngest member of the Peenemünde team. "The Russians had no such hesitations."

However, the slim, lightweight Vanguard rocket could carry only a small payload. Deputy Secretary of Defense Donald Quarles reported to Eisenhower that the United States could proceed quickly with an orbital mission but not with a satellite that would have much scientific worth.

For the army missile group, the selection left them grumbling, but there was also legitimate concern within the army team about the navy's chance of success. The Vanguard rocket was complex and risky; it would ultimately require tests and failures to be a reliable launch platform for satellites. Conversely, the army's Juno rocket was a tested, reliable choice.

"When Sputnik went up, we all collectively blew our tops," said Major General John Zierdt, chief of the Army Missile Command. "We had known for some time that we had the ability to put an object in space." However, that claim had not been tested.

A meeting with his science advisers reinforced what the president already knew—that the development of national space programs needed to be removed from the military branches and their incessant rivalries and installed under the administration of a civilian agency.

But before final plans could be formulated, *any* part of the government—military or civilian—needed to get an American satellite into orbit. The navy group assured the president that it would be ready for launch by December. The army group at Huntsville under General John Bruce Medaris and von Braun would be the backup. Eisenhower announced that Vanguard would launch in December.

It was a national disaster.

6

A DULL THUD

"I am not attempting today to pass judgment on the charges of harmful service rivalries, but one thing is sure: whatever they are, America wants them stopped."

—President Dwight Eisenhower

On December 6, the media of the world were invited to Cape Canaveral to watch America catch up with the Soviets. The payload was modest: the Vanguard TV3 (short for "test vehicle") was a three-pound, six-inch-diameter aluminum ball spiked with six antennae. Inside was a simple set of sensors to measure the abilities of the satellite to link to earth stations. The launch would be carried nationally on television.

At 11:44 a.m., the booster ignited, but the journey lasted only three feet. Two seconds after ignition, the rocket lost thrust and settled back on the launch pad, rupturing the fuel tanks and exploding in a spectacular ball of flame.

As the Vanguard blew up, the national audience could see the nose cone break away from the rocket. What viewers could not see was the satellite simply fall off the rocket and land on the pad—the only part of the launch vehicle that was not incinerated or severely damaged. As the flames dispersed, the satellite sat on the pad, plaintively chirping its beacon signal.

For an American television audience, a majority of whom did not know what a satellite was six months before, the sight of a missile erupting into a fireball the height of a 10-story building must have been truly shocking—a vivid image of the ill-defined U.S. space program.

The next day, newspaper coverage of the explosion was brutal; few U.S. newspapers could resist the temptation of playing off the Sputnik name, with headlines like "Oopsnik," "Kaputnik," and "Stayputnik." The *Los Angeles Daily Mirror*, at least, was more straightforward in its headline: "Satellite Flops."

On CBS News, Douglas Edwards called the explosion "a dull thud heard 'round the world."

And in other countries it was also viewed as a thud; the insults carried over to the foreign press. "Oh, What a Flopnik!" screamed the *London Daily Herald* above a photo of the exploding Vanguard, underlining the loss of American prestige on a global scale (see plate 4).

The Soviets rubbed plenty of salt in the wound; Khrushchev connected the failure of America's first launch with his own country's expansionist policies: "With America's failure," Khrushchev said, "it will not be able to stop the forward march of Communism."

For Eisenhower, the explosion confirmed his worst expectations about the confusion and disarray in his space program. For the man who, as supreme commander of Allied forces in Europe during World War II, had vast success in building consensus between high-strung military leaders from many nations during the most complicated and bold military offensive in history, the lack of focused effort within his own administration in successfully launching a single rocket was intolerable; something had to change, and quickly.

Even worse, Eisenhower's own science advisers continued to paint a happy face on the issue, highlighting the ongoing progress in the lab while excusing the lack of success in the air.

"It is our judgment that technically our missile development is proceeding in a satisfactory manner," wrote James Killian, the president of MIT on leave to serve as a presidential special assistant for science and technology.

"Although it is probably true that we are at present behind the Soviets," wrote Killian, "we are in this position largely because we started much later and not because of inferior technology. Our technological progress in the missile field, in fact, has been impressive.

"The so-called failures of flight test vehicles, to which much publicity has been given, are normal and unavoidable occurrences in the development of complex mechanisms, many functions of which can be tested only in flight."

It was all true, but in the post-Sputnik environment, completely useless. The message that *was* helpful, even if not specific, was Killian's appraisal of what could happen next: "We are confident," he said, "that the U.S. has ample technical competence in our ballistic missile technical groups to achieve satisfactory operational missile systems at an early date."

But to get the job done required a change; the navy—or rather the Naval Research Laboratory—had failed. Eisenhower finally recognized that the need for success in space outweighed his concerns about pampering the Soviets with a civilian rocket. The army received approval to proceed with a satellite launch at the earliest possible date.

In December, at a staged media opportunity, General Medaris gave the charge to Wernher von Braun.

"I promised the secretary of the army that we would be ready in 90 days or less," said Medaris to a grinning von Braun. "Let's go, Wernher!"

For von Braun, after more than 20 years of working on weaponry, the door to space was now open. Even though he remained in an army program, he was—finally—involved in a purely civilian project, and one with an A-plus priority. His goal: to prepare a launch vehicle that, at the very least, would not produce another ball of fire.

Johnson opened hearings of his Senate Preparedness Subcommittee on November 25, 1957, to review how America was faring in space in the wake of the Sputnik crisis. This group found "serious underfunding and incomprehensible organization" for the conduct of space activities. When Vanguard program director John Hagan was asked why his satellite had not been first in space, he replied that Vanguard could have beaten Sputnik if the U.S. mission had been given a higher priority. He had asked the administration for a higher priority two years before but received no response.

With Johnson reaping political hay from the aftermath of Sputnik, his potential as a presidential candidate continued to increase. But he was not alone in that objective, as another rising star in the Democratic Party was taking note as well.

Strangely, the junior senator from Massachusetts, who only four years later would become so closely identified with the U.S. space program that he would be considered the chief catalyst of its success, was not yet convinced of the importance of space. Senator John F. Kennedy was already becoming a high-visibility example of a new breed of young, dynamic politician voicing progressive concerns about critical issues at home and abroad.

Kennedy, with a full agenda of issues, may not yet have been enticed by space, but he was carefully watching the issues surrounding the U.S. space program; like Johnson, he recognized the volatility of the Sputnik issue in shaping the Democratic assault on the presidency.

"Kennedy appreciated that Sputnik did indeed have the potential to be a campaign issue," said historian Robert Dallek, "but he had little personal or professional interest in the space program. Kennedy was focused on more traditional international issues, and on dealing with the complex domestic issues at home."

Kennedy would learn quickly.

⚮

Almost four months after Sputnik—which for Eisenhower must have seemed an eternity—but just eight weeks after Vanguard exploded, the United States finally reached space on January 31, 1958, with the launch and orbit of Explorer 1. Just as the von Braun team had predicted, their Juno 1 rocket worked flawlessly.

The Explorer satellite, a pencil-shaped, 30-pound, 80-inch-long tube, had been built at the Jet Propulsion Laboratory in Pasadena under the direction of University of Iowa scientist James Van Allen and was loaded with test and measurement instruments. Already the U.S. space program was being billed as a cooperative effort, "a three-way collaboration," reported a Universal-International newsreel, "between private industry, academic science, and the military."

For von Braun, it was a major victory, and a highly visible one. At the press conference after the launch, he joined project developers Van Allen and William Pickering in posing for celebration photos, holding a mock-up of Explorer above their heads. Von Braun would soon be a national hero and an acknowledged leader and spokesman for the U.S. efforts in space.

With Explorer 1, the value of the American version of a space program became almost immediately apparent. The Soviet Union, with a mania for concealing its failures in space, would also often hide the fruits of its successes, delay announcements, and shade the truth about its achievements. For the Americans, Explorer's scientific benefits became available immediately and to everyone.

During Explorer's 111-day mission, its instruments measured temperatures, listened for the impact of cosmic dust particles, confirmed the existence of Earth's magnetic field, and had many other successes. And the primary finding was produced by the main science instrument on Explorer 1: a detector designed to measure the radiation in Earth's orbit. When the instrument became overloaded, Van Allen proposed that it had been saturated by a belt of charged particles trapped by Earth's magnetic field. The layer of particles was named the Van Allen Belt in honor of the discoverer.

With the success of Explorer, said Eisenhower, finally getting the point, "Americans stand a little straighter, and they walk a little more confidently."

The findings of Explorer 1 set a pattern for the conduct of America in space—launching satellites with experiments that produced valuable insights about the physical world that were available for all to see and use. As the motto of a new organization soon to be created by Eisenhower would describe its mission, it was "space for all humanity."

America was space crazy; there were soon songs about spaceships, wacky hairdos with satellites dangling from entangled wires, and Boy Scout programs offering merit badges in rocketry. Youth groups formed rocket clubs, with young Americans launching their own miniature rockets just as von Braun had—although far simpler than the early German efforts—30 years before.

"More and more teenagers," reported *News of the Day* in the trite language of newsreels, "are passing up rock and roll for a rocket role."

But in spite of the new enthusiasm, Americans knew they were behind; even two years after Sputnik, 43 percent of the country still thought the Soviet Union would send a man to the moon before the United States could.

The score in the race into space was thus far Soviets 2, the United States 1. But to von Braun, who had launched a satellite that immediately demonstrated solid scientific worth, the United States had taken the lead in harvesting the nonmilitary benefits of orbital missions.

"We have firmly established our foothold in space," said von Braun. "We will never give it up again."

⁓⊗⁓

Van Allen's radiation theory would be confirmed two months later, when—finally—on March 17, the navy reached orbit with the launch of Vanguard 1. Similar in size and shape to Vanguard TV 3 and the first satellite to use solar cells for part of its power, Vanguard 1 performed basic research experiments, sending back information about the density of the upper atmosphere. And a test of tracking systems sent results that wowed every child in 1958 who was studying geography: by measuring changes in the pull of gravity, Vanguard proved that the world is *not* round; our globe is slightly—very slightly—pear-shaped.

Khrushchev could not resist insulting even the successful U.S. missions, calling Vanguard a "grapefruit satellite." Reports from Moscow said the jab was a dud, because most Russians did not know what a grapefruit was.

The scientific mission of Vanguard 1 ended 20 days after launch, and the solar-powered transmitter finally faded away in 1964. However, because of its unique orbit, Vanguard continues to orbit Earth today. After all the difficulties of launching an orbital mission, the navy program produced a satellite that now has the intriguing distinction of being the oldest object in space—an honor that will hold for a very long time. As of its 60th birthday in 2018, Vanguard 1 had orbited more than 235,000 times; the satellite will continue to circle Earth until at least 2198.

⌒∞⌒

With the United States achieving its first success with orbiting satellites, Eisenhower could turn to identifying the best direction for the U.S. space programs. The president knew that if the United States was going to continue making headway with civilian objectives in space, then interservice rivalry had to be eliminated.

Two steps in 1958 would set the direction for America in space: on January 7, Eisenhower announced the formation of ARPA, the Advanced Research Projects Agency. Housed within the Department of Defense, and managed a variety of ventures in collaboration with academic and industry partners, ARPA was created to be "a single control for our most advanced development projects"—in other words, to avoid Soviet surprises.

"I am not attempting today to pass judgment on the charges of harmful service rivalries," said Eisenhower, in his 1958 State of the Union Address, "but one thing is sure: whatever they are, America wants them stopped."

Eisenhower knew that the endless military rivalries and service branch scent marking continued to stall progress in space. His science advisory committee lobbied for a civilian space agency to manage all the scientific programs. The president agreed.

On July 29, Eisenhower signed into law the National Aeronautics and Space Act, which brought together the best elements of the military programs and people into an agency managed by civilians.

On October 1, the new organization absorbed the NACA, which ceased operating under its own name after 43 years, and the three research laboratories at Langley, Ames, and Lewis, and smaller test facilities. Also incorporated were the Naval Research Laboratory, earlier projects by the air force, and the Army Ballistic Missile Agency, including von Braun's team; three decades after his schoolboy dreams, von Braun would be working on peacetime space projects. Later in the year, the Jet Propulsion Laboratory, which was operated by Caltech, became part of the group as well, and space projects managed by ARPA would also soon be transferred.

For the former NACA research centers, the meaning of the change was obvious.

"We would keep doing some aeronautics work," said Peterson, "but we knew that we had a new priority: the space program."

Previously, the National Advisory Committee for Aeronautics had been known by its initials: "N-A-C-A." The new organization, the National Aeronautics and Space Administration, would also be recognized by its initials, but pronounced as a single word: "NASA."

The creation of NASA settled the issue of who would manage U.S. projects, but it in no way determined the future directions for America in space.

ARPA had coordinated and funded millions in projects, including research on technology for space, ballistic missile defense, and solid propellants—and a top-secret milestone orbital mission at the height of U.S. concern about success in space (see page 204). But it would soon move on to other priorities, including support for work on some of the vexing problems affecting the growth of a young industry: computers. Those issues would be part of the story of the next decade.

Whether in a panic or not about Sputnik, there was plenty of finger pointing about the reasons why the Soviets had beaten the United States into space. One frequently addressed reason was flaws in the U.S. education system.

"The public demanded to know why our space scientists had failed to keep pace with the Soviets, and many critics were quick to place the blame on inferior schooling," wrote Peter Dow in *Schoolhouse Politics*. "In the mid-1950s, the popular press teemed with articles extolling Soviet educational practices and questioning our own."

It was yet another blame game that Eisenhower could have avoided by being more concerned about being first rather than second-but-better. In December, a Gallup poll showed 70 percent of respondents agreed that American high school students must now work harder to compete with the Russians.

"The education issue was a field day for certain interest groups," said NASA historian Lee Saegesser. "One could get quoted in the papers or invited to testify in front of a congressional committee just by coming up with some statistic which showed how bad our schools were compared to those in Russia."

Of course, part of the issue was money, and the National Education Association (NEA) beat the drum about deplorably low teachers' salaries as a reason for America's second-place status. At a time when the average American factory worker earned almost $5,000 a year, "any nation that pays its teachers an annual average of $4,200," reported the NEA, "cannot expect to be first in putting an earth satellite into space."

The furor would ultimately produce benefits for American education. As a direct response to fears of falling even further behind the Soviets, in September 1958, Congress passed the National Defense Education Act, which injected funds into every level of American education: resources for K–12 schools and higher education, college loans for 1.5 million students, and matching funds to states that increased their own spending. In 10 years, more than $3 billion would be channeled into education for American students—including money to train 15,000 PhDs annually—precisely the type of support that Vannevar Bush had envisioned.

Yet critics could point to the act as another example of how Congress could be spurred to fund major reform only for military reasons and not at other times for the general public good—in fact, the first line of the act declared "the security of the Nation requires the fullest development of the mental resources and technical skills of its young men and women." It was the first significant improvement of U.S. education on a national level since 1917, and the act marked the first time *ever* that the U.S. government subsidized higher education for nonveterans.

As usual, Jim Crow politics were partly to blame for a national ill. Obstructionist Southern legislators had for years resisted federal funding for education because of its possible use as leverage to require desegregation as part of the deal.

The effects of the act were broad and deep.

"The act served two purposes," wrote Stephan Schwegler in 1982. "First, it was designed to provide the country with specific defense-oriented personnel. This included providing federal help to foreign language scholars, area studies centers, and engineering students. Second, it provided financial assistance—primarily through the National Defense Student Loan program—for thousands of students who would be part of the growing numbers enrolling at colleges and universities in the 1960s."

And the growth in college attendance was extraordinary; when added to the growing number of veterans who attended college with support from the GI Bill, it resulted in by far the largest increases in college attendance in the nation's history. In 1940, about 500,000 Americans attended college—15 percent of the college-age population. By 1960, however, college enrollment expanded to 3.6 million—21 percent of the college-age population. And by 1970, 7.5 million students were attending colleges in the United States, or 40 percent of college-age youths.

That dramatic change in college attendance would soon resonate in other ways, as the next—and much larger—generation of college students became an incubator for many of the counterculture and social protest movements across the 1960s.

The act was a far-reaching achievement, but not without a sinister element: when enacted three years after the anti-Communist hysteria that was promoted in congressional hearings by Senator Joseph McCarthy, the "better dead than red" sentiment continued to fester; the act required that anyone receiving funds swear, in writing, a disclaimer against the overthrow of the U.S. government.

Institutions across the country protested; eventually, 32 colleges and universities would refuse to participate in the act's student loan program in defiance of the oath. The requirement of an oath would be overturned by court ruling in 1962, but until then it represented yet another dark memory of the witch hunts that had plagued the nation in the 1940s and 1950s.

In spite of the prominence of the first U.S. launch successes, the public was still generally uninformed about space but was nevertheless fascinated by the country's new adventures in science and technology. Eisenhower released "Introduction to Outer Space," a publication produced by the Government Printing Office in 1958 that for 15 cents would give curious Americans a general idea about the future of the nation's efforts in space.

Originally, the report had been written by the president's Science Advisory Committee to give Eisenhower a broad view of the country's plans. The president considered the report so informative that he ordered it to be made available for the public.

"This is not science fiction," wrote Eisenhower in the introduction. "This is a sober, realistic presentation prepared by leading scientists."

If Eisenhower found the report as enlightening as he stated in the introduction, his understanding of a comprehensive space program and its goals was even less than the Democrats might have imagined.

While modestly useful for an uninformed reader—one section was titled "Why Do Satellites Stay Up?"—the report painted a fuzzy picture about specific goals and objectives for American advances in space.

The timetable in "Introduction to Outer Space" was not broken out by years or even by general targets—the reason, said its authors, was "there is yet too much uncertainty about the scale of the effort that will be made." Instead, the report includes a list of unspecified "scientific objectives"; for instance, "physics" was an objective. The objectives were listed under four vague headings: "Early," "Later," "Still Later," and "Much Later Still."

While the intent of "Introduction to Outer Space" was admirable, the goals represented precisely the type of unfocused, unchallenged thinking that Eisenhower's successor would reject in favor of a new, direct, and unforgettable call to action. The vast majority of the thousands of NASA technicians and administrators were talented, ambitious, and eager to succeed in developing their country's space program; three years later, a new president would blaze a trail for them.

⟨∞⟩

By the end of 1958, the tally of launches had tilted in favor of the United States: the American program moved ahead more quickly than the Russians', with 23 attempts at orbital launches. But the U.S. program had only five successes and 16 complete failures (along with two partial failures). The Soviets would mount only five launches in 1959, with one success and four complete failures.

And the U.S. space program was also proceeding on a plan for manned missions: on December 17 came the official announcement of Project Mercury, which beginning in 1961 would launch astronauts into space—first in brief test launches and then in orbital missions. But Mercury's flights were the only plans that the U.S. space program had at the time for manned missions; after Mercury, nothing firm was announced.

The next year, the Soviets would jump ahead impressively in one area: Luna 2, launched in September 1959, would pass a new milestone by leaving Earth's gravity and crashing (deliberately, for an experiment) into the lunar surface—the first manmade object to reach another celestial body.

In September 1959, on Khrushchev's only visit to the United States, as gifts for Eisenhower he brought along replicas of the Soviet pennants that Luna 2 had just taken—just crashed—to the moon; the president no doubt accepted the pennants with gritted teeth behind the smile. If Americans thought they had jumped ahead of the Russians, they were quickly learning that competition would continue.

As a political objective, as a measure of national honor, and as a gateway to scientific achievement for the public good, the space race was on.

On December 20, six weeks after Richard Nixon lost the 1960 election and a month before Kennedy would take office, space exploration was on the agenda for an Eisenhower cabinet meeting—in particular for the NASA budget as the Kennedy administration began. Discussion of a manned lunar landing stalled when science adviser George Kistiakowsky told the group that a full-scale mission to land on the moon would cost from $26 to $38 billion; to approve such a pricey agenda was, as a legacy of the Eisenhower administration, an unacceptable option. Eisenhower closed the subject with a question: "Can anybody tell me what is the best space program for $1 billion?"

The unspoken answer was "not much."

However, there was agreement on some points: the Apollo spacecraft program would continue to develop—it had been announced on July 28—and von Braun would work on the Saturn project, a large-scale rocket for Apollo. But in November 1960, NASA's plan for the next 10 years called for an orbital mission *around* the moon but not a landing.

"There are too many imponderables in a manned lunar landing," the report stated, "to warrant further investigations in the near term."

According to the plan, no more manned missions would be planned until Mercury was finished—a potential delay of years.

"As a tactical error, that decision ranked with the reasoning for delaying the Vanguard launch," said Dallek. "The idea that Americans would care about an astronaut going around the moon and not landing was no more impactful—perhaps *less* impactful—than sending an unmanned mission that actually landed on the moon."

John F. Kennedy would inherit a space program that his senior adviser Theodore Sorensen called "disorganized." Before the election, Kennedy's staff strongly criticized the current NASA structure as well as the previous NACA operations, calling it "an old line government activity" and "simply not technically competent to deal with space age problems."

It was an unfair assessment, especially given the dramatic growth and improvement in U.S. achievements in space since the humiliating 1957 explosion of Vanguard on national television. Under NASA, the space program had become a productive enterprise—at least as far as the unmanned missions were concerned—with a regular schedule of launches of satellites for orbital projects and probes beyond Earth as well. These included Pioneer 4, a March 1959 launch that became the first spacecraft in the U.S. program to escape Earth's orbit on its journey past the moon and around the sun, and Pioneer 5, launched in March 1960, which explored space between Earth and Venus.

But, as demonstrated in the last meetings with Eisenhower about space, what NASA *did* lack was the vision to move ahead with a dynamic agenda and specific goals that would inspire America—the type of clarion call to the nation to achieve the seemingly unachievable that would soon become part of the American experience under the new president.

A new approach would be needed to engage the young president in the excitement of space. But even then, and long after he had committed the nation to the most daunting peacetime goal in the nation's history, Kennedy would still be left with concerns about the importance of the effort.

7

THREE STEPS AHEAD
OF A PACK OF HOUNDS

"We are neither making maximum effort nor achieving results
necessary if this country is to reach a position of leadership."

—From an April 20, 1961, memo from Vice-President Johnson
to President Kennedy about the status of the U.S. space program

When in his inauguration speech in January 1961, John F. Kennedy
said, "the torch has been passed to a new generation of Americans,"
he was not referring specifically to American efforts in space, but he might
as well have been. The new 43-year-old president had inherited a program
that had the potential to represent the nation as the dominant power in
space but as yet had none of the direction or focus that it needed to achieve
great things.

For years, Kennedy had harbored doubts about the benefits of space,
and in the transition before the beginning of his presidency he was still uncertain about how the United States would fare in the ongoing space race.

"It was a difficult competition for the United States," remembered
Theodore Sorensen, a senior adviser to Kennedy throughout the 1950s
and into his presidency, of the space race. "Our competitor could advance
in secret, largely uninhibited by press criticism, public opinion, legislative
priorities, or constitutional and budget limitations."

In particular, Kennedy's team knew that the money for the space
program would be a major concern for their boss when compared to the
dramatic need for social programs at home and economic aid to other
countries.

But in the years since Sputnik, Kennedy had begun to see both the
benefits and problems of being a competitor in space. He had always

understood the scientific importance of orbital missions, and he knew that the ongoing psychological battle for global supremacy with the Soviets would require more than just a regular schedule of successful satellites.

"The impression began to move around the world that the Soviet Union was on the march, that it had definite goals, that it knew how to accomplish them, that it was moving and that we were standing still," candidate Kennedy told an audience in Albuquerque. "That is what we have to overcome."

After the election, Sorensen and other Kennedy aides met with the science officials to explore how the potential benefits of a space program could be measured against the billions that the program required.

"I was deeply impressed by the scientific by-products that could come from that exploration," said Sorensen, "not only advances in communication, health, information, astronomy, and meteorology, but possibly the unlocking of mankind's oldest mysteries: the origins of the universe, of the planet Earth, and of life itself."

Satellites had their place, Sorensen noted, but what about a program of manned missions beyond Project Mercury?

"That project, they agreed, was so large, so complex and so far off, requiring so many new scientific and engineering developments," remembered Sorensen, "that the United States might have time to . . . undertake new developments, components, and studies, and thus possibly have as much chance as the Russians had to be the first to achieve this goal.

"That ray of hope, after all the previous pessimistic answers, caught my attention," Sorensen said.

It was the idea of sending astronauts to the moon, Sorensen knew, that could be the key.

"The very notion of a manned flight to the moon, as impossible as that seemed, was one that I knew would engage President Kennedy's keen interest," Sorensen said. "It embodied everything he had said for a year and longer about striving to get this country moving again, about crossing 'new frontiers.'"

Kennedy had also learned to appreciate the space program as a measure of American prestige on a global scale—a tangible gauge of American "can do" that could help neutralize the sting of other American transgressions, such as the lack of progress on civil rights.

Also urging on the president-elect was his running mate. Lyndon Johnson had made a strong showing in the 1960 election primary season, but in the end it was the dynamic senator from Massachusetts who won the nomination.

As senators and presidential competitors, Johnson and Kennedy had viewed each other cautiously; Sorensen knew that Johnson had considered Kennedy to be a "young whippersnapper." (Johnson was nine years older than Kennedy but seemed much older.) Kennedy in turn said that Johnson was "a son of a bitch, but he's got talent."

But then—surprising many—Kennedy chose Johnson as his running mate.

"Johnson was a vice-presidential candidate who could carry the south that Kennedy needed to win," said historian Robert Dallek. "And he needed Johnson just as much once they reached the White House, so Johnson could push through the administration's high-priority projects."

And one of Johnson's favorite agendas continued to be the space program.

"Johnson helped Kennedy appreciate that the space program had benefits beyond science," said Dallek. "Pushing forward with manned missions had economic benefits for the country, and—if we succeeded—would be a status booster in our psychological war with the Soviet Union."

The contrast in appearance and style between the two new leaders of the United States was striking. Johnson was rough and unattractive but thoroughly connected to the Washington political scene and a bridge to Southerners in Congress; Kennedy was handsome, urbane, and—even after 14 years in Congress—still viewed as something of a Washington outsider. Johnson had taken leadership of the space program in the Senate; now Kennedy would be the standard-bearer as president. But both men were focused, forceful, and optimistic in their objectives; they had been political competitors, but now they would be partners in leading the nation into a focused manned space program.

As the new administration settled in, plans for space moved quickly. In February 1961, Kennedy named Johnson to chair the President's Space Council, making the vice-president his ramrod to push ahead the planning for space. Johnson would work closely with James Webb, the newly appointed administrator of NASA. A former marine and director of the Bureau of the Budget for President Truman, Webb was the physical definition of a square-jawed administrator and the type of tough, no-nonsense manager who could go toe to toe with the new president and speak his mind—precisely what Kennedy wanted.

On April 12, the United States was again beaten by the Soviets when Yuri Gagarin became the first human launched into space, and in the same mission also the first person to orbit Earth. On April 20—three days after the failure of the CIA-led invasion of Cuba at the Bay of Pigs, and with foreign perceptions of the United States at their lowest—Kennedy wrote to Johnson to request a tough appraisal of the status of the space program.

In a one-page memo, Kennedy took on the hard issues: in sum, did the United States have a chance of beating the Soviets with *any* space-related project—a trip to the moon, a lab in space, or as Kennedy put it, "any other space program which promises dramatic results in which we could win?"

After inquiring about a series of other difficult issues involving space, Kennedy closed by asking the central questions: "Are we making maximum effort? Are we achieving the necessary results?"

Eight days later, Johnson responded. A detailed survey would follow later, but building on input not only from NASA but also the military branches and the private sector, the broad answers Johnson supplied that point by point responded to Kennedy set the tone for the next steps for the United States in space.

The Space Council, Johnson reported, agreed that the Soviets were ahead of the United States, in particular they cited the Soviet advances in world prestige gained through "impressive technological accomplishments in space."

Even though the United States has greater resources than the USSR for attaining space leadership, Johnson said, the United States "has failed to make the necessary hard decisions and to marshal those resources to achieve such leadership."

"This country should be realistic and recognize that other nations, regardless of their appreciation of our idealistic values, will tend to align themselves with the country which they believe will be the world leader—the winner in the long run," Johnson wrote. "Dramatic accomplishments in space are being increasingly identified as a major indicator of world leadership."

Johnson emphasized that the nation needed to move ahead now, otherwise it would never catch up. He also focused on manned moon landing as "an achievement with great propaganda value."

The effort would require more resources, Johnson said, and needed to move ahead as soon as possible with "a bold program."

Answering Kennedy's specific question, Johnson replied that beating the Soviets was possible, and many programs would promise "significant world-wide advantage over the Soviets—not just a manned program, but satellites for communications, navigation, and mapping—all programs where the Soviets were lacking."

As to the question of whether the United States was making "maximum effort," Johnson was blunt: "We are neither making maximum effort nor achieving results necessary if this country is to reach a position of leadership," he told the president.

Johnson had also met with von Braun, who followed up with a letter to the vice-president with his own appraisal of the moon-landing issue.

"We have a sporting chance," von Braun told Johnson. "With an all-out crash program I think we could accomplish this objective in 1967–1968."

For Kennedy, the message was clear: for the United States to establish itself as the global dominant power, the nation needed to either fully commit to a grand agenda for the space program or give up the fight.

"Kennedy was focused on winning hearts and minds in the Third World, while Khrushchev was trumpeting the idea that Communism was superior to American free enterprise," said Dallek. "After failures like the Bay of Pigs, Kennedy wanted to re-establish the idea that his administration was a fresh take on domestic and international affairs. He was going to demonstrate that his new frontier was exactly that—it was a breakthrough in the way America would conduct itself on the world scene."

In his response to Kennedy, Johnson told the president, "The American public should be given the facts as to how we stand in the space race, told of our determination to lead in that race, and advised of the importance of such leadership to our future." A month later, Kennedy would do precisely that in a May 15 speech to a joint session of Congress that would become known as the Urgent National Needs speech.

"The idea was to create a new sense of possibility," said Dallek, "presenting his ideas as an opportunity for progress, especially alongside the Soviets who were so boastful about what they were achieving in space and how they had eclipsed the United States."

Although decades later Kennedy's speech would sometimes be remembered as his "moon speech," the subject of America in space was only one of nine—and the last—major agendas that he presented that day to Congress. But it was perfectly timed, because 10 days before, America had finally sent an astronaut into space. On May 5, at 10:34 in the morning, a Redstone rocket carrying Alan Shepard in a tiny Mercury spacecraft launched America's first manned mission.

Shepard's journey was a brief suborbital flight, lasting only 15 minutes before the Mercury spacecraft splashed down in the Atlantic within sight of its recovery ship, but it was enough.

Shepard was met at home with ticker-tape parades and a meeting with the president, but after Gagarin's flight—which was not only a first flight but an orbital mission as well—Shepard's achievement was viewed as yet another second-place finish for the U.S. program.

Two years later, the Soviets would yet again beat the Americans to a space milestone, but this time the United States would need decades to catch up. On June 16, 1963, the Soviets launched the first woman into space: Valentina Tereshkova, who flew for almost three days aboard Vostok 6. In the male-dominated NASA culture, it was an ignored milestone that would not be matched for almost 20 years: Sally Ride flew aboard the space shuttle Challenger on June 18, 1983.

In May 1961, the time had come to start catching up with the Soviets.

To formulate his thinking, Kennedy brought together viewpoints from his Space Council as well as experts from across the country.

"The president fired off a constant stream of written questions to them on costs, risks, manpower, alternatives, and administrative responsibility," said Sorensen. "He heard from hundreds of individuals in the process of making his decision—scientists, engineers, experts of all kinds—and became convinced that the United States must not remain second in this race."

Ultimately, however, in the president's speech, the text on space was deliberately short on details but long on ideals, as Kennedy, in only a few sentences, clarified what the problems had been in the years since Sputnik, why America was behind the Soviet Union, what it would take to move ahead, and what the target date should be—all packaged in the form of a national call to action. (For the full text, see page 278.)

"Now it is time to take longer strides," Kennedy said, "time for a great new American enterprise—time for this nation to take a clearly leading role in space achievement, which in many ways may hold the key to our future on Earth.

"I believe we possess all the resources and talents necessary. But the facts of the matter are that we have never made the national decisions, or marshaled the national resources required for such leadership. We have never specified long-range goals on an urgent time schedule.

"Recognizing the head start obtained by the Soviets . . . and recognizing the likelihood that they will exploit this lead for some time to come, we nevertheless are required to make new efforts on our own. For while we cannot guarantee that we shall one day be first, we can guarantee that any failure to make this effort will make us last.

"We take an additional risk by making it in full view of the world, but as shown by the feat of astronaut Shepard, this very risk enhances our stature when we are successful. But this is not merely a race. Space is open to us now; and our eagerness to share its meaning is not governed by the efforts of others. We go into space because whatever mankind must undertake, free men must fully share."

And then Kennedy came to the point of the message.

"I believe that this nation should commit itself to achieving the goal, before this decade is out, of landing a man on the moon and returning him safely to the earth.

"No single space project in this period will be more impressive to mankind, or more important for the long-range exploration of space; and none will be so difficult or expensive to accomplish."

Kennedy may have deliberately underestimated the price tag to soften the blow, saying that the moon mission would cost "seven to nine billion dollars additional over the next five years." Softened or not, the amount of money involved was shocking; even at the price tag that Kennedy described in his speech, the moon mission would be the largest expenditure in the federal budget for a single project.

But Kennedy was clear in his vision.

"If we are to go only halfway, or reduce our sights in the face of difficulty," he said, "in my judgment it would be better not to go at all."

Within weeks, Congress would increase NASA's budget by 89 percent and double it the following year. With a total of 15 minutes of experience in manned spaceflight, the United States had committed to spending billions for a lunar landing in less than nine years. The countdown clock was already ticking.

But would it really be possible to land on the moon in less than nine years?

To most Americans, the Urgent National Needs speech was doubly surprising—first Kennedy announced the moon objective on behalf of the nation, and second he declared a specific deadline: *before this decade is out.* Kennedy had lobbied for the deadline to be 1968, so it would occur within what he assumed would be the second term of his administration. But more reasonable voices at NASA prevailed, and Webb wisely asked for the extension.

Beginning with his Urgent National Needs speech, then later in several venues (including a major policy address to come at Rice University), Kennedy introduced the purpose of the moon mission to the American public as an irresistible invitation to pick up his gauntlet and do the impossible.

And "impossible" was what many thought it was—including many within NASA, who still wondered if landing a human on the moon was possible in any time frame.

"Kennedy's speech shocked me, and I was relatively close to what was going on," said Bill Stoney, who seven years later would become director of engineering for Apollo.

"I thought: wow—can we even conceive of doing this?" Remembered Bill Lucas, who directed the materials division at the Marshall Space Flight Center, "Reality sets in for a moment—how are we going to do that? It was a mixture of exhilaration and maybe even depression."

Even some in NASA's senior management were caught off guard. Robert Gilruth, at that point still leader of the Space Task Group at Langley, was flying over the Midwest in a NASA plane during the speech and knew that Kennedy was planning something dramatic, but Gilruth had no idea of the enormity of the announcement to come.

"An accelerated program, yes," recalled Gilruth. "A lunar landing, yes—in an orderly fashion, with time to work through all the difficulties that such an enterprise was bound to encounter. But not *this*."

Christopher Kraft, part of Gilruth's group who would become NASA's first flight director, remembered that he was "paralyzed with shock. My mind was going off in a hundred different directions."

Said historian Peter Westwick, "It wasn't just a case of 'Kennedy gives a speech and then we go to the moon.' For a lunar program to even get started required relying on decades of research and development, and then—bringing together the research of thousands of scientists with the engineering skills of industry, all of whom would have to pool their skills in this giant endeavor. It was a tremendous challenge."

For Jack Boyd at the Ames Research Center, the lunar program would offer the NASA centers the opportunity to flex their research muscles.

"We were confident we could do anything we put our minds to," said Boyd. "We didn't think it would be easy, but we thought we could make it. We were already doing research on guidance systems and blunt bodies and lifting bodies—now we would have a chance to apply it."

However, for some who would soon join NASA, the concern about the deadline was outweighed by their enthusiasm as young engineers involved in the most exciting venture imaginable.

"I was so excited," said George Phelps, an engineer who in 1963 would join North American Aviation, builder of the second stage of Apollo, "because I knew I was going to be a part of it."

Donald Binns, who also joined North American in 1963, said, "I didn't realize the magnitude of the challenge, or some of the technical requirements, but I still felt we could do anything at the time."

Bob Schwinghamer, who in 1966 would become a technical adviser in the engineering lab at the Marshall Space Flight Center, summed up the feelings of thousands of engineers, managers, and technicians who would work on Apollo: "We were all young," said Schwinghamer. "We didn't know what failure meant. We knew we could do it."

But whether a moon landing came in 1967, 1968, or the end of the decade, the deadline set by Kennedy would continue to echo long after his death in November 1963. For *everyone* at NASA—from senior administrators to the astronauts to the engineers and on down the line—Kennedy's deadline would be the overriding objective guiding the mission. As a result, the American space program not only moved ahead with the most daring scientific and engineering objective ever attempted, but also had an unbreakable deadline to get the job done.

On September 12, 1962—16 months after his speech to Congress—Kennedy amplified the purpose of the moon mission in a speech at Rice University in Houston. Speaking to 40,000 people in the university's football stadium, Kennedy made clear that a manned mission to the moon was more than just a lofty goal that drew on the talents of current scientists and engineers; it would represent the United States as the standard-bearer for peace and liberty around the world.

For the mission to succeed, Kennedy said in the late summer heat, it would involve creating a whole new structure for American engineering and scientific skills, with an impact that would last for generations after the mission ended.

"This generation does not intend to founder in the backwash of the coming age of space," Kennedy said. "We mean to be a part of it—we mean to lead it." Space, Kennedy said, would not be governed by conquest, "but by a banner of freedom and peace."

"We have vowed that we shall not see space filled with weapons of mass destruction but with instruments of knowledge and understanding."

But the American goals for space could only be accomplished, Kennedy emphasized, "if we in this nation are first, and, therefore, we intend to be first.

"In short, our leadership in science and in industry, our hopes for peace and security, our obligations to ourselves as well as others, all require us to make this effort, to solve these mysteries, to solve them for the good of all men, and to become the world's leading space-faring nation."

"But why some say, the moon?" Kennedy said. "Why choose this as our goal? And they may well ask why climb the highest mountain, why, 35 years ago, fly the Atlantic . . .

"We choose to go to the moon in this decade and do the other things, not because they are easy, but because they are hard, because *that goal* will serve to organize and measure the best of our energies and skills, because *that challenge* is one that we are willing to accept, one we are unwilling to postpone, and one which we intend to win." (Italics are Kennedy's emphasis.)

Kennedy emphasized how science and education "will be enriched by new knowledge of our universe and environment, by new techniques of learning and mapping and observation, by new tools and computers for industry, medicine, the home, as well as the school." He was also eager to point out that the space effort would create many jobs—especially in Houston, where the Manned Spacecraft Center, the home-to-be for astronaut training, research, and flight control, was being built on land donated by Humble Oil Company through Rice.

Finally, Kennedy closed with a idealistic vision of the journey that America would attempt, not hesitating to quote a bold adventurer from another era who had perished trying to achieve his objective.

"The great British explorer George Mallory, who was to die on Mount Everest, was asked why did he want to climb it," recalled Kennedy. "He said, 'Because it is there.'

"Well, space is there, and we're going to climb it," the president concluded, "and the moon and the planets are there, and new hopes for knowledge and peace are there. And, therefore, as we set sail we ask God's blessing on the most hazardous and dangerous and greatest adventure on which man has ever embarked."

As he had done in front of Congress, at Rice, Kennedy had again matched the rewards to the difficulties of the task. But even at that point, after the dynamic vision of the Rice speech, and with the space program already moving ahead full force, Kennedy still privately harbored misgivings about the importance of pushing ahead. He believed in the moon mission and would continue to describe it as a bold national endeavor. But in meetings with his senior advisers—and even while encouraging the program to move quickly—he would voice concerns about its significance to the nation.

⌦⊗⌫

Kennedy was so thorough in creating his vision of the lunar program as an American objective that it is often forgotten that on two occasions he was willing to give up competition with the Soviets and partner with them in a cooperative space mission, inviting Khrushchev to unite in a joint moon effort. While discussing space at the summit meeting between the two leaders in June 1961, Kennedy offered, "Why don't we do it together?" At first Khrushchev seemed interested, but on the second day of the conference, he declined, saying that a disarmament agreement had priority over creating a partnership for space.

More than two years later, this time in a speech on September 20, 1963, to the general assembly of the United Nations, Kennedy again suggested a partnership in a joint expedition to the moon.

"Why should man's first flight to the moon be a matter of national competition?" asked Kennedy. "Surely we should explore whether the scientists and astronauts of our two countries—indeed of all the world—cannot work together in the conquest of space, sending some day in this decade to the moon not the representatives of a single nation, but the representatives of all of our countries."

The idealistic Kennedy, said John Logsdon, founder of the Space Policy Institute at George Washington University, "never gave up that hope even as he approved the peaceful mobilization of the substantial human and financial resources needed to meet the lunar landing goal he had proposed."

However, the idea of a joint United States–Soviet space mission faded away after Kennedy was assassinated—yet another question mark in the president's legacy about a visionary project that might have been.

Two months after the Rice speech, Kennedy's uncertainty about the space program would become clear in a November 21, 1962, meeting in the Cabinet Room with Webb, presidential science adviser Jerome Wiesner, budget director David Bell, and other aides.

The meeting, which was tape-recorded, began as a review of budget priorities for the space program but soon evolved into a philosophical discussion—often heated—about the priorities and direction of the space program. (The text below is edited—for the full transcript, see page 278.)

President Kennedy: Do you think this program is the top-priority program of the Agency?

James Webb: No, sir, I do not. I think it is one of the top-priority programs, but I think it's very important to recognize . . . [that] several scientific disciplines that are very powerful . . . converge on this area.

Kennedy: Jim, I think it is the top priority. I think we ought to have that very clear. Some of these other programs can slip six months, or nine months, and nothing strategic is gonna happen . . . But this is important for political reasons—international political reasons. This is, whether we like it or not, in a sense a race. If we get second to the moon, it's nice, but it's like being second any time. So that if we're second by six months, because we didn't give it the kind of priority, then of course that would be very serious. So I think we have to take the view that this is the top priority with us.

Everything that we do ought to really be tied into getting onto the moon ahead of the Russians.

Webb: Why can't it be tied to preeminence in space—

Kennedy: Because, by God, we've been telling everybody we're preeminent in space for five years and nobody believes it . . . I do think we ought to get it really clear that . . . this is the top-priority program of the Agency, and one of the two things, except for defense, the top priority of the United States government.

Now, this may not change anything about that schedule, but at least we ought to be clear, otherwise we shouldn't be spending this kind of money because *I'm not that interested in space*. I think it's good; I think we ought to know about it; we're ready to spend reasonable amounts of money. But we're talking about these fantastic expenditures which wreck our budget and all these other domestic programs, and the only justification for it . . . to do it in this time or fashion, is because we hope to beat them and demonstrate that starting behind, as we did by a couple years, by God, we passed them.

After a little more back and forth, Kennedy excused himself and left the Cabinet Room, but the others remained for a discussion that revealed Webb's own concerns about the management and direction of NASA.

Webb: Now, let me make one thing very, very clear. The real success of this program and what it does for this administration in terms of prestige and for the country in terms of a position of preeminence is going to depend not so much on these target dates but how this program is run.

David Bell: I don't think that the president or any of us has any illusions about that. We all think it's being run very well.

Webb: Well, it's not being run *too* well!

Bell: You're improving it every day.

Webb: We're running fast and trying to stay ahead.

Bell: But . . . none of this should be interpreted as a challenge to the basic management.

Webb: All I'm trying to say is, Dave, that we are running about three steps ahead of a pack of hounds. And we have got some real vulnerabilities to validate the capacity to do this thing which is almost beyond the possible anyhow.

Bell: That's perfectly clear. But our problem is that we all work for the president, and as far as he's concerned, as he very clearly expressed this morning . . . the manned lunar landing program is the number-one-priority program.

Webb: I fought tooth and toenail here to avoid this implication that . . . we are just a one-purpose agency going to the moon. And I hate to see that.

Nine days later, Webb complied with Kennedy's request by sending a detailed letter that described NASA's priorities—with the moon program, of course, being number one—but with a strong endorsement that the rest of NASA's agenda was not only important to establishing the U.S. program as "preeminent in space" but also included key programs that would affect the success of a lunar landing, including among many others, research on crew safety, guidance, and topography.

Webb's letter convinced Kennedy. The moon program would continue as scheduled, with no additional push for an earlier date.

"Ultimately, Kennedy agreed with Webb on all of his major points," said historian Dwayne Day. "By the summer of 1963, he also publicly agreed that America sought to become preeminent in all important aspects of the space program."

But Kennedy would never fully appreciate the broad benefits that would come to the nation as a result of a full-fledged lunar program—that by advocating spending on space, he was creating a new infrastructure for technology inventiveness and increased support for education that would strengthen the nation's place in the world, perhaps even more effectively and with longer effects than the lunar program itself could sustain.

"Kennedy's reasons for America going into space were entirely based on the need to protect America's national security interests," said Dallek. "He had little interest in space for its scientific value—although he certainly understood why others felt strongly about this—but he didn't consider a strong connection between the space program and long-term benefits for the country, other than the jobs it would create. He saw the science that was gathered only as a benefit to speed the moon program along.

"The one who saw it was Lyndon Johnson," said Dallek, "because Johnson could see how the space program would create intellectual and economic benefits that would open a new era for the American economy. But at the moment, Kennedy was opening the door, giving Americans a sense of beginning to become a new progressive nation, especially in terms of technology. This perception would become enormously important to the nation."

But was it all worth it? Critics of the space program asked—with plenty of justification given the number of domestic priorities in need—why should America spend billions on space, just to beat the Soviets to the moon, as a tool to impress other nations of America's primary position on the planet? And others would ask, why not spend the same money on foreign aid?

The political objectives of the space program might have been handled by venturing down other paths—such as huge increases in foreign aid—but those avenues were no guarantee of success either, and writing checks all over the world would not have created a unifying national goal and knowledge-building at home.

Kennedy's misgivings about the budget for space no doubt continued for the rest of his short life. But he also recognized the undeniable realities of working with the legislative branch of government on money matters: one of the hard facts of congressional dealings is gaining the momentum needed for multibillion-dollar commitments of federal dollars to cover years of funding for new programs that do not directly involve war or urgent national security.

As the National Defense Education Act in 1958 demonstrated, even improving education for millions of young Americans—a seemingly obvious priority—had been politically impossible until defense became part of the issue. For the new president to go to Congress and ask for billions to change the world would have been politically unfeasible.

"I partly agree with those who said these enormous financial resources—tens of billions of dollars in 1960s currency before it was over—may have been better devoted to combating our own planet's ills and helping our own country's poor," said Sorensen, even though he had led the group that encouraged Kennedy to propose the lunar mission.

But, Sorensen also said, "I do not believe for a moment that those billions would have been approved by Congress for compassionate purposes, nor do I believe that Congress would have voted for the many less dramatic science programs proposed as alternatives by many scientists. The moon shot was the making of America's superiority in space and all the scientific, diplomatic, and national security benefits that followed."

With the goal for the moon landing set by Kennedy, the Mercury program unfolded with a new and focused purpose, moving through six missions for the single-astronaut spacecraft that would serve as the prelude to the two-person Gemini missions—10 manned missions for the two-person spacecraft that would test many of the methods that would be needed for the Apollo flights, especially the complex docking maneuvers that would be required for Apollo.

The seven original Mercury astronauts—along with Shepard, Virgil "Gus" Grissom, John Glenn, Walter Schirra, Gordon Cooper, Scott Carpenter, and Deke Slayton—were national celebrities from the moment they were announced in April 1959, claimed as heroes before they had the opportunity to achieve heroic feats.

The astronauts were kept on a constant regimen of training and publicity. To keep morale high among rocket builders and engineers during the high-pressure grind of manufacturing, astronauts frequently visited the production plants, meeting with staff, keeping up spirits, and creating an in-person reminder of the importance of their work.

After the two suborbital flights by Shepard and Grissom, the Mercury spacecraft was shifted to an Atlas booster—a larger and far more powerful rocket—for the orbital missions (Gemini would launch aboard the Titan rocket). Both the Atlas and Titan were proven military vehicles originally designed to carry nuclear weapons; Eisenhower's fears about the crossover of military and civilian rockets were long forgotten.

On May 15, 1963, astronaut Gordon Cooper became the last American ever launched into space alone, completing 22 orbits—more than triple the previous best in the Mercury program—a successful finale of the Mercury program. Because Mercury was originally planned in the Eisenhower era with no specific follow-up program, there was an 11-month lag until Gemini could gear up with two unmanned missions.

After two unmanned test missions, Gemini III began the most aggressive period in the history of the American manned space program. Beginning with Gemini III on March 23, 1965, and concluding with Gemini XII on November 11, 1966, NASA launched 10 manned missions in 19 months, in a compressed schedule to test many of the skills and tools needed for the Apollo flights, such as docking and the rigors of long-duration flights (the round trip to the moon would require up to a 13-day mission).

And while the Gemini missions proceeded, the Saturn program was gearing up for its first test manned mission in January 1967. The evolution of American progress had been astonishing.

"In 10 short years," said space historian Roger Bilstein, "the builders of Saturn progressed from the small, single-engine rockets like Redstone to the giant vehicle with clustered engines that [would] put man on the moon."

And even though in 1965 the Saturn V was still in its development stages, at that point there was every reason to think that America would not only reach the moon by Kennedy's deadline but would complete it with more than a year to spare.

8

NO CHOICE BUT TO BE PIONEERS

"There was just so much we didn't know."

—Joe Garvin, director of the lunar module program,
Grumman Aircraft

Beginning in 1961, and continuing for the next eight years, the Apollo program would become an endless series of ventures into the unknown—thousands of individual questions without precedent, and answers that came with the expectation that the solution would lead to yet another problem.

Kennedy, in one of the rarely replayed passages of his Rice University speech, outlined the extent of the challenge: "We shall send to the moon, 240,000 miles away . . . a giant rocket more than 300 feet tall . . . made of new metal alloys, some of which have not yet been invented . . . capable of withstanding heat and stresses several times more than have ever been experienced . . . fitted together with a precision better than the finest watch . . . carrying all the equipment needed for propulsion, guidance, control, communications, food and survival, on an untried mission, to an unknown celestial body . . . and then return it safely to earth . . . re-entering the atmosphere at speeds of over 25,000 miles per hour . . . causing heat about half that of the temperature of the sun . . . and do all this, and do it right, and do it first before this decade is out. Then we must be bold."

Bold indeed. The mission to the moon would require the largest rocket ever designed—a mammoth three-stage vehicle, 363 feet tall and weighing 6.5 million pounds on the launch pad, comparable in weight, as von Braun liked to say, to a medium-size navy cruiser. The scope of the attempt was staggering: compared to the previous manned U.S. missions, the Saturn V rocket for the Apollo program was a behemoth—three times bigger and five times more powerful than its next-largest cousin. The five F-1 engines in the first stage of the Saturn V on liftoff would produce 7.7 million pounds of thrust—more than 160 million horsepower—as they burned almost 30,000 pounds of fuel per second.

The Saturn V was the most complex mechanical device yet created, some 3 million parts comprising 700,000 components that not only had to function properly but also had to work in perfect harmony and be timed to the millisecond (as examples of the precise synchronization that is visible on the exterior of the rocket, watch close-up footage on YouTube of the Apollo launches, which shows the rocket still attached to hoses, cables, and gantries until the merest fraction of a second before the Saturn V started to rise).

The project would test every level of the American engineering and technology sector: dozens of main contractors, hundreds of subcontractors, thousands of suppliers, and more than 400,000 people in both the government and private sectors, all working toward a single objective. The Saturn V rocket would become the pinnacle of America's 20th-century achievement in technology, but it was the peak by necessity; for all involved, there was no overstating the point that only perfection would ensure success.

With such technical complexity in close proximity to more than five million pounds of propellant composed of refined kerosene and liquid oxygen, the Saturn V was the riskiest flying object imaginable. Sitting in the command module above the launch pad, the three astronauts were strapped to the top of a pillar of fuel with the explosive potential of 4,000 pounds of TNT. A launch failure like the Vanguard explosion would have produced a fireball the size of a skyscraper larger than any building in Florida.

And it was not too far-fetched to consider that a single faulty bolt might cause a potentially lethal mission failure; in 1968, the flight of Apollo 6 (an unmanned test mission critical to the program schedule) was nearly cut short when two engines in the second stage shut down. The primary issue with the J-2 engines was precisely the type of seemingly minor issue that creates nightmares for rocket scientists: the flight was almost aborted because a small flexible fuel line slightly thicker than a drinking straw broke; for the next launch, a stiff pipe solved the problem.

With so much at stake, the primary components on Apollo were built with redundant or backup systems. But even so, 99.9 percent reliability of 3 million parts still meant the potential failure of thousands of components.

"We all recognized that if any one of the major components could not be perfected, then we weren't going to the moon," said North American engineer Jerry Blackburn. "They had to work."

What did it take to build a rocket that could take three men to the moon and back? The question represented thousands of obstacles in 1961—an endless and growing list of issues involving mechanical engineering, physics, materials science, thermal properties, vibration, propulsion systems, and computer systems, to name just a few.

"At the start of the lunar program," said historian Peter Westwick, "there were unknowns about almost every aspect of space flight. The scope of the challenges in the Apollo mission was remarkable. By 1961, NASA had already produced some successes with its satellite projects and the early Mercury missions, but they paled in comparison to the challenge of flying to the moon, landing on the surface, and then returning to Earth."

On top of the other issues, add the even more confounding problem of including humans in the mix and the difficulty of ensuring that three astronauts have the life support required to survive for up to two weeks in the vacuum of space. (For more on the spectrum of issues involving the creation of the Saturn V, see page 86.)

"There was just so much we didn't know," said Joe Garvin, director of the lunar module program at Grumman from 1961 to 1971.

And the deadline—"before this decade was out"—brought with it an additional pressure: with so many unique problems to solve and new components to develop from scratch, the overall goal required the completion of thousands of independent deadlines, all in a long chain and with each main deadline dependent on many other smaller ones.

As a result, each primary system of the Saturn V, such as the individual rocket stages, the command module, the lunar module, and many others, could not be finished until all the components—in some cases parts produced by thousands of individual manufacturers—came together, step by step. In the rush to maintain the production schedule, the Saturn V represented the most intricate jigsaw puzzle imaginable. But in this puzzle, each piece required the successful assembly of the piece next to it before it could be assembled.

The technical challenges of the mission were compounded by the logistical problem known to any vendor who solicits federal business: low bids win contracts.

A story that has long circulated in NASA circles—possibly apocryphal and sometimes told citing a different astronaut but nevertheless accurate in sentiment—recalled that when reporters asked Alan Shepard what he thought about as he sat atop the Redstone rocket, waiting hours for liftoff, he replied, "All I could think of was that every part of this ship was built by the lowest bidder."

As a result, the Saturn V was constructed by dozens of major manufacturers who bid successfully, many of them concentrated in southern

California, but others located in cities scattered across the country. For instance, the Saturn V started life as a design by von Braun's team at the Marshall Spaceflight Center in Huntsville, Alabama, but the massive first stage was constructed by Chrysler (later Boeing) at the Michoud Assembly Facility in Louisiana. The second and third stage were built in California: the second stage by North American Aviation in Seal Beach and the third stage just down the road in Huntington Beach at Douglas Aircraft.

Twenty-five miles inland, the command module was constructed by North American at its facility in Downey; farther north in the San Fernando Valley, the 11 main engines needed for the three Saturn V stages were produced by Rocketdyne in Canoga Park. Meanwhile, across the country in Long Island, New York, work on the lunar module was underway at Grumman Aviation.

Beyond all the other issues, the greatest impediment to success of the Apollo program was the pressure—the unrelenting crush of work, the ceaseless drive to push ahead that was needed to maintain the project schedule for launch in the 1960s. The problem was particularly acute at NASA; suppliers, at least, had provisions for overtime pay and mandatory annual leave for some levels of staff. Within the NASA program management, however, for many staff 100-hour work weeks were not uncommon, seven-day schedules were routine, and vacations were almost nonexistent for years.

The strain on personal relationships was widespread at NASA. The personal cost of Apollo would be measured in hundreds of failed marriages or broken families.

"The level of personal commitment to the mission was almost unbelievable," said Westwick. "The toll on relationships was relentless, with many families that rarely saw their spouses or parents. The personal sacrifices by workers on the Apollo mission represent a lesser-known cost of the program."

The pressure took on many other forms, not least of which were the many conflicts among the high-powered personalities within NASA. In spite of the "all systems are go" culture that NASA presented publicly, in 1961, the most fundamental questions about the moon mission were laden with uncertainty; resolving the issues would reveal bitter turf wars and deep divisions.

Perhaps the most important decision of all was the most fundamental question about how the moon mission would work. Years earlier, the natural assumption among many within NASA was that when the time eventually came for a lunar landing, the vehicle to do the job would mirror every science-fiction vision of how a spacecraft should look and function: a giant, slim rocket—like an overgrown V-2—that would launch from Earth, and all or part of it would fly to the moon, land tail first, and then blast back to Earth.

It was a plan filled with pitfalls—not least of which was the tremendous amount of fuel required for the round trip as well as such incidentals as how astronauts would descend 100 feet or more from the spacecraft to the ground. Another alternative would have involved two rockets with parts for a vehicle that would rendezvous while in orbit around the Earth.

John Houbolt, an engineer at Langley, had other ideas.

"They were going to send a vehicle the size of a 100-foot rocket to the moon with absolutely zero help and land it backwards," Houbolt recalled in 2008. "I said, 'It cannot be done.'"

Houbolt lobbied for another method—a single rocket with several stages that would boost the crew into Earth's orbit and start them on their journey to the moon with two small spacecraft: a main capsule to carry the crew and a lander that would make the descent to the surface. The lander would then launch from the surface and dock with the main ship for the return trip to Earth, with the lander ultimately left behind.

The concept was called "lunar-orbit rendezvous." It was not a new idea, having been first suggested in 1916 by Russian scientist Yuri Kondratyuk and later considered by von Braun's own mentor, Hermann Oberth. But in the late 1950s, von Braun preferred the direct method, as did most of the NASA leadership.

Although engineers in the Space Task Group had earlier studied—and rejected—the lunar-orbit rendezvous concept, Houbolt felt there was no other workable choice. And Houbolt—whose actual job was studying rendezvous methods for future space stations—was speaking up about an issue outside of his field, further diluting his credibility in the silo-driven structure that often governed thinking at NASA.

Houbolt may not have been the most tactful of advocates, but he had the data to make his case. Nevertheless, the reaction to his research among others at NASA was harsh and ugly.

"His figures lie," shouted Max Faget, designer of the Mercury spacecraft at a gathering of NASA engineers and administrators. "He doesn't know what he's talking about." Said another angry engineer, "Houbolt has a scheme that has a 50 percent chance of getting a man to the moon and a 1 percent chance of getting him back."

But Houbolt pushed and pushed, and then—after creating reports on the feasibility of lunar-orbit rendezvous with the data to back it up, which were read and rejected—pushed some more.

"Houbolt didn't say it was one way," said Langley engineer Bob Causey. "He didn't say it was the best way; he said it was the only way."

Why did so many within NASA resist Houbolt's ideas?

"The only thing I can come up with," recalled Houbolt, "is the syndrome of 'NIH'—not invented here."

Houbolt wrote directly to associate administrator Robert Seamans twice, and he would not let up, beginning his second attempt—the week before Kennedy's Urgent National Needs speech—by saying, "Somewhat as a voice in the wilderness, I would like to pass on a few thoughts that have been of deep concern to me over recent months."

Houbolt finally got Seamans's ear.

"I had to meet with this guy," remembered Seamans, "to get him off my back."

But by then, the hidebound Eisenhower leadership at NASA was departing, and new thinking was coming into the agency. At last, Houbolt's proposal was taken seriously.

By some estimates, more than 1 million staff hours and three years of analysis had gone into reviewing the options for planning the mission. But von Braun, eventually realizing that Houbolt's method was the only viable option, surprised his own team by endorsing the recommendation, and in 1962 Webb made the choice to go with the lunar-orbit rendezvous.

In hindsight, the decision was critical to the mission's success.

"Had the lunar-orbit rendezvous mode not been chosen," said George Low, who would be NASA administrator at the time of the moon landings, "Apollo would not have succeeded."

The decision was perhaps the most important of the mission. But there would be many more weighty decisions to come, as NASA carefully inched forward.

The major hurdles showed up early in the program. Three months after Kennedy's Urgent National Needs speech, NASA awarded the first contract of the moon mission for a project that was at the top of the list of "must-function" components: the computer that would provide guidance, navigation, and control for the voyage.

Computers were not new in 1962; IBM, Scientific Data Systems, and other companies were already building computers to run, among many jobs, accounting for industry and calculations for academics. What was new was the idea of shrinking some of that processing power from devices that filled a large room into a lightweight component that could fit into a briefcase.

But NASA's usual computer contractors such as IBM were not chosen to design the Apollo guidance computer; instead, the contract was awarded to an unexpected source: the Draper Instrumentation Laboratory at MIT, chosen for its 30-year track record in developing instrumentation for navigating and tracking aircraft.

The Apollo guidance computer—known at NASA as AGC, would be the first computer to use integrated circuits for processing. But each computer would also require information storage. The method available at the time used a process so physically complicated that in retrospect it seems implausible that it could have worked: information was stored in "rope memory," the technique of recording data within the patterns of thin wire threads that are hand-woven through tiny magnetic cores.

While by 1962 standards, rope memory could contain large amounts of information in a small space, the technique was a mind-numbingly complex method of data storage. Teams of women used long needles to hand-weave thousands of feet of wire as thin as sewing thread into hundreds of tiny holes in the magnetic cores. (See plate 8.)

"The supervisors responsible for overseeing the careful integration of changes and additions to the software were known as 'rope mothers,' regardless of their actual gender," said David Brock, writing for the Institute for Electrical and Electronics Engineers.

However, the administrator ultimately responsible for the rope mothers was, in fact, a woman: Margaret Hamilton, who had been a programmer developing air-defense systems, moved to the Apollo project, and became director of the software engineering division at the Draper Lab. (See plate 9.) For her work on Apollo, and for representing "that generation of unsung women who helped send humankind into space," Hamilton received the Presidential Medal of Freedom from President Barack Obama in 2016.

"From my own perspective, the software experience itself—designing it, developing it, evolving it, watching it perform, and learning from it for future systems—was at least as exciting as the events surrounding the mission," Hamilton said. "There was no second chance. We knew that. Coming up with solutions and new ideas was an adventure. Dedication and commitment were a given. Mutual respect was across the board. Because software was a mystery—a 'black box'—upper management gave us total freedom and trust. We had to find a way and we did. Looking back, we were the luckiest people in the world; there was no choice but to be pioneers."

The result of the wire weaving was a maze of metal threads and cores attached to metal frames that were loaded into cases called modules. Each frame could contain as many as 512 cores woven with a half-mile of wire. Fortunately for the sanity of the rope mothers and their teams, the even more complex wiring required to link the modules to each other could be completed with machines. The full code developed by Hamilton's team is now available to anyone (see page 279).

The process was not only detailed but also meant that no changes could be made in the information stored in the rope memory without rewiring a module. And there was no margin of error either; a single thread woven in the wrong direction meant reweaving was required.

Each moon flight would carry two 70-pound computers for routine use: one in the command module and the other in the lander (a separate computer mounted in an instrument ring at the top of the third stage governed the Saturn V from launch into orbit). An additional backup computer was aboard but was not used except for an emergency abort during a landing attempt.

Today, questions about the power of the Apollo computer continue to rank among the most popular questions asked by visitors to the Kennedy Space Center (for *the* most common question about the Apollo mission, see page 90). While the performance of the Apollo guidance computer cannot be matched directly to today's computers, comparing some of the physical characteristics from then and now shows just how limited the computer resources actually were.

Each Apollo guidance computer was capable of roughly the processing performance of the earliest personal computers that would become available in the early 1980s, such as the Apple II or Commodore 64; a typical coffeemaker today has more computing firepower than the Apollo spacecraft.

More impressive, though, is comparing the hardware. The Apollo computer contained the equivalent of 12,300 transistors; an Xbox One game console, which debuted 50 years later, has 5 *billion* transistors. A basic Android phone with 16 gigabytes of memory has almost 8 million times the storage of the Apollo computer; that single phone has more computing power than the entire two-story computing center for the Apollo mission.

With such restricted computing assets, the question then became how to use every scrap of the data storage resources.

"It's difficult for most people who are not computer engineers or assembly language programmers to imagine how you could do anything with such limited resources," said historian Paul Shillito.

As primitive as this early computing technology may seem now, the builders had no choice. The Apollo guidance computer had barely the computing capability required for the mission. Creating a more advanced system would have required years of delay or hundreds of pounds of additional equipment. The computer needs for Apollo stretched to the limit.

The challenges of onboard computing would test the NASA staff for the duration of the Apollo missions. Eventually the decision was made to use the land-based IBM computers for course calculations and then send them to the command module computers.

The onboard computers had to be capable of working on their own in case the link to Earth was broken. And there was no option other than the independent use of the computer on the lunar module; because of the lag in communication caused by the 1.5-second delay in transmitting signals from Earth to lunar orbit, the computer on the lunar module had to be operated from the craft. And as with everything else on board, it had to work; without the onboard computers functioning properly, the spacecraft would be adrift and helpless.

Just the physical act of building some components was a study in contrasts; for those delicate components that were constructed in clean rooms, technicians who bathed infrequently were preferred because of the reduced risk of contamination caused by flaking skin. At North American Aviation in surfing-crazed Seal Beach, when new materials were needed to create a thin honeycomb layer of insulation for the second stage of the Saturn V, the company turned to local surfboard makers who used the same material.

"They did a great job," said project engineer Donald Binns of the surfing fabricators. "The only downside was when the surf was up, there was a big absentee problem."

For young engineers, the Apollo program was an opportunity beyond any expectations; the average age of a flight engineer in Houston was 26. Just as young were many engineers involved in design and production: for instance, Saverio "Sonny" Morea, who in the mid-1950s had worked as a novice engineer with the von Braun team while serving in the army, continued at Marshall in civilian life. When development of the Saturn rocket began, Morea—still in his twenties—was named project manager for the program to develop the F-1 engine. Morea would later assume other key roles, including managing the fixes needed for the J-2 engine from the second stage when problems surfaced during Apollo 6, and then moving on to direct the development of the lunar rover vehicle—all before he was 35.

Every step of the mission produced new questions and surprising answers. One of the most basic: How to make a spacesuit that could survive the rigors of space, protect the astronaut, and still be flexible enough to be used in a working environment? Would it look like spacesuits in the movies or comic books? Who would, or could, make them?

The answer was seemingly the unlikeliest of sources: International Latex Corporation in Dover, Delaware, best known for manufacturing Playtex bras and girdles, produced the model A7L spacesuits for the astronauts of Apollo. Using 11 layers of material, a team of seamstresses often required three months to produce a single suit. Staff supervisors—always alert for the tiniest hole that would kill an astronaut in the vacuum of space—would allocate pins, one at a time, for workers to use only while sewing and then return them to a central repository.

And the most important issue of all—and decades later, still the most popular question asked by wide-eyed youngsters visiting space museums: How do astronauts in space go to the bathroom? For Alan Shepard on the first Mercury mission, the seemingly endless delays for his 15-minute flight that led to an overwhelming need to urinate made the answer easy: *just go*—which Shepard did, shorting out sensors in his spacesuit but causing no further damage. However, for the orbital missions for Mercury and Gemini that involved more time in space, and for the even-longer Apollo missions, the answer was less obvious.

The unglamorous, yet vital, responsibility for developing "waste management systems" went to a team led by Don Rethke, an experimental engineer at Hamilton Standard in Connecticut. Known to his colleagues as "Dr. Flush," Rethke would point out to inquiring minds that at the time of the Apollo program, "there was no cosmic commode." For solid waste collection, the solution to a 20th-century problem required a timeless solution: a system of plastic bags secured with tape.

The bag system was generally effective, but as the description on the display of a waste bag (unused) at the National Air and Space Museum discretely points out, the system was "far from perfect." More than once on missions, the system did not work as effectively as had been hoped; in the weightlessness of space, astronauts could be heard trying to capture a "floating turd" that had unexpectedly become a mission priority.

The system of liquid waste was simpler, requiring only a condom-and-tube arrangement similar to systems used for patients in long surgeries. However, the condom system revealed the macho nature of the astronauts; when the condom sizes were originally designated as small, medium, or large, all the astronauts, regardless of their actual physical features, chose large, with the mismatch producing messy results. Only when NASA changed the sizing to large, gigantic, and humongous did most of the astronauts accept the inevitable and select large.

"'Large' still worked," said Rethke with a smile.

❦

Planning the mission accounted for every practical precaution to protect the astronauts, but during construction, there was little about the Saturn V that was not dangerous—its components were a maze of wires, chemicals, solvents, pumps, and gases.

The Saturn V was like a high-tech version of the Amazon jungle—for those who did not use caution, almost any part of it could kill or maim.

The components and chemicals used in a Saturn V could freeze, deafen, deform, or vaporize anyone who was in the wrong place at the wrong time. For example, in testing or launch, the five F-1 engines in Saturn's first stage could produce 220 decibels of sound; 150 decibels can rupture eardrums. Even a mile away from a test firing, the F-1s generated 135 decibels of sound—louder than standing on the deck of an aircraft carrier 50 feet from the takeoff of a navy jet—a sound level that can cause instant hearing damage.

For the lunar module, the required fuel was a horrifyingly caustic mixture of Aerozine 50 and nitrogen tetroxide, two chemicals so volatile that they ignite on contact to make a powerful rocket propellant—efficiency that was essential for the weight-critical lander.

Still used today as a rocket fuel, the chemicals are lethal. The list of warnings on the side of the fuel tanks reads like a catalogue of human disaster: besides being flammable (of course) and corrosive, they are carcinogens that will damage the liver, blood, kidneys, skin, eyes, and nervous system, and are reproductive toxins as well. Five parts per million will rot human lungs. With no surprise, the tanks are also identified as "highly toxic."

But the practical concern about the fuel for the lunar module was its corrosive properties. The mixture is so destructive that the engines installed in each lunar module could not be fully tested with fuel in advance; the final assembly would not be fired at all until the mission itself, when two men in the lunar module were betting their lives on their operation.

"The first time these engines would have been fired would be when they were fired on their mission," said Lynn Radcliffe, manager of the White Sands test facility for Grumman from 1963 to 1967. "They had to be perfect."

The lunar module itself was a risk-laden venture. A spindly, fragile-looking craft with an aluminum shell the thickness of three layers of the metal of a soft-drink can, the first time astronauts would fly the lunar module in an actual landing would be on the descent to the moon.

The astronauts trained to fly the craft for hundreds of hours in a flight simulator, but for real-life operations, they had to use test vehicles, the first of which was called the lunar landing research vehicle. A frame of tubes laden with fuel and a motor, nicknamed the "flying bedstead," the craft was ungainly. Two of them crashed during testing, nearly taking the pilots with them (including Neil Armstrong); only last-second ejections a few hundred feet from the ground saved the pilots from a death in flames.

A successor, the lunar landing training vehicle, was somewhat more stable (only one failed, with pilot Joe Algranti ejecting a half-second before the crash).

Years later, Armstrong said the trainers did "an excellent job of factually capturing the handling characteristics of the lunar module." But all involved had to wonder: Would the real lunar module be any better? The Apollo crews would not know for certain until they were descending to the moon.

⚬⚮⚬

Each element of the Apollo program demonstrated how every question became a chain of problems and solutions: working a problem would produce a solution, which then led to another problem and more solutions, and on and on.

Consider one example of a single issue that created a series of unprecedented problems and solutions, the first question being, where should the Saturn V rocket be assembled and housed before launch? In Florida, with a climate that ranges from swamp heat to hurricane-force winds, outdoor assembly was not feasible. To put together the Saturn V stages and Apollo spacecraft—in mission terms, the "stack integration"—NASA constructed the Vehicle Assembly Building, which was completed in 1966.

Built by Morrison-Knudsen, an Idaho-based company that had participated in the construction of Hoover Dam and the San Francisco–Oakland Bay Bridge, the 526-foot-tall Vehicle Assembly Building was, still is, and probably always will be the most voluminous single-story building on Earth; it is capable of holding the Statue of Liberty inside with 220 feet overhead to spare and could easily fit the field at Yankee Stadium on top of its eight-acre roof. The interior is so voluminous that the building can generate its own weather; on especially humid days, rain clouds form near the roof—a problem kept under control by 10,000 tons of air-conditioning equipment.

But when fully assembled—rather, stack integrated—the Saturn V was still more than three miles from Launch Pad 39A (or 39B for Apollo 10); how to get it to the launching site? Moving the 6.2-million-pound rocket in its upright position to Launch Pad 39A required yet another goliath of engineering: the launch vehicle crawler-transporter, a huge movable platform on which the Saturn V sat, along with the launch umbilical tower and the mobile launch platform that held the stack.

Created by the Marion Power Shovel Company of Ohio—a principal supplier for equipment used to excavate the Panama Canal—the crawler-transporter featured a 90-feet-square deck, a platform the size of a baseball infield that had more than enough room for the Saturn V and accessories.

The crawler-transporter was driven by eight bulldozer-style tracks, but each of these tracks alone, at 41 feet long, was longer than a conventional bulldozer. The tracks were driven by electricity generated by the vehicle's two 2,750-horsepower engines that together burned 150 gallons per mile, or .007 mpg.

The crawler-transporter moved slowly and carefully but nevertheless required yet another mission-critical solution: How to ensure that the Saturn V was stable on the journey to the launch pad, its thousands of fragile components remaining absolutely vertical and jolt-free? The solution was stabilizers built into the crawler-transporter that gave new meaning to the word "level." The Saturn V was maintained in vertical position so carefully that the tip of the escape rocket atop the spacecraft more than 360 feet above the platform base never wavered by more than a foot.

Then, how would the crawler-transporter move across the Florida marshlands? With a combined weight of more than 16 million pounds, the crawler carrying the Saturn V, tower, and platform would crush even the strongest conventionally paved road. The answer was the construction of a purpose-built route—the "Crawlerway." The two-lane road surface—one lane for each side of the tractors—extended from the Vehicle Assembly Building to Launch Pads 39A and 39B.

To support the tremendous weight, the Crawlerway was constructed with four layers a total of nearly eight feet thick, starting with a base of compact fill that was topped with select fill and crushed stone and then overlaid with a four-inch layer of smooth river gravel from Tennessee (yet another state thus involved in the Apollo program), a material chosen for its antispark properties.

Such adventures in colossal engineering were not glamorous elements of the lunar mission, but they were innovations—some still in use today—that were vital to the success of Apollo.

9

GO

"If we die, we want people to accept it. We are in a risky business and we hope that if anything happens to us it will not delay the program. The conquest of space is worth the risk of life."

—Gus Grissom, after the Gemini III mission, March 1965

November 9, 1967
Cape Kennedy, Launch Pad 39A
6:55 a.m.

To NASA, 1967 was the most demanding year in the agency's history. The previous year of flight with the Gemini spacecraft had proceeded with great success: five orbital flights had verified the ability of spacecraft to dock in orbit and confirmed the physical endurance required for a trip to the moon and back. During the flight of Gemini XIII, the final mission of the project, the spacecraft docked with a test Agena target vehicle while astronaut Buzz Aldrin set a record for an "extravehicular activity"—a spacewalk that lasted five and a half hours.

NASA was ready to proceed with the Apollo program, which was set to begin in February 1967. Veterans Ed White and Gus Grissom, along with rookie Roger Chaffee, were scheduled to fly the Apollo command module aboard a Saturn 1-B rocket—at 223 feet tall, much smaller than the Saturn V that would make the journey to the moon—to test the spacecraft and its service module in Earth orbit.

But in January, luck ran out.

The unyielding pressure and the myriad unknowns in the program caught up with the mission: during a routine test of Apollo's internal power, with the three astronauts closed inside the spacecraft and pure oxygen pumped into the cabin filled with volatile fabrics and fluids, something went wrong: a spark—probably caused by faulty wiring, but no one would ever learn for certain its actual source—was accelerated by the pure oxygen, flashing into a raging fire in a few seconds. The cumbersome hatch—a frequent complaint of the astronauts—could not be opened fast enough from the inside; in moments, Grissom, White, and Chaffee were dead.

The astronauts and the engineers who supported them knew the inherent risks of flight testing; many had seen pilots die in crashes. But Apollo 1 was different: that three astronauts were killed in a spacecraft sitting idle on the pad, with nearby ground crew unable to reach them, was almost beyond comprehension.

The fire was especially traumatic because all involved—especially the astronauts—knew that the command module was an accident waiting to happen.

At a meeting in August 1966 between the astronauts and program manager Joseph Shea, the crew had described the issues: too much flammable material in the spacecraft, the unsolved issue of the door, and a host of other problems with the design and workmanship. The concerns were nothing new, but nevertheless, Shea—with a close eye on the calendar—approved the command module for flight.

A few days later, when posing for their official crew portrait with a model of the command module, Grissom, White, and Chaffee asked for an additional image: the trio bowed their heads with closed eyes in mock prayer over the model (see plate 6). The astronauts sent the photo to Shea with an inscription: "It isn't that we don't trust you, Joe, but this time we've decided to go over your head."

The astronauts continued their preparations for Apollo 1, working with the unshaken confidence that test pilots maintain, hoping that their belief in the mission and faith in their ground-based colleagues would carry them through.

"If we die, we want people to accept it," Grissom had said in 1965 at the time of the first Gemini mission. "We are in a risky business and we hope that if anything happens to us it will not delay the program. The conquest of space is worth the risk of life."

The fire produced other casualties. For many engineers, Apollo 1 became the breaking point; they departed the project for engineering jobs with less at stake. Shea became dependent on drugs and alcohol and never fully recovered from his guilt about the fire; he was shifted to Washington and resigned from NASA six months later.

Formal investigations by Congress and NASA's internal review followed quickly—along with the inevitable finger pointing: NASA accused North American of shoddy workmanship; the company shot back with accusations about program management and unrealistic expectations. But the reality was that everyone was to blame; the three astronauts were victims of the mission itself and its crushing schedule.

"We had taken too much for granted," said Gene Kranz, Apollo flight director.

It was time to do it right. The reviews produced 125 recommendations for revisions to the command module: reinforced joints for fluid lines, fire-resistant Velcro fasteners, nonflammable cooling liquid, flame-retardant paper for onboard flight documents, and on and on. The engineers worked the problem; the result was a better, smarter, safer spacecraft. But the modifications would take time; manned missions were delayed by 20 months.

The wiggle room that some had seen in Kennedy's original declaration, "before the decade is out" (does that mean the end of 1969 or 1970?), had long disappeared; to everyone involved, the deadline meant 1969.

And so the program—and the pressure—continued, but now with an undercurrent of sharp new awareness about Apollo and its cost in lives. Apollo 4 (so designated in a revised numbering scheme) was scheduled to launch in late 1967 as an unmanned first test of the Saturn V. To maintain the pace, Apollo 4 would need to be an "all-up" mission, a test of all the rocket stages and the spacecraft as well (an original Apollo 1 would be used, with some modifications). The launch would be the first time that the massive first and second stages had ever flown.

The test would determine if the Saturn V was ready for a mission to the moon and whether the program would succeed or fail.

⸙

On November 4, 1967, at 6:58 a.m., Apollo 4 was two minutes from launch—a Saturn V ready to fly for the first time. Jack King, the "voice of Apollo" at Kennedy Space Center, in his crisp Boston accent, read down the countdown for Apollo 4 as the nation watched.

"All the launch support operations look well at this time with 90 seconds and counting. . . . Our status board still shows we are Go at this time."

Across the country, tens of thousands of engineers, technicians, designers, and contractors who had devoted their careers, most of their personal lives, and much of their sanity to the project were watching the progress of the launch.

"Everyone who had made contributions to the program—we were all flying with Apollo 4 that morning," said engineer Jerry Blackburn.

"At 50 seconds and counting, we have transferred to internal power . . . the transfer is satisfactory. The 6.2-million-pound Saturn V launch vehicle now on its own power at 38 seconds and counting."

Bill Lucas, director of the Propulsion Lab at Marshall, was following the countdown, saying, "I think this is okay. It has to be."

"Stages reporting ready to launch . . . T minus 15, 14, 13, 12, 11, 10, 9 . . . ignition sequence starts . . . "

At 8.9 seconds before launch, inside the first stage the giant turbo pumps roared to life, forcing 15 tons per second of RP-1 fuel and liquid oxygen into the F-1 engines.

"Five, four . . . "

A sequence of automatic operations triggered ignition, and the five engines fired instantly, in two seconds generating 7.5 million pounds of thrust—160 million horsepower—as flames blasted out of the nozzles.

"We have ignition . . . all engines are running . . . "

High above the launch pad, a blizzard was falling, as giant sheets of ice—caked on the skin of the Saturn V because of the super-cooled liquid oxygen within—shed off and tumbled in a storm, vaporizing in the growing inferno below.

A sequence of procedures started with perfect precision, all designed to occur in the milliseconds before launch: the umbilical hoses and cords ripped from connectors on each stage, the eight gantries swung away, the giant hold-down arms securing the rocket slammed back, and Saturn V was loose, for a fraction of a second rising so gradually that many onlookers thought it was the prelude to a fall to the pad and a massive fireball.

"What's wrong—it's never gonna go," shouted Lucas. "C'mon—go, go, go, *go* . . . "

Lucas, and thousands of others, lived a lifetime in a moment. And then in two seconds, Apollo 4 was rising.

"We have liftoff . . . we have liftoff at 7 a.m. Eastern Standard Time!"

Over the intercom and King's excited shouts, the flight team in the control room could be heard cheering.

In the predawn darkness of California, project engineer Donald Binns was yelling, "It's working, it's working, it's working!"

The previous Mercury and Gemini launches had been colorful visual shows but nothing as overwhelming as this. The warnings to onlookers and the media about the force and power of the Saturn V were wildly underestimated; the F-1 engines shot smoke and flame for thousands of feet in every direction as the rocket rose. Saturn V was a spectacular brute, climbing slowly through a flood of fire.

"The tower has been cleared. The tower has been cleared."

Four hundred feet above the pad and 10 seconds into the flight, the Saturn V was already 300,000 pounds lighter. As Apollo 4 rose, the gush of flame below it extended almost 800 feet—more than twice as long as the rocket was tall.

"We were all just transfixed," remembered instrumentation engineer Frank DeMattis.

In the CBS Broadcast Center, the structure shook so violently that Walter Cronkite and producer Jeff Gralnick held up their huge viewing window to keep it from falling. The normally reserved Cronkite was shouting with excitement as ceiling tiles fell around him while Apollo 4 climbed.

"My golly, the building is shaking here—the building is shaking!" Cronkite yelled above the building rattle. "It's terrific—the building is shaking! This big blast window is shaking, we're holding it with our hands! Look at that rocket go! The roar is terrific! Look at it go!"

For the closest spectators about three miles away, the launch was visually stunning but silent—for 20 seconds. Then the sound and shock wave flashed across the wetlands, shaking the ground with earthquake force and punching the spectators like a blow to the chest.

"The sound was so crushing that it felt like it was inside of you," remembered Blackburn.

The thousands of onlookers stood in awe, all heads moving upward as Apollo 4 thundered higher and farther down range.

And then, in little more than a minute, the rocket was flying out of sight, leaving behind a vapor trail high in the sky and a fading rumble that soon diminished into silence.

In less than two minutes, the Saturn V was accelerating past 6,000 miles per hour. Two minutes and 48 seconds after liftoff and 42 miles high, the massive first stage was jettisoned, the F-1 engines flaring out, their extraordinary job now done, as the five J-2 engines in the second stage fired to life. Apollo 4 was streaking across the Atlantic and on its way to its first orbit.

The Saturn V was a success.

Apollo 4 splashed down in the Pacific 8 hours and 37 minutes later, the mission a triumph. The Saturn V had achieved all its goals, demonstrating that the giant rocket was ready for a series of launches to prepare for an ultimate step to a moon landing. The setbacks and tragedy of the last 11 months would be remembered, but the goal was now again in sight. NASA had two years to go until the deadline.

⸙

On January 22, 1968, Apollo 5—a smaller Saturn 1B—would perform as well as its predecessor, carrying the still-unperfected lunar module for testing during an 11-hour mission. On April 4, the program had a modest setback with Apollo 6, the final unmanned mission, with vibrations at launch and performance problems with two of the second-stage engines— the problems described earlier about a broken fuel line—but the mission was still a partial success.

The issues were fixed in time for Apollo 7 on October 11, a Saturn 1B that would carry astronauts for the first time—this mission a 10-day journey in Earth's orbit—giving NASA the confidence to attempt a mission around, but not yet landing on, the moon. The program continued from then on with the Saturn V.

On December 21, 1968, Apollo 8 launched carrying astronauts Frank Borman, Jim Lovell, and Bill Anders—the first humans to leave Earth's orbit and enter outer space to travel around the moon.

At the end of a year of tragedy on many fronts—riots, escalating war in Vietnam, and the assassination of Martin Luther King Jr. and Robert Kennedy—with the journey of Apollo 8, Americans began to personally appreciate the nation's ventures into space, during the most emotional moment of the program. On Christmas Eve, the command module orbited 60 miles above the moon, its television camera pointed at the surface. As the spacecraft approached the lunar sunrise, Anders said, "The crew of Apollo 8 has a message that we would like to send to you."

With millions watching close-up images of the moon, Anders's voice crackled through with the first lines of the Old Testament—the Book of Genesis.

"In the beginning, God created the heaven and the Earth," Anders read. "And the Earth was without form, and void; and darkness was upon the face of the deep."

Lovell and Borman in turn continued the reading, with Borman concluding, "And from the crew of Apollo 8, we close with good night, good luck, a Merry Christmas and God bless all of you—all of you on the good Earth."

Forty years later, John Noble Wilford, science writer for the *New York Times*, remembered the moment. "My father and other ministers, priests, and rabbis never read the Scripture to a more rapt audience," Wilford recalled. "This message, truly from on high, was like a gift of hope: There is still beauty to behold, still an aspiration to goodness and greatness.

"Those who believe in other gods, or no god at all, shared in the spirit of the moment, its solemnity and its evocation of wonder."

Apollo 8 also broadcast grainy TV images of Earth; for the first time, humans saw video of their planet from space. On the return of Apollo 8, NASA released a color photograph taken by Anders of Earth as the planet rose over the lunar horizon (see plate 10). Informally titled *Earthrise*, the photograph showed Earth as a bright, blue, cloud-shrouded orb, radiant in the blackness of space—a vivid, eye-opening tribute to humanity's only home.

"It was ironic that we had come to study the moon," said Anders, "and it was really discovering the Earth."

Photographer Galen Rowell would later call *Earthrise* "the most influential environmental photograph ever taken." Four decades after Apollo 8, historian Robert Poole described *Earthrise* as a landmark moment in the growing awareness of the global environment.

"It is possible," said Poole, "to see that *Earthrise* marked the tipping point, the moment when the sense of the space age flipped from what it meant for space to what it means for Earth."

On Christmas Day 1968, poet Archibald MacLeish described the views from Apollo 8: "To see the Earth as it truly is, small and blue and beautiful in that eternal silence where it floats, is to see ourselves as riders on the Earth together."

⚮

The final year before the deadline began with the March 13 launch of Apollo 9 for a 10-day mission in Earth's orbit that tested the complete spacecraft, with the command module and lunar module docked. Two months later, Apollo 10 flew in a full dress rehearsal of a moon landing, orbiting the moon, docking, and releasing the lunar module to fly tantalizingly close—less than 10 miles—from the lunar surface.

With the success of Apollo 10, the U.S. space program was as ready as it could be for a mission to land on the moon. Apollo 11 would proceed with launch in July 1969.

10

A MAGNIFICENT SIGHT

"This has been far more than three men on a mission to the moon. More still, than the efforts of a government and industry team; more, even, than the efforts of one nation. We feel that this stands as a symbol of the insatiable curiosity of all mankind to explore the unknown."

—Buzz Aldrin

Tranquility Base, the Moon
July 21, 1969
02:56:15 Universal Time Coordinated (Greenwich Mean Time)*

Two men walked on the moon, and the world stopped.

Apollo 11 had been yet another perfect launch for Saturn V. Mitch Evans and more than 1 million spectators on the shore of the Indian River lagoon, along with hundreds of representatives of some 70 countries and 5,000 reporters, watched the Saturn V take off within two seconds of its scheduled launch time.

Astronauts Neil Armstrong, Edwin "Buzz" Aldrin, and Michael Collins enjoyed a perfect flight in their command module named Columbia (for *Columbiad*, the huge cannon shell that carried fictional 19th-century space travelers in Jules Verne's *From the Earth to the Moon*). Stowed away below the service module was their lunar module, nicknamed Eagle.

On one of the legs of Eagle was a plaque that would be uncovered by Armstrong when he reached the lunar surface. Below two drawings of Earth, the plaque was inscribed:

---

*Because there are no time zones in space, this chapter uses UTC time—also known as Greenwich Mean Time—for all notations.

HERE MEN FROM THE PLANET EARTH
FIRST SET FOOT UPON THE MOON
JULY 1969, A.D.
WE CAME IN PEACE FOR ALL MANKIND

On the flight, Armstrong carried with him pieces of fabric and wood from the Wright brothers' 1903 flyer; he also had an astronaut pin that would have flown aboard Apollo 1.

After the 76-hour journey to the moon, the docked command module and lunar module established lunar orbit. Twenty-four hours later, the lunar module broke away and departed for the surface. Then, in a 2-hour-and-45-minute descent that seemed to take days, Armstrong searched for a suitable landing location, rejecting the original site until—with less than 30 seconds of fuel remaining—he found a flatter location on the dark, basaltic plain on the Sea of Tranquility (as viewed from Earth, in the upper right quarter of the moon).

And then, 102 hours and 45 minutes into the mission, the call came from Neil Armstrong: "Tranquility base here—the Eagle has landed."

"Roger, Tranquility, we copy you on the ground," came the reply from Charles Duke, astronaut and spacecraft communicator during the landing. "You got a bunch of guys about to turn blue. We're breathing again. Thanks a lot."

In Mission Control, the tension was overwhelmed by joy.

"All hell broke loose in Mission Control," remembered flight director Christopher Kraft, "cheering and waving small American flags, handshakes all around, complete pandemonium from people who had held it in and did their jobs in the face of historic stress."

In the Bronx, where the Yankees were playing the Washington Senators, a message went up on the scoreboard, "They're on the moon," as the game was halted for a moment of silence followed by singing "America the Beautiful."

Newspapers published a photo taken in front of Neil Armstrong's home with the moon overhead.

And at a community center on the North Carolina coast, a group of friends in their late seventies—high school classmates from the early years of the 20th century—watched the two men on the moon as they remembered when another pair of aviation pioneers, Orville and Wilbur Wright, came to the windswept dunes nearby 66 years earlier to become the first to fly.

"For millions, the concerns of men on earth remained undwarfed by the accomplishments of mankind in space," wrote reporter Lawrence

Van Gelder, "when personal cares stood suspended and all hopes and fears seemed to focus on the Sea of Tranquility."

In spite of the delays, the pressure, and the extraordinary demands of creating the most technically rigorous experiment in history, the nation had responded to Kennedy's challenge: eight years and two months after the declaration to Congress, 400,000 people across the country and three astronauts in Apollo 11 had succeeded in landing on the moon—with five months to spare.

❦

Armstrong and Aldrin required almost six hours to thoroughly check and test their life support systems in preparation for their walk on the moon. Then Armstrong wiggled through the hatch and started down the ladder on the lunar module's leg. Armstrong took care deploying equipment, including the TV camera that would broadcast his descent. He paused on one of the lander's footpads, and then at 2:56 a.m. on Monday, July 21, Coordinated Universal Time—11:56 p.m. the night before in New York, almost noon in New Delhi, or just before dawn in Moscow—he stepped onto the moon's surface, saying, "That's one small step for [a] man, one giant leap for mankind."

On small televisions at markets in India, on a giant screen for 150,000 in a park in Seoul, on radios in Norway as Laplanders herded reindeer under the nighttime arctic sun, in Australian courtrooms during recess, and at military bases in Vietnam—the world came together for two men on the moon.

"For a moment," recalled one reporter, "earthly concerns fell away."

In Moscow, Soviet citizens were photographed watching excerpts of the moon walk. Seemingly reluctant to acknowledge the inevitable, Soviet media buried the story late in broadcasts, but Russians were seen celebrating and congratulating Americans. "It's a great day!" said one Muscovite.

Some 600 million people—one-fifth of all people on Earth—watched the television broadcast of Armstrong and Aldrin walk on the moon, while millions more in less-developed areas listened on radio.

Said one moist-eyed viewer in front of a TV store in Boston, "Perhaps more than any other time in recent history, everyone on Earth was one people."

Later that night, in Arlington National Cemetery, where an eternal flame burned at the grave of John F. Kennedy, a visitor left a small bundle of flowers. Attached to the bouquet was a note: "Mr. President, the Eagle has landed."

But for some in America, life in this new chapter of the space age had to go on as usual.

"Moon or no moon," said cheese manufacturer Peter Maggio in Philadelphia, "we have to go on making cheese. After all, we can't turn the cows off."

And not all were celebrating; in Los Angeles, New York, and other large cities, antipoverty groups protested the expense of the moon program.

"The poor," said Manuel Aragon, director of the Economic and Youth Opportunities Agency, "will have no holiday from hunger. It is a hollow victory for the United States to win the space race, but fail in its efforts to train the unemployed, educate its young, or rebuild its cities."

And more than a few antiwar advocates pointed out the clash of values that Apollo represented for America. The tragic irony was impossible to ignore: the country that was advancing the cause of humanity on another world—the message attached to the leg of the lunar module said the astronauts "came in peace for all mankind"—was at the same time escalating a hopeless war in Asia.

After only a few minutes on the lunar surface, Armstrong completed perhaps the most prudent procedure of the Apollo program: with a specimen bag looped on a stick, Armstrong gathered a handful of the lunar soil and stowed it in a pocket in his suit; it was the just-in-case guarantee that if the crew needed to depart quickly in an emergency, they would have, at least, one bit of the moon to take home.

During their excursion on the lunar surface, the astronauts planted an American flag, collected almost 50 pounds of rocks and soil samples, shot dozens of photographs, and set up instruments to measure moonquakes and a laser ranging experiment to measure the ever-changing distance from the earth to the moon (an experiment that continues to this day). They also explored the smooth, powdery surface of the Sea of Tranquility; Aldrin ventured almost 200 feet from the lander, looking back to photograph the most isolated outpost ever known.

"Isn't that something?" said Aldrin as he stepped onto the surface. "Magnificent sight out there. Magnificent desolation."

Armstrong agreed. "It has a stark beauty all its own," he said, looking out over the lunar surface.

The astronauts left behind mementos for eternity: an olive branch made of gold, a mission patch from Apollo 1, and Soviet medals honoring two fallen fellow astronauts: Vladimir Komarov, who was killed in April

1967 during a reentry malfunction—the first human to die in a space flight—and Yuri Gagarin, the first astronaut in space and in orbit, who had died in March 1968 during a routine training jet flight.

Also placed on the surface were friendship messages from the four presidents involved in the space program (Eisenhower, Kennedy, Johnson, and Nixon) and leaders of countries around the world and lists of leadership in Congress and NASA. The messages, explained a NASA briefing document, were etched on a disk the size of a 50-cent piece made out of silicon—"a non-metallic chemical element found abundantly in nature and used widely in modern electronics."

After a little more than two hours exploring the lunar surface, Armstrong and Aldrin returned to the lunar module to prepare for the trip home. The exploration was brief, but it was a beginning; there would be more missions and longer excursions to come.

After twenty-one and a half hours on the moon, Armstrong pushed the button to ignite the never-before-fired ascent engine; it worked. In five hours, Armstrong and Aldrin rejoined Collins in the command module; six hours later, on July 22, Columbia left lunar orbit on the return voyage to Earth.

⟡

The mission insignia for Apollo was the only design created for an American space mission that did not feature the names of the astronauts. When planning for the first moon landing had begun, the crew decided that their individual names should not be included on the insignia so that the mission would, said Collins, "be representative of everyone who had worked toward a lunar landing."

On July 23, the last night before splashdown, the Apollo 11 crew sent their final television broadcast home, in which Collins commented: "The Saturn V rocket which put us in orbit is an incredibly complicated piece of machinery, every piece of which worked flawlessly . . . We have always had confidence that this equipment will work properly. All this is possible only through the blood, sweat, and tears of a number of people . . . All you see is the three of us, but beneath the surface are thousands and thousands of others, and to all of those, I would like to say, 'Thank you very much.'"

11

A SENSE OF POSSIBILITIES

"Somewhere, something incredible is waiting to be known."

—Sharon Begley, *Newsweek*

On a warm summer night in 1961, two months after Kennedy declared a mission to the moon as a national goal, presidential adviser Theodore Sorensen sat on the front steps of his home in Washington, staring up at the heavens, and wondered about the wisdom of creating a program to send humans to the moon.

"Was it really possible," Sorensen remembered thinking, "or was it all crazy?"

Sorensen, like President Kennedy, had continued to be troubled by the enormity of the cost of going to the moon; although he was one of those who had lobbied Kennedy most strongly to endorse a moon shot, Sorensen could not help but continue to think that perhaps the money could have been better spent.

"I partly agree with those who said these enormous financial resources—tens of billions of dollars in 1960s currency before it was over—may have been better devoted to combating our own planet's ills and helping our own country's poor," he would recall.

"The 'moon shot' was the making of America's superiority in space, and all the scientific, diplomatic, and national security benefits that followed."

But later, Sorensen believed the lunar program was worth the effort, as he would find greater value in the role of the space program in inspiring change on Earth.

"The most important test of President Kennedy's global greatness was not whether he could get a man to the moon and back but whether he could achieve peace on planet Earth," Sorensen said. "The lunar landing program, by accelerating and organizing our effort to avert the Soviet militarization of space, and by increasing the possibility of international scientific cooperation, including work with the Soviet Union, helped his efforts for peace."

Dwight Eisenhower's goal of eliminating rivalries within the U.S. military by creating a civilian agency had longer-term benefits that, during the Kennedy years and beyond, reinforced the global opinion of the United States as a peaceful, open nation committed to progress.

"As a civilian agency with a mandate to discover useful knowledge and disseminate it to the world," said science historian Matthew Hersch, "NASA stood in stark contrast to the secretive and quasi-military Soviet space program, which shielded its rockets, spacecraft, and cosmonauts from public view.

"By exploring space peacefully, in unarmed craft, and then showing the world its technology, its moon rocks, and its heroic personnel, the United States convinced much of the nonaligned world that America's vision for the future was superior, and that Americans could accomplish anything to which they devoted their energies."

In the end, the space race did not matter; by the late 1960s, the Soviet Union had given up trying to send astronauts to the moon. The Soviets maintained an active lunar program for years, but the manned element of their program petered out in the late 1960s when the development of their rockets and spacecraft stalled and then proved unworkable.

The Soviets expanded their robotic mission program to the moon, eventually completing successful landings of probes on the lunar surface. Among those missions was Luna 16, which became the first robotic probe to land on another celestial body and then return a sample to Earth; in September 1970, Luna 16 picked up 3.5 ounces of lunar soil from the Sea of Fertility, doing so after Apollo 11 and 12 had already done the same job with astronauts.

The Soviets' robot missions also included two robotic rovers—the first in November 1970 and the second in January 1973, which puttered around the lunar surface processing soil samples and transmitting thousands of images back to Earth.

In a one-horse race long before Apollo 11 launched, the United States continued its peaceful quest for the moon on behalf of humanity and the advancement of science. However, it was a mission for peace that for years would continue to clash with the heartbreak of the Vietnam War. On July 30, 1969, when the first photographs shot by the astronauts on the lunar surface were published on the front page of newspapers, they appeared side by side with coverage of President Nixon traveling to Vietnam to review the progress of the war that would not end.

⚬✖⚬

In the post-Apollo era, it became easy to tally the tangible by-products of the nation's journey to the moon, and there were many: the spin-off companies, the lasting economic benefit to communities across the country, and the new products—spin-offs as diverse as advances in solar cells, fire prevention fabric, medical monitoring, insulation, and freeze-dried food, among hundreds of others—that evolved as a result of the nation's journey to the moon.

The economic jolt provided by the space program produced a trail of benefits—not only for the results it achieved but also for the technical possibilities that it illuminated; for example, the process of creating the Apollo guidance computer, with its razor-thin margin of capabilities needed to support the moon missions, became a high-profile inspiration within the computer industry to create new generations of components that were more powerful, smaller, and cheaper.

And the country's growing needs for digital technology created a thriving market, and competition, in the creation of semiconductors and related hardware for the computing industry. U.S. government projects, primarily defense and space, were the world's largest purchasers of semiconductors—accounting for almost 70 percent of all sales—spurring production and shrinking prices. In 1962, the average price of a computer chip was $50; by 1973, the price had fallen to $0.63 cents. The path was clear for the emergence of new and cheaper types of computers that did not yet exist, including computers for individuals; soon to come were the first personal computers in the 1970s and 1980s—and the Internet was not far behind.

Beyond shrinking the costs of digital technology, Apollo proved to be a powerful catalyst for American enterprise long after the missions were over, with important links to the development of Silicon Valley and later the Internet.

"Many people point to guys working in their garages in the Silicon Valley as the starting point for the technology industries of the 1980s," said space historian Roger Launius. "But much of the innovation of that era had already come from scientists and engineers trained to work in the space program; after Apollo, these people dispersed and went everywhere—to companies, to universities, to think tanks—taking with them the knowledge they had gained from working on the space program.

"We saw a blossoming of technology in the 1970s," continued Launius, "that was in no small part the result of the base of knowledge that built up during the space program, and that was pushed by Apollo."

Equally important is the role of the space program in transforming how organizations make critical decisions: the concept of a "combat information center" that originated within the U.S. Navy was refined by NASA into "Mission Control," the central hub seen by generations of television viewers watching space missions and the classic image of a team of engineers riveted to their consoles, with information flowing to and from experts who pool their specialized knowledge to make command decisions. Mission control became the model for decision making at many levels of industry and government, from metropolitan emergency centers to police operations to industrial disasters.

Possibly the greatest value of Apollo to the future of America was the sudden, abrupt focus of technological inspiration needed to create the lunar mission; the largest financial outlay ever made by a peacetime nation played a pivotal role in creating a national core of science and technology—in the private sector, universities, and independent laboratories. The advancements of space have over the decades spread into a wide range of industries, including many enlightened enterprises that are both profitable and progressive, such as companies involved in precision medical equipment and alternative energy sources. And the development of the Internet itself was possible largely because of Americans' growth in technological leadership—progress that occurred in part because of the flourishing of the space program.

While one can also point to the growing needs of national defense as a catalyst for economic growth, it was the research and development across the spectrum of science required for Apollo, compressed from decades into a few years in the 1960s, that acted as a formidable accelerator in moving ahead the nation's capabilities at a breakneck speed.

But the enduring advances are less tangible, and also broader: it can be said that one of the most important benefits of America's programs in space was the transformation of how the nation thinks and learns. After World War II, the United States, pushed by people like Vannevar Bush, spawned a deliberate effort to build the long-term strength of the country—in war or peace—by changing the nature of the ways that America creates new knowledge and educates its citizens. That effort succeeded, and the space program was one of the early beneficiaries; today more people go to college and learn more in a broader range of disciplines than ever before.

The Apollo program was a success in its age, but to many it seems disheartening that the American space program no longer captures the emotions of the entire country as it did when astronauts first went to the moon in the summer of 1969. Yet it could also be said that superior achievement has truly found a place in the American culture when the feat becomes so commonplace that it is no longer noticed.

For instance, until 1957, no craft had orbited Earth in space until Sputnik stunned the world, and 12 years later astronauts walked on the moon to global acclaim; today, the world shares an international space station, corporate-owned satellites are launched on rockets that return to their launch pads in minutes, and private ventures are booking tickets for journeys into space to come; the miracles of one age become lasting successes where they seem routine in the next.

Yet perhaps most important of all, decades after the last astronaut departed the moon, is the sense of possibility that the Apollo program continues to inspire. For those intrigued by science, or simply by the lure of the unknown, the achievements of Apollo demonstrate the wonders to be discovered, the unknowns to explore, the obstacles to overcome—whether in space or on Earth.

"When we all think about our Earth in our post-Apollo age, by comparison with the moon, we see it as even more life-giving," wrote Jack Boyd in 2003, then 56 years after he first joined Ames. "Before Apollo, school kids imagined the Earth like a brown Mercator projection lined with political divisions. After Apollo, we envision the Earth—as first did the Apollo astronauts—as that fragile orb of interlaced green, blue, and white suspended in the black vastness of space, a frightening thin layer of atmosphere keeping it alive. Life on Earth now inspires even more wonderment."

COUNTERCULTURE

One Week of the Darkest and the Brightest

"The story of counterculture is the story of baby boomers."

—Ken Paulson, educator and columnist

In late December 1966, *Time* released its first publication for the coming new year, an issue that annually since 1927 has featured the magazine's "Man of the Year." The choice of Man of the Year goes, as *Time* reports, "to the person or idea or thing that, for better or worse, has done the most to influence the events of the year."

For most of the years that the Man of the Year had been awarded, the recipients had been individuals whose impact spanned the events of the 20th century, from Lindberg to Hitler to Churchill to Roosevelt, although in a couple of years the designation went to a group, such as Hungarian freedom fighters who battled in the country's 1956 uprising. But for 1966, the honor went, for the first time, to an entire generation: the *Time* Man of the Year for 1966 was those Americans under 25 years old—the young people in the United States who, the magazine reported, "had already shown they would remake the world."

"In the closing third of the 20th century," *Time* wrote, "that generation looms larger than all the exponential promises of science or technology: it will soon be the majority in charge.

"Never have the young been so assertive or so articulate, so well educated or so worldly," *Time* reported. "Predictably, they are a highly independent breed, and—to adult eyes—their independence has made them highly unpredictable. This is not just a new generation, but a new kind of generation."

A new kind of generation to be sure. The real impact of young people in America was just beginning to be heard, not only through the success of young Americans in the mainstream of life in the United States but also with even stronger voices in the counterculture that was developing across the country.

ᑫ⊗ᑐ

How does counterculture emerge? Books, college courses, and academic careers are built on exploring that question. But the most basic answer is that every culture produces countercultures—to challenge, to question, and to defy mainstream society.

In post–World War II America, issues and ideas—a rapidly expanding young population, growing questions about the personal values of the previous generation, and a host of social ills and injustices—converged to spawn a new counterculture: the moment was right for protest, change, and rebellion.

"Some of counterculture comes from the deep psychological needs of people to rebel, to create an identity," said MIT sociologist Gary Marx.

"An important factor had to do with the end of World War II—the triumphs, and the economic expansion," Marx continued. "Depression-era people had to struggle and were focused on obtaining some kind of economic security. Suddenly the next generation saw more affluence, and affluence meant that there was no need to struggle.

"Once you had that security," said Marx, "you had the leisure to engage in alternative kinds of ideas."

And in the 1960s there were more people to consider these ideas—an abrupt result of the baby boom after World War II. By the middle of the decade, there were nearly as many Americans under 25 as over 25. By 1970, 100 million Americans would be 25 or younger.

"The story of counterculture is the story of baby boomers," said Ken Paulson, dean of the College of Media and Entertainment at Middle Tennessee State and former editor of *USA Today*. "With baby boomers, you have a generation that for the first time didn't have to go to work at 16. They had far more free time and far more disposable income. They had discovered that by sheer numbers they can drive demand for the things they care about."

College also represented more time for reflection and discussion and increased opportunities to examine new ideas, question the status quo, and explore the unconventional to make a better world. In 1960s America, counterculture became a mix of social activism, environmental awareness, and expanding demands for civil rights, social equality, and the rights of women.

Counterculture of the 1960s not only represented activism about national issues but also could inspire rejection of social norms.

"There were at least two very distinct countercultures, especially here in California," said Stanford cultural historian Fred Turner. "One centered in Berkeley—the new left, doing politics to change politics; and the other centered in San Francisco—wanting to avoid politics, celebrating consciousness, psychedelia, and transformation of consciousness."

But overarching all other social issues and counterculture grievances was the war in Vietnam. American involvement in Vietnam had started in the mid-1950s, with support by advisers for South Vietnamese regimes against Communist incursion; that policy grew into full-scale military involvement by the early 1960s. Through four presidential administrations, as the United States become increasingly entangled in Southeast Asian affairs, Vietnam became a seemingly unsolvable political and strategic travesty. For growing numbers of Americans, it was a conflict with none of the clarity and noble mission of World War II, no end in sight, and progress measured only in terms of the growing death toll. By 1969, almost 50,000 Americans had died in Vietnam, and troop strength was at its highest: some 520,000 men and women. Everyone in America knew someone fighting in the war, or who had died in the war, or who might be drafted to fight in a country they did not know and for a cause they did not understand.

In the 1960s, college campuses became the focal points for dissent and protest. The free speech movement—which had developed at UC Berkeley in 1964 as a response to, of all things, the university's policies that restricted political activities on campus—took root as the first significant civil disobedience on college grounds; most other major universities would soon follow with their own protests.

With the rejection of mainstream social ideas came the casting off of many social conventions: the visible declarations of 1960s counterculture were obvious—suits and wingtips were replaced by jeans and sandals. Women rejected designer fashion for the natural look. Hair became the great indicator of male counterculture involvement: the crew cut—perhaps the most observable symbol of straitlaced American convention—was defied by long hair. And rejection of traditional escapism, such as alcohol, led to abuse of other drugs, in particular marijuana, and substances with more disturbing effects, especially psychoactive drugs.

And then there was the most tangible denunciation of all: complete rejection of society and dropping out entirely. The hippie living in a commune—although only a minor percentage of counterculture lifestyle choices—became the high-profile symbol of counterculture values.

But often lost in discussion of 1960s social clashes was the discontent experienced not only by the young but also by older generations—some of whom were frustrated, as in any era, by their own unmet expectations. But unlike dissatisfied Americans of previous decades, many adults in the 1960s were merely bystanders as young people found enlightened paths in a free-thinking counterculture that their parents did not understand and could not experience. Hostility within older generations toward the younger that seemed like disapproval was instead often resentment; the result was greater distance between the young and those who preceded them.

CBS News tried to make some sense out of the impact of counter-culture with a project called Generations Apart, an ambitious exploration of the generation gap as seen through national surveys and interviews with both young and older Americans. Hosted by reporter John Laurence, the results of the project were aired in three broadcasts in late May and June 1969. The results were a vivid reminder of the change experienced in America brought on by counterculture values and differences between the generations.

The episode of Generations Apart titled "A Profile in Dissent" was particularly hard-hitting and described how young people (17 to 23) and parent-age Americans viewed social change and political controversy.

"It is a time of dissent for many of America's young," said Laurence. "The collision of events that they could not control has caused a challenge to values they cannot accept."

"The majority are quiet as they always are, ready to conform as they always are," admitted Laurence. "But a growing minority is shaking up society and raising their voice. There is a swelling tide of dissent among the young in America today. It is surging up against some of the most basic institutions of adult society."

The survey showed a widening generation gap on a range of fundamental issues involving sex, religion, drugs, and money. The program's most startling finding was the broad rejection of the most basic ideals of middle-class values: 6 out of 10 young people said they want "something different in life" from what their parents wanted.

"Will they find the definitions for the 'something different' that they are searching for?" Laurence asked of a new generation of Americans. "Only the young can tell us. And maybe not even the young can say for sure how they are going to shape this society, until they are older."

The counterculture of the 1960s would continue to evolve into the early 1970s, but in 1969, two events in particular—only a week apart—would symbolize both the worst and the best of the era: the first demonstrated the tragic vulnerability of some who sought alternatives to mainstream America, and the second showcased the new generation at its best.

II

MANSON

August 8–10,[1] 1969: The Manson "Family" kills seven in Los Angeles

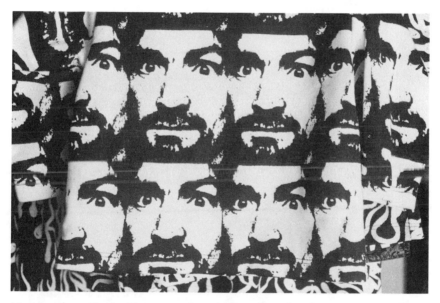

Mass murderer Charles Manson on dress fabric at Amoeba Boutique in the Haight-Ashbury district of San Francisco, 1994. Decades after the Tate-LaBianca murders, Manson's portrait remains an iconic image of the 1960s. PHOTOGRAPHY BY PAUL SOUDERS COPYRIGHT © PAUL SOUDERS | WORLDFOTO.

---

1. Note: Some accounts of Charles Manson include differing dates for the Tate-LaBianca murders because of the timing of the crimes. The killers who struck at the residence of Sharon Tate set out on Friday, August 8, but committed their crimes after midnight, making August 9 the official date of the murders. The same issue affects the second night; the killers started out for the crime site on Saturday, August 9, but the murders occurred after midnight on August 10.

12

LIKE MOTHS TO A FLAME

"How the hell did I brainwash 35 girls in less than a year? That's impossible. You're making me out to do the impossible. You don't understand you are making me a legend."

—Charles Manson, 1988

10050 Cielo Drive, Los Angeles
Saturday, August 9, 1969
9:15 a.m.

Sunset Boulevard unspools across Los Angeles in a twisting path that starts near downtown and ends at a parking lot on the Pacific Ocean—a 24 mile road that is a virtual driving tour of the cultures and industries that make up the city.

Any summer morning in August, Sunset Boulevard is busy in both directions, but two police cars had no trouble making their way east to Benedict Canyon Drive, where they headed north toward the hills. The neighborhood south of Sunset, with its large mansions and broad streets, was a sharp contrast from the north, where the roads soon narrowed, leading to many isolated, rural-in-the-city enclaves built against the foothills of LA that are described locally as "canyon living."

The patrol cars from the Los Angeles Police Department were responding to calls from residents who were trying to soothe a local housekeeper who had been screaming about discovering bodies and blood when she arrived for work at 10050 Cielo Drive, a snug, low house built in the French-country style that was common in the hilly neighborhoods. The first two officers on the scene questioned the housekeeper at a neighbor's house where she had run, then they went up to 10050.

They found a nightmare.

✽

All day Saturday, the news from Cielo Drive came in bursts of bulletins about the carnage. A body in a car, lying on the front seat. Two bodies strewn on the lawn, mutilated and so soaked in blood they were unrecognizable. Inside the house, a pregnant young woman with a rope around her neck and her body covered with stab wounds. Near her was the body of a man, shot, stabbed, and also soaked in blood. Written in blood on the front door was the word "pig."

Five dead. No explanation.

The police speculated that the August 9 murders of actress Sharon Tate, Abigail Folger, Jay Sebring, Steven Parent, and Wojciech Frykowski might be "ritualistic slayings." Perhaps the murders were somehow drug related— a deal gone bad. Or maybe there was a connection to one of the victims that would turn up in the investigation. But in any case, the police said, the circumstances of the crime seemed so unusual that it was almost certainly an isolated incident.

And then it happened again.

For weeks, the murder of seven on two nights in Los Angeles defied reason or explanation. And months later, when it became clear that the murders were the responsibility of a crazed career criminal leading a band of young drugged-out social rejects, the story seemed to confirm the worst fears of mainstream America about the evils of 1960s counterculture. But when the full story became clear of how Charles Manson created a distorted vision of race war, it would change forever how America viewed crime and murder.

✽

Charles Manson's life played out as a long trail of dysfunction, mostly of his own doing but all of it, as he would say his entire life, the fault of society and everyone around him.

Manson was born on November 12, 1934, just after the worst days of the Depression. His mother, Kathleen, was a petty thief and a drunk; his father disappeared when he learned Kathleen was pregnant. Much of the time Kathleen left Manson with friends and babysitters. She was imprisoned for a minor infraction when Manson was three, and he was sent to live with his aunt and uncle; it was the beginning of a childhood marked by temporary homes and family separation and later by minor crimes and arrests.

Manson's home life was anything but stable and loving, but many suffered worse in the prewar late-Depression years. Yet later in life, Manson would take any opportunity to shift responsibility for his actions away from himself and onto others—especially his mother, in many interviews calling her a prostitute (which she wasn't) and uncaring (she later dutifully followed him to some of his prison assignments to remain near). She would live long enough to see her son become a mass murderer.

"The only thing my mother taught me was that everything she said was a lie," Manson said, as he damned her with the ultimate responsibility for his lifetime of failure. "And I learned never to believe anyone about anything."

It was a pattern that Manson would exploit to explain his fate, and he absolved himself of responsibility by convincing others to do his dirty work—including killing for him.

"At six years old in the first grade, he was talking the girls in his class into beating up boys he didn't like," said Manson biographer Jeff Guinn. "Then when the principal came to ask Charlie, 'Why did you do that?' Charlie's response was, 'It wasn't me; they were doing what they wanted. You can't blame me for that.' The exact same defense he uses all those years later."

Such manipulation became the early stages of the mantra that Manson would chant the rest of his life—that society was to blame, and that he was a product of the jails and the brutality of incarceration. Manson never framed his life in terms of his own deeds, only in terms of the penalties exacted on him by others, saying (in various incarnations) statements like, "my father is the jailhouse. My father is your system."

While Kathleen was serving time for petty theft, Manson skipped school. Before he was 10, he was stealing from stores and his own family.

When Kathleen could no longer control Manson and was unable to place him in a foster home, she sent him to Gibault School for Boys, a Catholic-run institution for delinquents in Terre Haute, Indiana. Manson escaped and returned to her, but she sent him back. He stole a gun; at 13, he committed his first armed robbery. By 14, Manson was living on his own, little more than an animal, surviving on income from thievery.

From his early teen years, Manson's life could be tallied as a cycle of crime, jail, release, and jail again. Crossing state lines with stolen cars and a string of robberies made him a federal convict; at the National Training School for Boys, a social worker classified him as "aggressively antisocial."

After more time in a juvenile center, Manson was sent to Boys' Town, the legendary center in Indiana founded by Father Edward Flanagan to care for children by teaching self-support and social preparation. (Spencer Tracy won an Academy Award playing Flanagan in the 1938 film about the institution, called *Boys Town*.)

In 1949, Manson's enrollment at Boys' Town was a newsworthy event.

"Charles Manson, 14, a 'dead-end kid' who has lived in an emotional 'blind alley' most of his life, is happy today," reported the *Indianapolis News*. "He's going to Boys' Town." Manson told judge Joseph O. Hoffman, "I think I could be happy working around horses and animals. I like animals."

Boys' Town was—and is—a haven for wayward children who are willing to accept guidance to find their paths. But by that time, Manson was already finished as a redeemable member of society; he lasted four days at Boys' Town before escaping. The next 20 years would get worse.

Manson's crimes became more serious: more federal convictions and additional offenses even while in jail, including the attempted rape of an inmate. At 17, Manson had been described as "criminally sophisticated." Later, a prison report found that he had an "unstable personality." And yet Manson was returned to society again and again, each time escalating his crimes.

Marriage—first at 20 and again at 25—did nothing to temper him; Manson spent much of the 1950s in jail. By 1959, he had graduated to pimping and forging federal checks. After his arrest for violating federal probation, the penalty was particularly stiff: in 1961, he was sentenced to 10 years in the McNeil Island Federal Penitentiary in Washington state. The time in federal prison was not completely wasted; he learned to play the guitar to accompany himself as he sang. By the time of his 30th birthday—celebrated in jail—Manson had spent more than half of his life in confinement.

In June 1966, Manson was sent to Terminal Island near Los Angeles; in spite of his history as a repeat offender, he was eligible for early release. As his freedom drew near, for once Manson's judgment was sound: he supposedly pleaded for permission to stay inside, telling his jailers that prison had become his home. (The story may have been just another way for Manson to blame society for what he later did; in 1986, he told a reporter that once he was released from prison, his overwhelming priority was to stay out.) In March 1967, Manson was free again.

In another era, Manson might have continued the pattern of life as a petty habitual criminal who lived in a constant rotation of repeat offenses and detention. But in 1967, his jailers overlooked the deeper development of Manson's character; prison had served as the ideal training ground for Manson to hone his talent for manipulation, for refining his flexibility to adapt to any situation, and for polishing his skill in drawing people close by sizing up their strengths and weaknesses and capitalizing on both. Manson had developed the tools of a sociopath that were ideal to gather prey in the innocent counterculture lifestyle of the 1960s.

With nowhere else to go, Manson followed the advice of a friend from prison and headed north to San Francisco, then about to become the focal point of counterculture during the Summer of Love—that colorful celebration of youth, music, and drugs in the Haight-Ashbury district. By mid-July, more than 100,000 young people had come to "The Haight" that summer.

San Francisco, wrote Guinn, "always attracted those who didn't fit in anywhere else." It was the perfect destination for Manson.

"What we saw at its peak was literally thousands of flower children attracted to this movement—like moths to a flame," said David Smith, founder of the Haight Ashbury Free Clinics of San Francisco. "There was a philosophy here that was totally revolutionary that they had not heard, and this was the epicenter of it. A lot of very young, creative, exploring people came. But then you started to see a shift—where more disturbed, sicker, more drug-involved people started to come."

And taking on the trappings of counterculture California was simple.

"It was a scene," said Roger Smith, Manson's parole officer in San Francisco, "that if you grew your hair and talked the talk, you fit in."

At 33, Manson was older than the typical flower child but just mature enough to ensure the respect of the locals. Always malleable in a situation to suit his needs, Manson discarded his short-haired tough-guy look; in its place appeared shaggy longish hair and a short beard (see plate 12). Superficially, Manson looked like a hippie, but he shared none of the counterculture philosophy. Under the skin, he was a hunter—a diabolical, methodical wolf, welcomed into a flock of vulnerable sheep.

San Francisco in 1967 was the destination of many who were seeking a better way—a life of love, sharing, and caring through an alternative lifestyle. But it was also a destination for the dispossessed—the confused, the disenfranchised, the lonely looking for someone to listen and to understand—perfect prey for a seemingly sympathetic opportunist who was a shrewd judge of human frailty as he looked for sex, a roof over his head, and a place to plot his future as a musician bigger than the Beatles.

"Psychopaths are incredibly charming and persuasive," said David Wilson, professor of criminology at Birmingham City University. "To get you under control, to court you, they appear to give their complete and utter attention."

In San Francisco, Manson began his conquest step by step. A few weeks after his release from Terminal Island, he met Mary Brunner, a library assistant at UC Berkeley. Manson charmed his way into Brunner's home, gaining a place to live; within days, they were sleeping together. Brunner became the first inductee into Manson's circle, soon to be known as the

Family; together they traveled between Los Angeles and San Francisco, building their circle with new recruits, mostly young women who were estranged from their families, lacking focus, and desperately in need of sympathy, love, and someone to tell them all the answers—precisely the façade of contrived emotional connection that Manson would provide.

Manson, said Roger Smith, his parole officer in 1967, "was glib, he was superficial, and he was very adaptable."

And Manson was also deeply compelling. Although short, only five-foot-three, Manson had a captivating aura and a dark intense stare; a reporter during the murder trial would call it "mad Rasputin eyes." But it wasn't just his appearance that connected Manson to his Family members; unknown to them, he could identify the needs of his followers, peel away their pretenses, and create an instant and lasting rapport.

Among the first who Manson found in Haight-Ashbury was Susan Atkins, who in her teen years had been abandoned by her father. Adrift like many others, Atkins wound up in San Francisco that summer. Drawn to Manson as he played his guitar near the park, Atkins was soon part of Manson's circle.

While living in Manhattan Beach on a trip south, Manson met Patricia Krenwinkel, who had dropped out of college. Plain-looking and with low self-esteem, Krenwinkel was an easy mark for Manson, who sized her up and told her what she was hoping to hear.

"I felt really loved by him almost immediately," said Krenwinkel, "because at that point, I was really desperate for someone to care."

The Family grew, adding mostly women members.

Much later, Manson would, of course, again absolve himself of responsibility for creating a group that would do his bidding.

"How the hell did I brainwash 35 girls in less than a year?" he asked a reporter in 1988. "That's impossible. You're making me out to do the impossible. You don't understand you are making me a legend."

But in a counterculture age of love and peace that also sheltered the forlorn and marginalized, for Manson it was indeed possible. In every age there are the neglected, the confused, and the misunderstood who are looking for love and leadership, and no doubt Charles Manson would have been able to find them in any era. But as Manson's plans played out—his vision, his survival methods, his ability to draw together a clan, and then using drugs to draw his followers even tighter to him—he developed a brand of manipulation that was possible only in the unique circumstances of the 1960s, as he preyed on the innocents of the counterculture and transformed children into monsters.

13

MESMERIZED

"Your children would come to me, because they had never had anyone tell them the truth."

—Charles Manson, 2009

As lonely, disillusioned teenagers, Leslie Van Houten and Suzanne Cosgrove didn't know each other, but the patterns of their early lives were so closely matched that they could have been sisters. Van Houten and Cosgrove are less than a year apart in age, and as children they lived in some of the same neighborhoods. In their youth they experienced many of the same tragedies and traumas, and both would spend time within a prison—although for vastly different reasons. But the stories of Van Houten and Cosgrove explain much about how some lives were shaped in the 1960s and how far wrong they could go; one of them would become a killer while the other persevered.

Seeing Leslie Van Houten as a 15-year-old in 1964, it would have been hard to imagine that the smart, friendly high school beauty queen would, five years later, be holding down a near-lifeless Rosemary LaBianca and stabbing her 16 times in the back.

Van Houten's decline into murder began with family tragedy, drugs, disappointment, rejection, and lack of focus. But she might have been just another confused child of the 1960s, looking for the way ahead, had she not met Charles Manson.

Born in 1949 and raised in Altadena, a comfortable suburb of Pasadena, as a teenager Van Houten was a student at Monrovia High School and was twice elected homecoming queen. Her father was supportive, but her mother had expectations for her daughter that Van Houten could not meet.

"Other kids had curfews and they had consequences—if you stay out to 11, you're going to be grounded for three weeks," Van Houten said. "My mom would say: 'I don't have to do that because you will never let me down.' And so I felt that I always had to anticipate what her expectation was of me."

Van Houten's life began to crumble in 1964 when her parents divorced; without focus or the guidance she needed, her world began to shift toward drugs.

❧

As a child, Suzanne Cosgrove had a desperate prayer: that the gypsies would come to take her away.

Cosgrove was born in 1950, a year after Van Houten, and her family lived in Westchester, a suburb near the Los Angeles International Airport. After her parents divorced in 1963, Cosgrove lived with her mother in, among other places, Eagle Rock—a few minutes from the Van Houtens in Altadena.

"I was a daredevil as a little kid," Cosgrove said. "I would climb walls and trees, and made up a lot of stories—pirate ships and dinosaurs."

But even as a child, Cosgrove felt a disconnect at home.

"Even when I was five or six years old, I really didn't feel like I belonged with my parents," Cosgrove said. "I wanted gypsies to come for me."

The problem was simple but tragic: her father was an alcoholic, the child of blackout drunks. Even when Cosgrove's mother encouraged him to attend medical school, partly as a distraction, the drinking didn't stop.

"Beer was his drink," said Cosgrove. "I don't remember seeing him sober until late in his life. He was a controlled alcoholic, even after he graduated from medical school."

"There was also lots of alcohol on Mother's side of the family," said Cosgrove. "They were always actively drinking when we visited. They would fight, or wind up passed out on the front lawn—lots of 'drunk stuff.' I used to listen to them and say, 'I never want to be like that.'"

By then, Cosgrove had moved with her mother across Los Angeles to Redondo Beach, where she started at Mira Costa High School.

At Mira Costa, Cosgrove met Sheila Elkind, and together they worked on *La Otra Vista*, the school's underground newspaper. But because the paper was "subversive," the school would not allow them to use a room for their meetings. Instead, the staff met at Sheila's family home in Manhattan Beach.

"That's now I met the Elkinds," said Cosgrove, "by working on an underground newspaper."

Cosgrove and Elkind were involved in many of the counterculture adventures of the 1960s, even at one point creating their own political party: the Love Party. But for Cosgrove's mother, a conservative Republican, politics and her daughter did not mix. It was one of many rifts that would develop between them.

"I used to tell my mother that I was going to visit Sheila, but we were really going to antiwar demonstrations," recalled Cosgrove. "My mother was very conservative and didn't believe in it."

Her mother had remarried, and in Cosgrove's teen years, the divisions between them deepened.

"I was becoming less and less controllable—my mother and I would fight all the time," Cosgrove said. "She was always complaining about me. At one point I asked her for my dad's child support money so I could move out on my own and finish high school, but she refused."

For Cosgrove, there was no good alternative: her mother was also drinking. Moving in with her father—who was either never at home while in medical school or else drinking himself to sleep—was no help.

But unlike many marginalized youth, Cosgrove did not want to be on her own; she needed a family.

"All I really wanted was a home," said Cosgrove. "I wanted to run away because it wasn't a home. I was actively looking for a way out."

⚬⚮⚬

When Van Houten's parents separated, she perceived her family's status in the community began to change.

"I became someone who lived in a single-parent household, which in that community had its own stigma," said Van Houten. "My dad told me he was leaving before my mom knew, which caused real friction between us. I was very close to him and resented her.

"All of those events began to lead me to a different group of people in high school. And so I began to hang around the kids that were smoking marijuana."

At 15, Van Houten smoked her first marijuana cigarette at home; her brother was already an active user.

"I started because [of the] curiosity of it—being rebellious was part of it," she said. "I loved how I felt on it—I felt more relaxed inside. And I liked the bit of change in reality that it gave me—it made me feel complete."

Van Houten wanted more; her interest in marijuana led her to students at school who pointed her in the right direction. Eventually their mutual interest led to LSD. When she tried acid for the first time, she was with her boyfriend, staying with a group of older college kids with a common bond whom she described as being "single-parent, marginalized people."

"I lied to my mom that I was staying at a girlfriend's house," she recalled. "I liked hallucinations and the out-of-body experience. We would read Timothy Leary's books and the whole idea was to find our inner deep self."

But that search produced no answers. Life for Van Houten was a constant cycle of drugs; in addition to the marijuana and LSD, she was a regular diet pill user, taking Benzedrine while in school to keep awake. Van Houten's pattern—from marijuana to pills to LSD to social dropout—was a model of drug abuse in the 1960s, the typical scenario featured in grainy health films shown in school that were often hooted at by students but too often turned out to be true.

"The main reason for my running away was because of my participation in dropping acid," she said. "I started when I was about 16. At the beginning I was going to school and more or less living within the structure of society, but the more I dropped acid, the harder it was to relate to different people other than the people who were dropping acid. Hippies were migrating to areas where they felt comfortable being with one another."

There was other turmoil in Van Houten's life. She became pregnant by her boyfriend, Bobby Mackie; her father invited them to live with him and the baby. She had stopped using drugs while she was pregnant, but her mother insisted she get an abortion, which was illegal at the time. The fetus was placed in a can and buried in the backyard.

"The abortion really left me feeling broken and brokenhearted," she recalled.

But Van Houten did graduate from high school in 1967. She then moved in with her father and began attending a business college, studying to become a legal secretary. At that time her mother tried to rebuild their relationship, but her attempts failed.

"Mom and I would meet once a week. She was trying so desperately to rekindle some sort of a relationship, and I just was not going to have it."

Lonely and resentful, Van Houten started to use drugs again.

In San Francisco during the summer of 1968, a chance encounter shifted the course of Van Houten's life: she met Manson Family members Catherine Share and Bobby Beausoleil. Share told Van Houten of a man in Los Angeles who could help her find a path.

"I really needed someone to have the answers," said Van Houten, "and . . . I was told [by Catherine that] Manson had the answers."

Traveling with Share and Beausoleil would lead Van Houten to a visit at Spahn Movie Ranch, a dilapidated movie set of a western town on the outskirts of Los Angeles where the Family was squatting. There Van Houten met Charles Manson and his followers.

"They said, 'do you want to come with us? We live for the day. You have to drop out of society. We have a good life, and do you want to come with us?' And I said yes."

But for Van Houten, the primary draw was Manson himself.

"I was absolutely intrigued and mesmerized by Manson," Van Houten said. "I believed that he was someone very special and extraordinary. I was caught and mesmerized by his mind and the things he professed. I was an empty shell of a person that was filled up with Manson rhetoric."

In Van Houten, Manson could see a bright new recruit.

"Leslie Van Houten is an example of how people can be very normal," said author Rick Ross. "But all of us had vulnerabilities, and Manson could smell it."

The Family was, Van Houten recalled, "embracing, friendly . . . I felt I belonged."

Not long after her visit to the ranch, Van Houten came again. This time she stayed.

❦

At 16, Suzanne Cosgrove had no place to go, and remaining at home was not an option. But unlike Van Houten, Cosgrove found stability, love, and acceptance.

In desperation, Cosgrove had turned to her friend Sheila Elkind to see if somehow she could help.

"I asked a tough question," Cosgrove said. "I asked if I could live with them."

The Elkinds—Rockie and Chuck Elkind, and their daughters, Nanette, Julie, and the eldest, Sheila—were everything that Cosgrove's family was not: open, liberal, and welcoming to all. In the mid-1960s, a party at the Elkinds in Manhattan Beach was a memorable celebration, often attended by several generations of family, friends, and neighbors representing many levels of mainstream and counterculture alike.

Sheila asked her parents, and they agreed: Cosgrove moved in with the family. She would stay for a year and a half.

Without the Elkinds, Cosgrove could have easily followed the same type of path that had led Van Houten into the abyss of the Manson Family.

"The Elkinds threw me a lifesaver, and I hung on for dear life," said Cosgrove. "They saved me—all of them."

⚬✕⚬

By 1968, Manson and the Family were living on the fringes, staking a permanent claim at Spahn Ranch while also traveling at Manson's whim to other parts of California.

"Your children would come to me," Manson said in 2009, "because they had never had anyone tell them the truth."

By "tell them the truth," Manson meant he was spoon-feeding them his brand of sociopathic understanding that was, to his rudderless recruits, precisely what they needed to hear.

"This is fate," remembered Lynette "Squeaky" Fromme of her meeting with Manson in 1967. "Charlie is exactly what I'm looking for."

In late 1960s America, recruiting women was easy; there were many who had lost their way, stalled in life by rejection and lack of direction. Bringing in men was even easier; with a clan of women willing to do Manson's bidding, he would pimp his most attractive Family members—he called them "front-street girls"—who willingly offered themselves as bait to attract men into the group.

Manson's primary disciple was a man—a recruit later described as "Manson's best piece of work" in transforming human beings into drugged killers. Charles "Tex" Watson was an honor student and former high school football star who was drawn in by Manson's women; he would become Manson's number-one follower, the go-to accomplice who would transform Manson's commands into action—including at least nine murders.

At first, Spahn Ranch was a happy setting—almost a summer camp, with everything a team effort. The ranch was isolated enough for Manson's indoctrination but convenient to suburbia for scrounging and drug deals.

Everything became a group effort. To eat, they salvaged food from dumpsters; in an era before thousands of homeless roamed Los Angeles, it was easy to find clean and edible food just past its expiration date that was discarded by supermarkets in the nearby San Fernando Valley.

And as the Family grew, Manson programmed them with his own form of brainwashing: a combination of their blind loyalty mixed with drugs and doctrine Manson used to depersonalize and then re-form his followers, by some estimates administering 300 LSD trips in two years that wiped clean their emotional and psychological slates so they could be filled with his dogma.

"The more you take acid, the more you become lost in [it]," said Van Houten in 1977. "While you are on acid, the less you are able to relate to others. I became totally immersed in the acid reality—it's a fairy-tale world."

According to actor Peter Coyote, an active participant in San Francisco counterculture in the 1960s, "the shadow side of psychedelics is that you are nakedly innocent and vulnerable. Someone can weasel their way inside your mind and alter your perspective."

In the Family, there were no watches, no calendar, and no birthdays—nothing but the Family. Manson's disciples were not permitted to leave the ranch without permission. In the evenings, the Family members played "games"—actually drugged-up role playing that was shaping their personalities and distancing them from their pasts and from reality.

"Every day," said Van Houten, "was a different role so we would get more out of ourselves. There was a time when Manson said to us, 'baa like sheep,' and we all did."

"We would not be sympathetic to anyone being homesick," Van Houten recalled. "If someone thought that I was missing memories of my childhood or something like that, then I would be mocked."

Family followers were given new names to fit Manson's mold for them: Susan Atkins became Sadie Mae Glutz, Patricia Krenwinkel was Katie, and Leslie Van Houten was Lulu.

In less than two years, Manson would create more than two dozen new personalities, stripped clean of their old values and morality.

"He had a way with words," remembered Krenwinkel. "He could be completely unpredictable, and he'd use that in different ways. He would have each one of the people at the ranch thinking the way he wanted them to. And if someone needed a compliment to be dependent on him, he would compliment that person. If another person always wanted to be accepted, he would put them down so they would try harder to be accepted."

As for Manson's relationship with Van Houten in particular, his ability to size up people was perfectly in tune with her need to be accepted.

"For Manson, I was basically 'what's her name,'" Van Houten recalled. "I think he knew that the more he didn't know me, the more important it was for me to make sure I impressed him."

Manson would form circles of Family members, making them stand naked while he critiqued them.

"I felt humiliated," Van Houten said, "but instead of reading the humiliation as 'for God's sake, get out of here,' I read it as 'I have to let go of all of my ego.' Everything that could have indicated to me that I needed to get out of there, I couldn't interpret it that way. I was interpreting it as self-judgment. . . . Because I so desperately wanted to be what he envisioned us being. . . . An empty vessel of—of him."

How did Manson succeed so completely?

Said Krenwinkel, "I tried to think, 'did he have a super power, or was it something else?' I just think he was a really good con artist, and he didn't have that hard a material to con. When you have a lot of young children that are dropping acid all the time, their minds are like clay."

And, remembered Krenwinkel, at Family get-togethers, there was LSD for all but one: Krenwinkel recalled that Manson never took any himself.

After the drugs did their work, there were different forms of manipulation. Soon there was physical abuse; a few months after Van Houten arrived, a group LSD trip went awry when Manson ordered everyone to not move during the experience. When a woman nicknamed Bo stood up, Manson smashed a chair over her. For Van Houten, it was a signal.

"I would see these things and become very complacent," she said. "I didn't want to be hurt."

Van Houten tried to resist—once. She told Manson she wanted to leave, but again he read her perfectly. He drove her to the top of a hill and told her to jump, and then he left.

"To leave was to die," Van Houten remembered Manson saying. "And I held on to that and I'm sure when the guys came to get me, I felt my feet were in cement, that fear of what would wait for me by leaving the group was what kept me attached there."

But soon the games grew darker; Manson would tower over the Family, arms spread, simulating the crucifixion. "I am Jesus Christ," he would tell them in their drug-induced state. "Would you die for me?"

14

A CARNIVAL RIDE
TO THE APOCALYPSE

"The idea that those people were not safe just sent shock
waves through the country, and woke up the country to the
fact that there was an evil lurking in it and an evil beyond
what anybody imagined."

—Janet Maslin, *New York Times*

Woodland Hills, California
May 23, 1969
2:08 a.m.

K aren Daniels was just settling into bed when she heard a scratching
sound.

Karen lived with her husband, Alan, and their six-year-old twins,
Bobbie and Will, in a two-story tract house in Woodland Hills, a suburb of
Los Angeles in the San Fernando Valley. Alan, a manager for General Motors
at the company's massive car assembly plant across the valley in Van Nuys,
traveled frequently for the job; in her low-crime, suburban neighborhood,
Karen felt no concerns spending many nights on her own with her sons.

Karen heard the scratching sound again.

Are the twins awake? she thought. She walked down the hall to check
on the boys; they were motionless—for a change—and asleep. In the
hallway, the house seemed quiet. Karen stood for a moment at the top of
the stairs, heard nothing, and returned to her bedroom.

Back in bed, Karen leaned toward her nightstand in front of a slightly
ajar window and listened at the narrow opening. The scratching sound
had stopped; now Karen heard something outside—*was it girls whispering*

135

and giggling? Yes, she was sure of it. She relaxed; it had to be the neighbor's 14-year-old daughter, who was having a weekend sleepover with her cousins from Santa Barbara. Surely the sound was floating over from the downstairs family room as the girls talked into the night.

But the next morning when Karen came downstairs early, something about the house did not seem right. A naturally tidy person in an ongoing struggle against the mayhem left by the twins, she was constantly cleaning up. The house was neat, but even so, Karen still felt uneasy. The throw pillows were on the couch; *I thought they were on the recliner last night.* The candlesticks were on the mantle; *weren't those on the dining room table?* The throw rug on the oak floor in the living room, which she had vacuumed the afternoon before, had been straight and neat; now it was pushed offline and wrinkled. *Were Bobbie and Will playing in the living room while I was in the garage doing the laundry?*

In the kitchen, an empty cookie package was stuffed in the trash can. Karen tried to remember; *I thought there were five cookies left after I gave the boys their snack.* She would have to remind the twins—again—that they needed permission to have cookies.

On the kitchen table, Karen's purse had fallen over, her wallet inside. She checked the contents; everything seemed intact, but in the cash slot she found only a five-dollar bill. *Didn't I have a 10, too?*

Karen looked at the casement windows at the front of the house; everything seemed secure. The back door was locked—it did not have a bolt, just a simple turn button on the knob—but outside, the screen over the sliding window in the door seemed slightly ajar. A week before, Karen had seen a rat skittering on the roof across the street—rare in the neighborhood, but not unheard of. *Maybe the scratching sound was a rat trying to get through the screen?*

Karen shook her head; it all seemed strange, but she saw nothing specific that truly concerned her. She could call the police, but what could she tell them? Perhaps it was just her imagination.

What could possibly be wrong?

❧

The events that led up to the massacres of August 9 and 10 began with the decline of Manson's dreams of a musical career and the rise of his vision of the apocalypse.

The women of the Family were accustomed to not only bringing in new recruits but also trolling for locals who could be conned for cash or other largesse. A few months before Leslie Van Houten arrived in 1968, the Family hooked a big fish. When two of the women were "hitchhiking," they were picked up by Dennis Wilson, one of the founding members of the Beach Boys. Wilson took them home, and after an overnight fling, they left. Later, Wilson returned to his house to find Manson and much of the Family in residence.

Incredibly, Wilson let the Family stay; the lure of an endless supply of women was too enticing to resist. Wilson later told a British music reporter about his "guests," and the story appeared under the headline "I Live with 17 Girls."

In the article, Wilson described "a guy named Charlie who had recently come out of jail after 12 years.

"When I met him I found he had great musical ideas," said Wilson. "We're writing together now. He's dumb in some ways, but I accept his approach and have learned from him."

The payoff for Manson was the door Wilson opened to the Hollywood music scene and his dreams of a recording contract. Wilson introduced Manson to Terry Melcher, a music producer and son of actress Doris Day. Melcher took a tentative look at Manson's music and singing, but the producer, who worked with such rock luminaries as the Byrds and the Mamas and the Papas, knew that Manson's talent was not marketable.

"Manson had nothing that would make you notice him as a musician," said Guinn. "He had great personality, he had charisma, but in a recording studio where the music has to carry you, it wasn't there."

For the self-proclaimed guru who commanded instant loyalty from his followers, the rejection was unacceptable—especially after the Beach Boys recorded "Cease to Exist," a revised version of a song Manson wrote. The rejection would become the start of a slide that would lead to murder.

Manson, like many fringe personalities, needed only a trigger to send his life—and the lives of his followers—into permanent turmoil; the moment came on November 22, 1968, when the Beatles released the *White Album*. The two-disc set—in a bare white sleeve with only the words "The Beatles" embossed on the front—represents what many consider the group's most wide-ranging artistic expression, with conventional pop songs and abstract compilations of sound.

Manson saw the *White Album* as a personal revelation—every track had significance that could be interpreted by him alone. Especially important was the song titled "Helter Skelter." Written by Paul McCartney, "Helter Skelter" is a noisy blast of instruments and shouted lyrics; McCartney intended "Helter Skelter" to demonstrate that the Beatles could produce a raucous tune; to Manson, "Helter Skelter" was a message of armageddon.

In England, "helter skelter" is the description of a carnival ride, but Manson believed the name and the lyrics were a description of hell. From his idea of helter skelter, Manson blended his lifetime of antisocial behavior and hate into a crazed, distorted plan that would inspire a massive race war between blacks and whites, with Manson and his followers somehow emerging as leaders of a new society.

"This music is bringing on the revolution, the unorganized overthrow of the Establishment," Manson told *Rolling Stone* a few months after his arrest. "The Beatles know in the sense that the subconscious knows."

Manson's plan for helter skelter was grotesque nonsense, but for the Family members, manipulated by drugs and with new personalities molded by Manson, it was the message that would guide the next stage of the Family's downfall.

Everything began to change for the Family early in 1969. After a temporary move to Barker Ranch at the edge of Death Valley, the messages at the evening meetings shifted from love to revolution.

"Manson began to talk about that blacks had been suppressed and mistreated by the whites, and that karma was changing," Van Houten said, "and the blacks needed to rise up and that we needed to prepare for a revolution.

"He said that he was going to have to take the lead and show the blacks how it needed to be done."

By the spring of 1969, the Family's training had grown more disturbing.

"Manson said that during the revolution that we would see a lot of very ugly things," said Van Houten, "and that we needed to get our minds adjusted to fear because he turned everything into living in fear.

"When we were on LSD, he would begin to talk about gruesome images," Van Houten said. "And then he began to talk about killing."

The Family's extracurricular activities became more sinister: car theft, petty robbery, and a unique form of home invasion Manson called "creepy crawling," which involved a small group of Family members sneaking into an occupied home in middle-class suburbia late at night. During a creepy crawl, the invaders stole little but left behind subtle hints of their presence to jangle the residents, such as slightly moved furniture or stealing some (but not all) money in the house; the 2:00 a.m. invasion of the Daniels residence in Woodland Hills was a textbook example of a creepy crawl.

Creepy crawling may have seemed harmless enough, but it was early indoctrination in creating willingness to commit crime more serious than the occasional petty theft or dumpster diving.

"It was like war," said Van Houten. "We were going through combat training at the ranch."

At the same time, Manson's impatience and anger about his stalled music career continued to deepen. Resentful about not getting a recording deal he thought he deserved, in March Manson decided to confront Melcher at home—the house on Cielo Drive. But Melcher had moved; instead, Manson arrived during the middle of a party hosted by the new tenant: actress Sharon Tate. Manson was turned away at the door; angry and resentful, he would not forget the rejection—or the address.

In late July, the LA Sheriff's Department discovered the body of Gary Hinman, a music teacher and drug dealer, at his home in Topanga Canyon in the Santa Monica Mountains. The murder, a stabbing, looked like a drug deal gone bad, with one exception: written on the wall near the body, in Hinman's blood, were the words "political piggy." Next to the words was a crude drawing intended to look like a panther's paw—the symbol of the Black Panthers. It was Manson's attempt to "show the blacks how it's done": the time had come for helter skelter.

⁓∞⁓

Over the August 8 weekend, members of the Manson Family killed seven: five at Cielo Drive and two at the LaBianca residence in the Los Feliz district near Griffith Park.

On the first night, Manson picked Patricia Krenwinkel and Susan Atkins to accompany Charles "Tex" Watson on the trip along with Linda Kasabian, a relative newcomer to the Family. Cielo Drive was a convenient choice, in part because of its private location and also as payback for Manson being snubbed there at the Tate party. Watson, on orders from Manson, knew what to do; to the group, Manson said, "Leave a sign—something witchy." They would follow his orders—with words written in blood.

The next morning, the police counted 102 stab wounds among four victims, with the fifth (Steven Parent) shot in his car. On the front door of Cielo Drive, they found the word "pig" written in Sharon Tate's blood.

Van Houten's part in the madness came the next afternoon. Earlier in the day, she had learned about the murders from Krenwinkel.

"It was sad and tragic that violence had to occur," recalled Van Houten, "but I wasn't questioning that it had to occur.

"I knew that she had crossed over and fully committed to the cause. I knew that I wanted to go and commit to the cause, too. I believed in it, and I wanted to go."

That afternoon, Manson stopped Van Houten in front of a building at Spahn Ranch.

"He said, 'Are you crazy enough to believe in me?' And I said 'Yes, I am.' And so I was told to get a change of clothes."

The violent wrath unleashed at Cielo Drive was matched the next night by the brutal horror left inside the residence of Rosemary and Leno LaBianca on Waverly Drive in the Los Feliz district of Los Angeles east of Hollywood—the house chosen because Manson had once attended a party next door. Manson and Watson entered the house first, tying up the LaBiancas. Then Manson went back to the car.

"Manson came back and pulled out Pat and I," Van Houten remembered. "And he told us to do everything that Tex said to do. And, we went into the house."

Inside, Krenwinkel and Van Houten found Watson with the LaBiancas on the sofa, trussed and with pillowcases over their heads. Watson sent Van Houten and Krenwinkel into the kitchen for weapons; they came back with a knife.

Watson ordered Van Houten and Krenwinkel to take Rosemary into the bedroom. Van Houten did not hesitate, she said, "to prove my dedication to the revolution and what I knew would need to be done to have proved myself to Manson."

In the living room, Watson executed Leno with a bayonet, stabbing him 12 times before carving the word "war" into his torso.

"The sounds of Mr. LaBianca dying came into the bedroom . . . a slow, guttural sound," said Van Houten. "And Mrs. LaBianca jerked up and began to call out—'What are you doing? What are you doing to my husband?' And I tried to hold her down. Pat took the knife and went to stab her, and it hit her collarbone and bent. I ran into the doorway and I said, 'We can't kill her.' And Tex came in. At that point, I was just staring off into a den that was across from the bedroom door . . .

"Tex was killing her, and then he turned me around, handed me a knife, and said, 'Do something.'"

Van Houten stabbed Rosemary 16 times.

"I felt," Van Houten said, "that I had to be a good soldier."

Watson showered while Van Houten changed into some of Rosemary's clothes. On the wall of the living room, Krenwinkel, using Leno's blood, wrote "Death to Pigs" and "Healter Skelter" (misspelling the name of Manson's vision). Krenwinkel jabbed Leno's body with a carving fork 14 times, leaving him with the utensil protruding from his stomach and a steak knife jabbed into his throat.

Then Watson, Van Houten, and Krenwinkel had a snack of milk and cheese and played with the LaBianca's dogs. They hid in the bushes nearby until daylight and then hitchhiked back to Spahn Ranch.

Back with the Family, Van Houten was numb to the horror of it all.

"I acted like it was a lot of fun," she remembered, "because everything at the ranch was supposed to be fun."

It would take years for Van Houten to fully comprehend the enormity of her crime.

⁂

In the months that followed the August 8 weekend, interest skyrocketed in the crimes that the national media would immediately dub "the Tate-LaBianca murders." However, with no significant leads in the investigation for more than three months, coverage of the murders stalled.

On August 9, as word started to spread on radio and television about the first night of murders, Los Angeles residents were concerned—anxiety that grew with the arrival of Sunday papers, with banner headlines about Tate and details about the savagery of the crimes. And when word came on Monday of the second set of murders, panic set in. With no suspects in custody, speculation was rampant: on the list of possibilities were mob hits, or a crazed killer like Richard Speck, the 1966 murderer of eight student nurses in Chicago.

Many celebrities who thought that Tate was the target left town; Steve McQueen, who had planned on being at Cielo Drive that night, may have escaped death when a chance run-in with a date sidetracked him to another destination; McQueen may have also been on a Family hit list for not helping Manson with a script idea; the actor began carrying a gun.

After a few weeks with no progress, actor Peter Sellers and several colleagues, including Warren Beatty and Yul Brynner, posted a $25,000 reward for information about the murders.

With the country already on edge after a year of violence in 1968 and the continuing strife and public protest against the war, reaction to the murders was broad and deep. In other cities, sales of handguns skyrocketed. Acquiring guard dog services required weeks on a waiting list, as did installation of security systems. In New York, enrollment doubled in training programs for dogs. One agency in Los Angeles reported more than 100 requests for guard dogs in Bel-Air, not far from the Tate murders.

Although the media immediately speculated about a connection between the Tate and LaBianca murders, weeks passed before the police would connect the methods of the crimes and the bloody scrawled words and acknowledge that the murders were related.

Los Angeles law enforcement were tracking Manson—although not for the murders. Suspected of auto theft and other crimes, on October 12, Manson and his Family were arrested at Barker Ranch; Manson was found contorted inside a tiny bathroom vanity. Taken to jail in Independence, a town in California's Owens Valley, at his booking, Manson listed his name as "Manson, Charles M., aka Jesus Christ, God."

Manson would never be free again.

Still not a suspect in the Tate-LaBianca murders, Manson would languish in jail for almost a month before suspicion would start to shift to the Family. On November 6, Atkins, already in jail for her role in Hinman's killing, bragged to fellow inmate Ronnie Howard about the Tate murders.

"We wanted to do a crime that would shock the world," Atkins told Howard, "that the world would have to stand up and take notice."

Howard told the prison authorities about Atkins's confession; the statements were confirmed a week later by Al Springer, a member of the Straight Satans Motorcycle Club who had been at Spahn Ranch visiting a biker pal when Manson bragged to him about "how we knocked off five of them, just the other night." Springer's friend Danny DeCarlo backed up Springer's story, reporting that Manson had said, "We got five piggies."

On December 8, Manson, Watson, Atkins, Krenwinkel, and Kasabian were indicted for the Tate murders; the same group, plus Van Houten, was also indicted for the LaBianca murders.

And with the indictments came a flood of news coverage—of Manson, his Family, and the twisted vision he had created, with much of the coverage examining not only the events of the murders themselves but also the circumstances of the extraordinary story that led up to them.

But it was more than the visceral shock of the murders that troubled America; Manson reinforced what many in mainstream America believed: that the counterculture of the 1960s was indeed as misguided by drugs and capable of subhuman behavior as they had feared.

Two weeks after the indictments, in coverage that resonated with many, *Life* magazine showcased the Manson story with a cover article that featured the iconic image of a crazed-looking Manson (see plate 11). Titled "The Love and Terror Cult," the *Life* article emphasized Manson's role in "the dark edge of hippie life."

"Long-haired, bearded little Charles Manson so disturbed the American millions last week—when he was charged with sending four docile girls and a hairy male acolyte off to slaughter strangers in two Los Angeles houses last

August—that the victims of his blithe and gory crimes seemed suddenly to have played only secondary roles in the final brutal moments of their own lives," *Life* reported. "The Los Angeles killings struck innumerable Americans as an inexplicable controversion of everything they wanted to believe about the society and their children—and made Charlie Manson seem to be the very encapsulation of truth about revolt and violence by the young."

What *Life* failed to acknowledge was that "violence of the young"—meaning violent crime within counterculture as a social phenomenon—was practically nonexistent.

The trial began on July 24, 1970. Watson had surrendered to authorities in his home state of Texas, and with delays in extradition, was tried separately. (Kasabian, who had no involvement in the murders themselves, later became the state's star witness.) As a result, the initial trial featured the daily imagery of Manson with his three compliant disciples. On the first day of the trial, Manson arrived in court with an "X" carved into his forehead, explaining the mutilation by saying, "I have X'd myself from the world. No man or lawyer is speaking for me." Soon Atkins, Krenwinkel, and Van Houten would carve their own Xs.

Even the atmosphere outside the courtroom attracted attention, with Manson followers stationed in a trial-long vigil at the corner outside the Los Angeles Hall of Justice, the women changing their clothes and physical appearance as ordered by Manson—including shaving their heads (see plate 13).

The press coverage reinforced again and again what large numbers in America wanted to believe: that the murders were part of the love and peace generation gone horribly wrong; many times the case was covered under headlines that contained the words "hippie trials." The coverage frequently missed the larger point: the murders had nothing to do with the peaceful sentiments of 1960s counterculture, but rather Manson had been able to prey on the confused and lonely, most of whom had become disconnected from families who could not understand nor relate to them.

"In court, Manson choreographed a spectacle that included his three co-defendants jumping to their feet and singing songs mocking the judge," wrote Linda Deutsch, who after the Manson trial would spend much of her career covering celebrity trials. "At one point, he propelled himself across the counsel table, brandishing a pencil and shouting at the judge: 'Someone should cut your head off, old man.'"

Judge Charles Older, a no-nonsense former pilot who had served in World War II with the volunteer Flying Tigers, earned praise from reporters and the lawyers for controlling the proceedings as much as he could. But Manson, said Van Houten, "was conducting the courtroom."

America was appalled—and transfixed.

"The idea that those people were not safe just sent shock waves through the country, and woke up the country to the fact that there was an evil lurking in it and an evil beyond what anybody imagined," wrote Janet Maslin of the *New York Times*.

The theater was made worse by the most unlikely of sources: the president of the United States. At a speech in Denver, Nixon described a fault of the "liberal media" by complaining how coverage of the case was trying to glorify the defendants. In the process, Nixon almost caused a mistrial by declaring that Manson was responsible for the murders.

"Here is a man who was guilty, directly or indirectly, of eight murders without reason," said Nixon. Chief prosecutor Vincent Bugliosi tried to keep the news from the jury, but Manson held open a copy of the *Los Angeles Times* with the headline "Manson Guilty, Nixon Declares." Older polled the jury and was assured they could continue.

Manson was upsetting in court, but the other three defendants were truly disturbing. Krenwinkel, Van Houten, and Atkins—arrogant, oblivious, shameless—were a daily visible display of Manson's control over them, and by extension their willingness to kill for him, seemingly puppet-like under his control.

The case culminated on November 17, with Manson testifying for more than an hour, outside the presence of the jury, summarizing all the blame he focused on society.

"I have ate out of your garbage cans to stay out of jail," Manson told the court. "I have wore your second-hand clothes . . . I have done my best to get along in your world and now you want to kill me, and I look at you, and then I say to myself, You want to kill me? Ha! I'm already dead, have been all my life.

"These children [indicating the female defendants] were finding themselves. What they did, if they did whatever they did, is up to them. They will have to explain that to you.

"I haven't got any guilt about anything because I have never been able to see any wrong . . . I have always said: Do what your love tells you, and I do what my love tells me . . . Is it my fault that your children do what you do? What about your children? You say there are just a few? There are many, many more, coming in the same direction. They are running in the streets—and they are coming right at you!"

After his rant was over, he told his co-defendants, "You don't have to testify now."

On January 25, the jury returned its verdict: guilty on all counts. On April 1971, they received the death penalty. Later, Watson was found guilty as well. On the day that Atkins, Krenwinkel, and Van Houten arrived in court to be sentenced to die, they were laughing and giggling in the hallway (see plate 14).

But there would be no death sentences for Manson and his followers. In January 1972, the California Supreme Court outlawed the state's death penalty. The sentences for the Tate-LaBianca murders were commuted to life in prison, creating a high-profile status for Manson that would continue to mutate for the next five decades.

"Had Manson's death sentence been executed, he would have been just a footnote to history," said Brian Levin, director of the Center for the Study of Hate and Extremism. "Instead, he became an icon of the age, and he would manipulate that role for the rest of his life."

While the others were serving life sentences, Van Houten got a break: because her attorney Ron Hughes had died during the original proceedings, she was granted a mistrial in 1977 and released on bail. As she prepared her defense, Van Houten worked as a legal secretary and lived in Echo Park—less than 10 minutes from the LaBianca house.

During the next 10 months before she was ultimately convicted with the same sentence as the others, Van Houten had the opportunity to see the real world as she contemplated her crimes—and her future.

"It took me a good two years to even begin to realize what had happened, and what I had been through," Van Houten recalled in 1977. "It took years to be able to start sorting out my mind and my thoughts and put them in the proper perspective.

"I knew I was going to have to answer for what had happened, and I began to try to figure out how I was going to live with what I had done. I take responsibility for the entire crime. I take responsibility for Mrs. LaBianca."

But Van Houten also feels accountable for another role: helping Charles Manson to become a symbol of hate and evil that he nurtured until the day he died.

"Part of my responsibility was helping to create him," Van Houten said, 25 years after the murders. "He is an opportunist of the cruelest, most vicious kind. I feel very responsible for creating a monster."

Charles Manson assumed a role as an elder statesman in the national dialogue about murder, violence, or anything else that reporters wanted to discuss, as he spouted a mixture of contrived philosophy and rage against society. Manson continued to absolve himself of all responsibility for the murders he ordered and the tragedy he inflicted on his followers, always blaming others—or the world—for everything he had done.

For instance, when in 1980 he was asked about his role in shaping his co-defendants, Manson retorted, "I didn't produce these kids. They are a product of their parents. I didn't recruit them, it was the other way around. I came out of prison a child and I was looking for guidance and a way to live. The children took me in. Through them I learned how to maneuver and exist in the streets without starving. At some point, I may have become a pivotal person to them, some place to always return to."

Manson never expressed remorse for the murders, twisting the issue into a distortion of the real world. In 1992, when parole board commissioner Ron Koenig asked Manson if he felt remorse for his crimes, Manson replied, "You say in your minds that I'm guilty of everything that you've got on paper. So therefore . . . I would need to have remorse for what you think is reality.

"I ask you back the same thing," Manson told Koenig. "You've been using me ever since I was 10 years old. You used to beat me with leather straps. Does anyone have any remorse that I've spent 23 years in a solitary cell? You only kept Christ on the cross three days."

Koenig said, "Mr. Manson, I think you answered the question."

Manson's deflection of blame would metastasize into an even broader conception about his role in society that has fascinated generations of scholars eager to analyze it: Manson was able to warp his already-distorted vision into a view of ourselves. For Manson, it was the ultimate manipulation—convincing the world that the human horror he had created of himself was a reflection of all of us: look in the mirror, Manson said, and you will see him.

"I am only what lives inside each and every one of you," he said in court. "Look straight at me, and you see yourself."

An entire era of Americans could not help but find Manson compelling—even those who already knew much about the best and the worst of American society.

"Years ago, I spoke at a book convention in Virginia," said Vincent Bugliosi, the prosecuting attorney who put away Manson for life. "I arrived at the station at the same time as William Manchester and Arthur Schlesinger, both Pulitzer Prize winners. The whole cab ride, Manchester and Schlesinger are tossing me questions about Charles Manson. That's all they wanted to talk about: tell me about him. Tell me about his eyes. Did you ever talk to him? How did he get control over these people?"

The control that Manchester and Schlesinger found so fascinating was an early indication of how a culture of violence inspired by Manson would begin to grow.

"The Manson Family both anticipated and inspired the growth of sinister cults in American life," said CNN legal analyst Jeffrey Toobin the week after Manson died in 2017. "In the decade that followed the Manson murders, the Symbionese Liberation Army kidnapped Patty Hearst, in Berkeley, and Jim Jones's Peoples Temple, in San Francisco, transfixed supporters, more than nine hundred of whom committed mass suicide in Guyana.

"Before Manson, it was more or less a given that criminals chose to associate with one another in gangs or in crime families," Toobin said. "But Manson told the world that people became criminals through the influence of others as well. Our fascination with Stockholm Syndrome and brainwashing owes much to what the world saw in the Manson case."

Manson can take credit for distorting the view of 1960s counterculture—a distortion that continues today. High-profile criminals had existed, of course, before Manson and his followers, but in 1969 never before had the public been exposed to evil with such depth and influence on others within the American experience; the "anti-society" in the Family that was capable of such savage violence revealed what many believed was the darkness of counterculture life in the 1960s. Even though Manson actually represented the antithesis of the peace and love that was the foundation of "flower power," he will be forever associated with a stereotype of the 1960s as an era gone horribly awry.

"Manson just played into the role of being the hippie cult leader, which he wasn't—Charlie was no hippie," said social scientist David Williams. "In the 1960s, there was already this fear in the more traditional part of society that the whole country was falling apart—that the hippies would overthrow culture, overthrow law, overthrow institutions, and they were outside the law—and he was one of them. So it isn't so much he himself as it is what he represented, that he was a hippie freak. But Manson wasn't a hippie—he was a psycho."

And Manson's packaging of his social and political message through murder continues to echo today.

"We've certainly known people before Manson who were mass killers, but Manson was killing to send a social and political message—the counterpoint to Richard Nixon's silent majority and law and order," said Brian Levin, a former police officer, lawyer, and director of the Center for the Study of Hate and Extremism in California.

"After Manson, the notion of symbolic violence really became a powerful statement," said Levin. "Terrorism has the same function that became a new cultural touchstone in the most horrendous type of way. We have never glorified mass murderers like Richard Speck, or Charles Whitman (who in 1966 murdered his mother and wife before shooting 15 others from a tower at the University of Texas). But with Manson, we see rock groups playing his songs, people wearing his face on their shirts, and artists using his image as cultural symbols.

"Had Manson been someone who just had a diabolical plan for murder and a few followers, I don't think it would have had the same kind of resonance," Levin said. "But he wrapped it in music, he wrapped it in the racial divisions, he wrapped it in kind of a youth culture, and he wrapped it in an anti-establishment kind of exercise. And as a social and political message, that resonated."

The electronic media also played a role in Manson's durability in the limelight. The Tate-LaBianca murders did not mark the first time in the 20th century that America had celebritized killers—criminals from Bonnie and Clyde to John Dillinger to Al Capone to Leopold and Loeb, each in their own way had been media darlings with their own folklore long before Manson. But the difference was that television news, for the first time, could bring a murderer's political message to tens of millions of people in one night.

"Even though viewers were appalled," said Levin, "Manson's messages stuck to the psyche."

Manson also represents a troubling reminder that a murderer with a political message can live forever; consider that on October 1, 2017, Stephen Paddock massacred 58 people and wounded more than 400 in Las Vegas by shooting them with semiautomatic weapons—the deadliest mass shooting in U.S. history. Yet Paddock had no known motive and left no message before he shot himself; since then his name has receded into the background in the national dialogue about the incident and questions about gun control. Yet decades after the Tate-LaBianca murders, Manson and helter skelter still resonate.

Manson may have played the ultimate cosmic joke on the world: the more we try to figure him out, the less we really understand him. However, when we see the real Manson, not as a larger-than-life philosopher about violence in America, and not as a guilt-inspiring reflection of each of us, but instead by pulling back the curtain and exposing the pure sociopath within, then the understanding of him becomes clear.

"Manson was not Jesus Christ or Satan," said Smith, Manson's parole officer before it all began. "He was a very odd, bizarre, little anti-social, who had some poor, confused, middle-class dropouts who decided to follow him. And he got into a situation where he had enormous power over these people, and he pulled it all together into this incoherent, hateful plan. There was no one there to say, 'Charlie, girls—this is crazy.'"

Plate 1. Vannevar Bush with his differential analyzer, an electromechanical device that helped provide solutions to complex equations. "No American," said Jerome Wiesner, science adviser to President Kennedy, "has had a greater influence in the growth of science and technology than Vannevar Bush." MIT MUSEUM.

Plate 2. Soviet leader Nikita Khrushchev, wearing the Kremlin as a crown and juggling Sputnik I. Khrushchev would use Soviet success in space, and America's early failures, to amplify ongoing social ills in the United States. TIME MAGAZINE ARCHIVE.

Plate 3. Space fight comes to Florida. A rarely seen "Bumper V-2"—an original German V-2 rocket topped with an American WAC-Corporal research missile—takes off on July 24, 1950. It was the first launch at Cape Canaveral, setting the stage for the future of America's space program. NASA.

Plate 4. America's first attempt to catch up with the Soviets' Sputnik satellite failed in spectacular fashion on December 6, 1957, when the Vanguard TV3 exploded on launch in front of a national television audience. The failure inspired a torrent of headlines that played off of the name "Sputnik," such as "Oopsnik," "Kaputnik," "Stayputnik," and this one from the *London Daily Herald*. NASA.

Plate 5. Wernher von Braun, director of the Marshall Space Flight Center, explains the Saturn launch system to President John F. Kennedy at Cape Canaveral, Florida, six days before the president was assassinated. Kennedy was the catalyst for America's program that sent Apollo to the moon, in spite of his own private concerns about the value of space. NASA.

Plate 6. Apollo 1 crew members (from left) Edward White, Gus Grissom, and Roger Chaffee. When the crew members met with program manager Joseph Shea, they expressed concerns about many problems with the design and workmanship of the Apollo command module. Afterward, they posed for this photo, sending a copy to Shea with the inscription, "It isn't that we don't trust you, Joe, but this time we've decided to go over your head." Five months later, all three were dead—killed in their spacecraft in a fire most likely started by a spark in faulty wiring. NASA.

Plate 7. The plumbing and wiring to power the engine for the third stage of the Saturn V—a very small example of the more than 3 million parts and 700,000 components required for Apollo to fly. NASA.

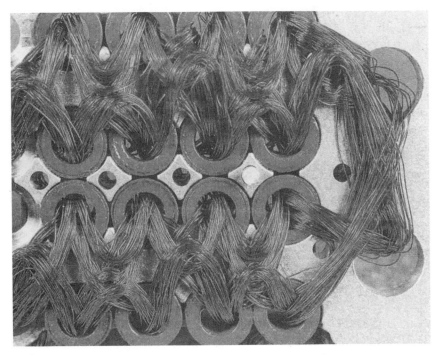

Plate 8. A detail of core rope memory used for the Apollo guidance computer, a mind-numbingly complex method of data storage that required teams using long needles to hand-weave thousands of feet of wire as thin as sewing thread into magnetic cores. In 1960s technology, it was the only practical method of computer storage that was small enough and light enough to go into space. NASA.

Plate 9. Computer scientist Margaret Hamilton with the navigation software that she and her team at MIT produced for the Apollo guidance computer. Hamilton coined the term "software engineering" and directed the program of that name at the MIT Instrumentation Laboratory while developing the on-board flight software for the Apollo space program. For her work on Apollo, Hamilton was awarded the Presidential Medal of Freedom by President Barack Obama in 2016. NASA.

Plate 10. This photograph of Earth rising over the lunar horizon, photographed on Christmas Eve 1968 by Bill Anders aboard Apollo 8, reveals the planet in all its delicacy. Informally titled *Earthrise*, the image has been called "the most influential environmental photograph ever taken" and is a landmark moment in humanity's growing awareness of the global environment. NASA.

Plate 11. Charles Manson in 1968. Often assumed to be a staged portrait (with the placard cropped out), this image is actually a mug shot from his arrest in Ventura County, California. The image appeared on the cover of *Life* in December 1969, introducing Manson to the world, as part of the magazine's exposé of Manson and "The Family." This shot would become one of the iconic images of the 1960s, as much a part of the era as photos of President Kennedy, Martin Luther King Jr., the Vietnam war, or the Beatles. VENTURA COUNTY SHERIFF'S DEPARTMENT.

Plate 12. The many faces of Charles Manson. Top row from left: at 14, already an armed robber, three days before running away from Boy's Town; at 21, a federal criminal. Bottom row from left: in 1969, after the Tate-LaBianca murders; a graphic created from Manson's 1968 mugshot (see plate 11). More than a half-century later, the graphic continues to appear on posters, signs, graffiti, and clothing ranging from t-shirts and dresses (see page 119) to baby outfits. SAN QUENTIN PRISON, TERMINAL ISLAND FEDERAL CORRECTIONAL INSTITUTION.

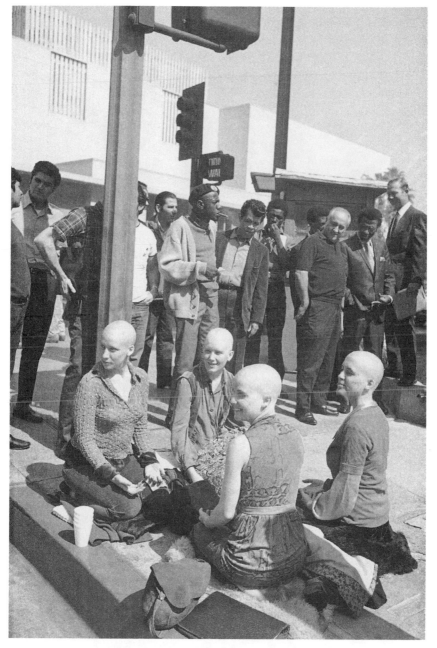

Plate 13. Four members of the Charles Manson "Family," with their heads shaved, sit on the sidewalk outside the Los Angeles Hall of Justice during the trial of Manson and his followers. The vigil served as an ongoing reminder to the world of the blind loyalty of Manson's followers to "Charlie." From left: Cathy Gillies, Kitty Lutesinger, Sandy Good, Nancy "Brenda" Pitman. AP IMAGES.

Plate 14. Susan Atkins, Patricia Krenwinkel, and Leslie Van Houten, Manson's co-defendants in the Tate-LaBianca murder trial, laughing on their way to court on March 29, 1971, knowing they were about to be sentenced to death (the sentences were later reduced to life in prison for all, including Manson, when the California death penalty was outlawed). Their in-court arrogance and defiance of the legal system contributed to denial of their paroles long after other defendants with similar criminal records were released. AP IMAGES.

Plate 15. The opening prayer at Woodstock by Sri Swami Satchidananda, who hoped for the 400,000 in attendance "peace and joy through celestial music." MARK GOFF.

Plate 16. Beth Henry (left) and Elizabeth Alexander, two friends whose lives were stuck in "nowheresville" who found direction for their futures after Woodstock. ELIZABETH ALEXANDER COLLECTION COPYRIGHT © MUSEUM AT BETHEL WOODS.

Plate 17. The mass of young humanity descending on the Woodstock Festival—before it was over, they would temporarily form the third-largest city in New York. AP IMAGES.

Plate 18. A rarely seen magazine ad for the Woodstock Music and Art Fair that appeared in the progressive publication *Ramparts* when the concert was still scheduled for Wallkill. Note the text describing the advantages of a country getaway for city dwellers ("walk around for three days without seeing a skyscraper or a traffic light"). At this point, several of the principal performers had not yet been confirmed, including Jimi Hendrix, Country Joe and the Fish, Ten Years After, and the Paul Butterfield Blues Band. WOODSTOCK ARCHIVES.

Plate 19. When the Woodstock concert was forced to move from Wallkill and the new site in Bethel near White Lake was approved, the promoters of Woodstock made their feelings clear about the local opposition. Woodstock Ventures announced the new site with this ad that portrayed the people of Wallkill as gun-wielding country hicks, along with an empty jug of moonshine. "Certain people of Wallkill decided to try to run us out of town before we even got there," the text of the ad began. "They were afraid. Of what, we don't know. We're not even sure that they know. We decided to switch now, and fight Wallkill later. After all, the whole idea is to bring you three days of peace and music—not three days of dirty looks and cold shoulders." WOODSTOCKWHISPERER.

Plate 20. The Pets.com sock puppet, the "spokesman" for the company that would become a high-profile symbol of the peak and burst of the dot-com bubble that evaporated billions in investments and destroyed thousands of jobs. HARLAN LEBO.

Plate 21. The test Amazon Go store in Seattle, Washington, where customers buy items simply by removing them from the shelf and then leaving. A convenience for buyers, the concept of "cashierless" purchasing raises questions about declining employment in a digital age. (TOP) BRUCE ENGLEHARDT, (BOTTOM) SIKANDER IQBAL.

III

WOODSTOCK

August 15–18, 1969: Woodstock brings together 400,000
for "three days of peace and music"

The Woodstock Music and Art Fair—"three days of peace and music" in rural New York that would name a generation. PAUL GERRY COLLECTION COPYRIGHT © MUSEUM AT BETHEL WOODS.

15

GRASSHOPPERS IN
THE GRAIN FIELDS

"The Woodstock Music and Art Fair, the three-day Aquarian Exposition at White Lake in Bethel, New York, will give you uncomplicated, unhurried, calm days of peace and music. Heavy traffic is anticipated, so leave early if you wish to arrive on time."

—New York–area radio commercial, summer 1969

August 15, 1969
Bethel, New York
11:00 a.m.

The hamlet of Bethel is a pastoral delight—the type of rural setting perfectly suited for a weekend drive to convince city dwellers that there are indeed places in America where the barns are bright red, the silos are shiny silver, and the herds of black-and-white Holstein cows compete with humans for the lead in total population.

In the case of Bethel, the contrast between city and country is especially pronounced, because the rolling hills in the Catskills are only 70 miles from New York—on a good day, just 90 minutes from the heart of Manhattan.

August 15, 1969, was not one of the 90-minute days.

From a New York State Police helicopter flying over Route 17B, the two-lane thoroughfare that cut through Bethel looked like an exodus from disaster: cars stacked against the shoulder for miles in every direction, an endless traffic jam of vehicles inching forward with little discernible progress, and tens of thousands of people carrying blankets and food, walking west.

The cars and people converged on Hurd Road, a narrow lane that branches north, leading through thick woods until it reaches a wide, alfalfa-covered summit that extends in a slope down into a broad bowl. On any day prior to this day, the view from the summit would have been a rural reverie of dairy cows grazing in the summer morning sun.

On August 15, however, the view from the summit was of thousands upon thousands of people, a mass of humanity filling an area the size of nearly 30 football fields—a crowd so large that it would soon be the size of a major city. At the base of the bowl was a large stage, the anchor point for, as the ads would say, "three days of peace and music": the Aquarian Exposition presented by the Woodstock Music and Art Fair, which in spite of its location in Bethel was soon to become known for all time as simply "Woodstock."

The Woodstock concert in the Catskills of rural New York on the August 15 weekend presented the paragons of 1960s rock music, from Jimi Hendrix to Jefferson Airplane to the Grateful Dead—in all, 32 acts playing day and night until Monday morning. But it was clear from the start that Woodstock would become much more than a concert: it was a weekend that would become a social and cultural milestone in the American experience.

The clash of values that surrounded planning the event almost sank the whole project, but by the time the concert weekend occurred—and in spite of crowds beyond any expectations, intolerable weather, a lack of food and water, and emergency resources strained to their limits, Woodstock was a symbol of how a whole community can become the best of what people are and what they hope to be. The 400,000 who attended would arrive enthusiastic and dry; they left muddy, hungry, and soaked—and part of the Woodstock generation.

⌒∞⌒

The often-told story of how four young promoters—Michael Lang, Artie Kornfeld, Joel Rosenman, and John Roberts—created the Woodstock Festival has several versions depending on the teller, but the basics are the same: after a twisty path of common contacts and references brought the four together early in 1969, they eventually circled in on the idea of a concert near the town of Woodstock that would draw on the musical talent that had settled in the area, including Bob Dylan, who had lived in Woodstock on and off since the early 1960s.

Dylan never became part of the project, but planning for a rural concert proceeded without him. Rosenman, Roberts, Lang, and Kornfeld formed Woodstock Ventures with a goal of staging a concert in the countryside in mid-August. For the next five months, the struggles to find a location for their concert would become a microcosm of cultural divisions that were also dividing the rest of late 1960s America.

In rural New York, opposition to counterculture interests was broad and deep. As Woodstock Ventures touted the virtues of their idea, problems at other events elsewhere in the United States amplified local concerns. On the June 20 weekend, a three-day rock concert at Devonshire Downs in suburban Los Angeles drew 60,000 spectators and deteriorated when police began fighting with gate-crashers. Spectators threw bottles, and events were soon out of control. More than 400 were injured and 165 arrested, and hundreds of teenagers sparked a mini-riot that (Catskills residents carefully noted) damaged a local shopping center and residences.

But to locals in New York, the problem was not the violence but *who* caused the violence.

"It was another case of hippies getting out of control," said one local.

Even good news about conduct at other events provided ammunition for the opposition. On the July 4 weekend, a pop festival at Atlanta International Raceway was held without major incident, but media reported the presence of "an impromptu but efficient commodities exchange in marijuana and LSD, where buyers and sellers let supply and demand establish prices."

The promoters took steps to placate local resistance that seemed unusual at the time but would later become integral to the Woodstock experience. For instance, in May, to ensure that the spectators could relate to the authorities managing the concert, Hugh Romney and his Hog Farm commune were hired to work at the festival for security and other support. Romney, better known as Wavy Gravy, described his communal colleagues as the "Please Force"—the name reflecting their low-confrontation method of keeping order.

When the traditional food services at the event fell apart as supplies ran low, the Hog Farm would step in to feed thousands with rice and vegetables, as well as with a grain and fruit cereal mix that had existed in Europe since the early 1900s but until Woodstock was unknown to most of mainstream America: granola. Romney—or Gravy—was also endlessly quotable at Woodstock; on the Sunday morning of the event he would wake up the crowd with the announcement, "What we have in mind is breakfast in bed for 400,000."

But new-age security measures did nothing to encourage local approval. The concert was still more than a month away, but it was already a focal point of issues that were splitting the nation: communities cited simple concerns about noise and trash, but underneath those concerns was a reaction against the young, the different, and the unconventional.

Woodstock, reporter Jim Miller would recall, was a lightning rod for reaction against counterculture—"a symbol for people who are hostile to the spirit of the '60s."

The outcome was, at that point, predictable: in Wallkill—about 40 miles from the town of Woodstock—a "concerned citizens committee" led the fight against the concert, stating that problems with the organizer's plans for traffic, health, and security had not been addressed.

"This thing could cause bedlam in my town," said Wallkill town supervisor Jack Schlosser. "The festival would come at the same time as the opening of a new Sears Roebuck in the area."

But the much broader issue at hand was not wanting "hippie types"— and everything negative associated with that characterization—descending on their community.

"Nothing against those people," said the owner of a grocery store, "but they say they'll bring 200,000 people into Wallkill for that festival and we just figure there won't be enough police and property will be damaged and the whole place [will] explode." One can only imagine the reaction had locals known the concert would attract twice as many spectators.

"It will be worse," said another local protester, "than grasshoppers in the grain fields."

Forty miles to the north, Saugerties said no as well. By then, with a month to go until the contracted concert dates for performers and no place to hold the event, cancellation seemed like the inevitable outcome. But the search continued. Looking farther south, 15 miles from the Pennsylvania border near Bethel, a potential location owned by local businessman Elliott Tieber turned out to be too small and too swampy, but Tieber knew a local real estate agent who showed Lang some potential sites.

Lang remembered the tour with the drama typical of the promoter-autobiographer. He recalled traveling the countryside on State Route 17B, when the searchers turned onto Hurd Road, driving north.

"About a quarter mile up, we broached the top of a hill and there it was," Lang reminisced. "'Stop the car!' I shouted, barely able to believe my eyes. It was the field of my dreams—what I had hoped for from the first. I left the car and walked into this perfect green bowl."

They had found a pasture of alfalfa owned by dairyman Max Yasgur.

Yasgur would have seemed the last person in Sullivan County who would have rented his land for a rock concert—seemingly much more a representative of the anticounterculture opposition. New York City bred, educated, and tough, Yasgur was an avowed Republican who supported the war in Vietnam—the touchstone subject by which all sympathy with counterculture or opposition to their ideals was usually measured.

But Yasgur also believed in the Constitution, free expression, and supporting people who got a raw deal.

"You're the people who lost your site in Wallkill, aren't you?" Lang recalled Yasgur asking him. "I think that you young folks were done a grave injustice over there. Yes, I'll show you my land—we might be able to strike a deal for your music fair."

Yasgur's field was ideal for a large-scale concert venue—37 acres of gently sloping hill that flattened into a stage area at the junction of two roads and perfect grassy seating at the top of the bowl for a huge audience.

It might have been said that Yasgur, who had heart problems, was driven by the financial incentive of a rental fee on top off his dairy business. But he would prove to be a stubborn defender of the concert and the problems that resulted from it. Ultimately, he rented the bowl and surrounding acreage for camping for $50,000.

When Yasgur learned that ticket sales had skyrocketed past the 80,000 mark, even he began to have doubts—until the real issue emerged the day before the meeting. On July 20, a crudely written sign appeared on Route 17B propped up on the road near Yasgur's dairy. Painted on an old tabletop, the sign read (with spelling errors shown):

LOCAL PEOPLE
SPEAK-OUT
STOP MAX'S Hippy Music FESTiVAL
NO 150'000 HiPPiEs HERE

Above the large sign was taped a smaller one that read, "Buy no milk."

When Yasgur saw the sign, he dug in his heels. The next day, at a meeting of the town and zoning boards, Yasgur was unflinching in his defense of not only the concert but also of the lifestyles of those who would be attending it.

"I hear you are considering changing the zoning law to prevent the festival," Yasgur said. "I hear you don't like the look of the kids who are working at the site. I hear you don't like their lifestyle. I hear you don't like they are against the war and that they say so very loudly.

"I don't particularly like the looks of some of those kids either," he said. "I don't particularly like their lifestyle, especially the drugs and free love. And I don't like what some of them are saying about our government. However, if I know my American history, tens of thousands of Americans in uniform gave their lives in war after war just so those kids would have the freedom to do exactly what they are doing. That's what this country is all about and I am not going to let you throw them out of our town just because you don't like their dress or their hair or the way they live or what they believe. This is America and they are going to have their festival."

Both boards voted unanimously to approve the event. The "Woodstock" concert would be in Bethel.

"The Yasgurs were decent, gentle, caring people," said John Roberts. "They came to our rescue."

Later, Yasgur steadfastly supported the concert and the young attendees.

"I never expected the festival to be this big," he later admitted to a reporter, "but if the generation gap is to be closed, we older people have to do more than we have done."

The new site was assured, and the promoters declared their frustrations with the locals by sharing some of their own stereotypes about cultural divisions: Woodstock Ventures placed ads in New York newspapers to inform patrons of the change of venue, with a headline that read, "To insure three days of music and peace, we've left Wallkill and are now at White Lake, NY" (a better point of reference than Bethel). The ad also included a drawing of two men, clearly portrayed as local hayseeds—one carrying an old-fashioned rifle, the other pointing a shotgun directly at the reader, with a bottle of moonshine at their feet. (See plate 19.)

"Certain people of Wallkill decided to try to run us out of town before we even got there," the text of the ad began. "They were afraid. Of what, we don't know. We're not even sure that they know.

"We decided to switch now, and fight Wallkill later. After all, the whole idea is to bring you three days of peace and music—not three days of dirty looks and cold shoulders."

With less than a month until the concert, planning proceeded in a near-panic, with stage construction, fencing, and food and sanitation to accommodate an audience of perhaps 50,000.

But ticket sales continued to climb. And climb. Unknown to most in Bethel, more than 180,000 tickets were sold. The promoters had a potential public emergency on their hands.

⌖

Even from high above the Catskills countryside, the Woodstock concert site is still strikingly distinct: on an aerial map, in the midst of a patchwork jumble of farmland, forests, and winding roads, the streets marking the borders of the concert bowl form the shape of a huge, wide arrow, like a left-turn sign on a freeway off-ramp.

Hurd Road extends north from Route 17B, forming the point of the arrow when it reaches West Shore Road. The concert stage was constructed 200 feet east on Shore Road.

The spectators began to arrive days early. By Wednesday, more than 30,000 people were on the concert site with nothing to do except what the concert ads promised: "walk around for three days without seeing a skyscraper or a traffic light. Fly a kite, sun yourself, breathe unspoiled air." But even so, there was no impatience, no discontent, as the spectators enjoyed the countryside and each other. And long before the live music began, they were entertained by a different type of musical genius: Bill Hanley, the incomparable engineer who specialized in audio for outdoor events and became known as "the father of festival sound," arrived in his sound truck, plugged in his equipment, and flooded the field with music.

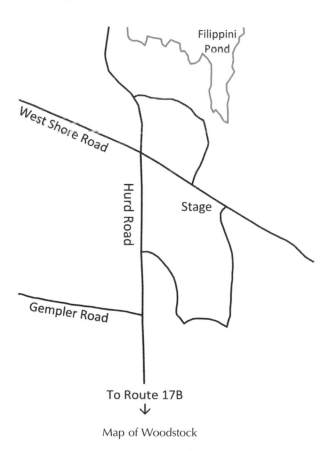

Map of Woodstock

On Thursday, the crowd continued to grow; most of the new arrivals struggled down Route 17B and abandoned their cars when it became clear that forward progress was impossible. West Shore Road was just as bad; by Friday afternoon, nothing for miles around the bowl was moving. But people kept coming.

From Friday, August 15, at 5:07 p.m., when Richie Havens stepped on-stage to perform on acoustic guitar, until 11:00 a.m. on Monday morning, when Jimi Hendrix finished "Hey Joe" as the last of the concert-goers departed, Woodstock would set the tone for a generation. The musicians would perform some 30 hours of music. The spectators would confront un-passable roads, heat, rain, winds at near-tornado strength, lack of sanitation, and little food. The music, everyone would later remember, was masterful—a concert for the ages. But what really mattered was a bigger issue: how 400,000 people would confront the problems—and each other—as they were changed forever by the experience.

16

OVERTAKEN BY THE FEELING

"I think my future came out of what I experienced at Woodstock. I don't know if I ever would have become a counselor or a social worker if I hadn't experienced at Woodstock what people could be. That weekend tapped into a part of me that I didn't realize was there; I absolutely got caught up in the Woodstock mentality—I began to believe in people."

—Beth Henry, Woodstock spectator

There are many voices of Woodstock, and in spite of "hippiefest" characterizations reported by newspapers across the country, most who attended did not fit that description. Many protested the war and attended marches for peace or civil rights, but they were not societal dropouts. They did not live on communes. They were not profound philosophers of their era. And other than smoking the occasional joint, most of them did not abuse drugs. The vast majority of the 400,000 at Woodstock were just young people challenged by a challenging age as they struggled to find direction in their lives. For many, they would find the beginnings of their focus at Woodstock.

Halfway up the sloping concert bowl and 300 feet from the stage, Charlie Maloney sat with Robert Donaghy and Cathy Capuano, soaked.

Going to Woodstock had been Donaghy's idea. Maloney lived in New York City, a June graduate of Archbishop Molloy High School in Queens. So when Donaghy, Maloney's cousin, suggested that they go to Bethel for a little music, their parents said go ahead.

"We had no idea what we were getting into," Maloney said.

Soon after they would know. Heading out on Thursday night, Donaghy and Capuano picked up Maloney after his shift at McDonald's, "and off we went," said Maloney. An hour outside of New York, they arrived at a service area on the freeway—a stop Maloney knew well from trips to his grandparents' vacation house—and when Maloney and Donaghy got out of the car, they looked at the hundreds of people there and then at each other.

"These were *not* tourists going to vacation houses," Maloney remembered.

Maloney and Donaghy were not prepared for the rigors of an outdoor festival.

"We thought we would be able to sleep in the car and buy food there," he said. "We didn't even bring a blanket.

"I had a lot of experience being out in the country, but I hadn't even considered what three days at a rock concert might be like."

Thursday night, the trio slept in their car on Route 17B when the road was shut down. On Friday morning, 17B was opened again, and they were able to get relatively close to the Woodstock site—eventually parking on Perry Road, only a mile and a half away. Soon after, clogged with cars, Perry Road was shut down as well.

"We got out of the car and had no idea where we were," said Maloney. "But when my cousin asked, 'Which way do we go?' it was obvious. I said, 'Just follow all those people.'"

A half-hour later, they reached the bowl. There were no ticket-takers, so Maloney gave his Friday ticket to someone collecting them; later he found out that some ambitious attendees were gathering up tickets, walking up to the main highway, and reselling them.

Maloney found a spot on the grass, the field already packed with more than 100,000 people, all with nothing to do while the construction crew frantically worked to build the stage and check the sound system.

"We were all just hanging out," said Maloney, "talking and enjoying being outside. I don't think anyone was particularly antsy for things to get started, and the stage announcements were a calming influence, as they read personal messages and kept us informed of what was going on."

The trio returned to the car to sleep, and on Saturday morning, they set out for supplies. They took a chance, driving west and north—away from the incoming New York crowds—and found clear roads. To the north, the locals had already heard about the brewing emergency around Bethel, and they extended a hand.

"Many of the local people didn't want the festival," said Maloney, "but once they realized that the crowd was having problems getting food and water, then everybody came together."

They ended up in Liberty, New York, where people in the local market and Woolworth's gave them discounts. A local travel agent let them use her phone to check in at home.

"They also gave us stuff for free," Maloney said, "like strips and strips of lollipops in plastic wrapped in cellophane."

Maloney stood on a street corner in Liberty, passing out lollipops by the dozens and greeting people going to the concert—in the process becoming yet another image of the generous spirit of Woodstock.

When they returned to the festival, two state troopers blocking Route 17B tried to turn them away. But Capuano was a nurse who could help in the medical tents, and the barrier opened; they were even able to return to the same parking spot as before. Back on the hill, they passed out oranges while others distributed apples. And when the rain came, they were drenched.

"People often ask me what was it like to be at Woodstock," Maloney said. "It was very simple: we came for the music and we left as a community. It was just togetherness. You know, if you needed something, someone would give it to you. If people had sandwiches, they would pass them down the line. If some had wine, they'd pass that; if people had a joint, they'd pass that, too. It was my first experience of group cooperation like that on any level."

But for Maloney, real-world commitments prevailed; late Sunday night, the three returned to the real world and to their jobs.

"It was time to go home—we all had to work on Monday," said Maloney. "But people say that when I got back, I was different on many levels. I think Woodstock made me a nicer person because of the sense of community that I had experienced there—unlike anything I could have ever known."

For the next four decades, Maloney held on to his memories as he built a career in hotel and restaurant management; there was a connection to Woodstock that would not let go. What Maloney called "a 45-year detour" would often lead back in a five-hour trip to the concert grounds.

"I came back to Bethel a number of times," Maloney remembered. "Whenever I returned, I was just overtaken by the feeling that was there."

And after the museum at the Bethel Center for the Arts opened, Maloney would return even more frequently. Oftentimes he would spend time meeting visitors near the monument to the festival at the corner of Shore and Hurd—a global assortment of the curious, or the nostalgia seekers, or the reverent who come, as Maloney said, "to feel the energy from the field"—families with grandparents and parents and children who have been hearing of Woodstock and needed to feel it firsthand. Maloney recalled a lone winter visitor from Saudi Arabia, standing in the snow silently staring across the bowl. More than a few times, Maloney would show the grounds to visitors from other countries who had flown to New York, come to the concert site, stayed for an hour, and then driven back to the airport to fly home the same day.

"I see people at the monument who have never been here before, and when they go onto the field, and their walk gets a little slower. Their smiles are a little more understated. Their talk is a little quieter. And that's just walking in there—*feeling it*. I've run into people that don't even want to walk on the field; they feel it's sacred ground.

"They all come to experience the spirit of Woodstock," said Maloney.

In 2013, Maloney came back permanently; he moved to Monticello, a village of 6,000 and the closest full-fledged community to Bethel. He became a docent at the museum for Bethel Woods Center for the Arts, sharing his experiences of Woodstock with a new generation learning to appreciate the spirit of the gathering.

To Maloney, "the spirit" represents a deep sense of community that more than 400,000 people could share in a challenging world.

"It's the feeling that there is hope, there is kindness in the world, for those who choose to experience it," said Maloney. "Things can be better. People can get along. We have work to do, but there's the goal. Maybe it's that they embrace the goal and then start on the journey to make the goal happen. So even if that makes somebody a little nicer, a little kinder to their fellow human beings, then Woodstock has succeeded in its purpose."

⚬∞⚬

Behind the stage and across West Shore Road, Elizabeth Alexander and her friends were sitting comfortably outside of their tent, enjoying the warm Saturday afternoon between performances. Had awards been given for planning attendance at a concert in the country, Lizzy and her friends surely would have taken a gold medal; her friend Richard Sender, known to all as Richie, planned the trip with military efficiency—right down to doing an overnight reconnaissance trip to Bethel the weekend before the concert and gathering up the camping equipment and supplies they would load into a U-Haul truck.

On Wednesday, almost 30,000 people were in the bowl, amusing themselves and relaxing in the sun the day before the concert; Alexander's group was close behind. Early on Thursday morning, Richie—tall, skinny, with chest-length hair—gathered his Woodstock excursion group at his home in Westwood, New Jersey. And then they were on their way—12 adventurers loaded with supplies to carry them through until Monday.

By Thursday afternoon, Richie, Alexander, her close friend Beth Henry (more about Beth later), and nine of their friends had arrived in Bethel at their prescouted location in a cozy spot in the woods next to Filippini Pond, a few hundred feet behind the stage. Richie had even arranged for a buddy to bring a motorcycle, so when friends inevitably got jammed up along the way, they could be rescued and brought through traffic.

"Our group was very, very well organized," Alexander, who was 19 at the time, remembered. "It worked out pretty well for us."

None in the group had tickets for Friday—"We got tickets for Saturday and Sunday," Alexander said, "because we didn't think the bands were all that great on Friday and we wanted to save some money. Then, seven dollars was a lot for 19-year-olds." Instead, they would spend the Friday enjoying having the tent setup, their cots and sleeping bags arranged, their food chilling in the lake, and their marijuana easily available.

Alexander and her friends were organized concert-goers, but for the other aspects of their lives, most of them were adrift. They had graduated from high school the year before, and Alexander and Richie used their first year out of school to take a trip across the country in a VW bus, taking time to explore their options. But at Woodstock, they still had no firm plans for the future, other than enjoying the music they were about to hear.

"I had really no direction at that point in my life," said Alexander. "All we wanted to do was sit around and get stoned."

Alexander was, at least, working—waiting tables at the Marshmallow Restaurant owned by New York Mets Art Shamsky and Phil Linz. In the year of the Miracle Mets—who had finished second-to-last place in 1968 but would rally spectacularly in 1969 take the National League pennant, and then shock the Baltimore Orioles for the World Series win—the Marshmallow was a bustling place. "But none of us were doing anything important enough that we couldn't get five days off to go to Woodstock," said Alexander.

Already Alexander was getting a sense of the genial feeling that would become part of Woodstock lore. On a Thursday afternoon walk down West Shore Road on her way back to camp, Alexander saw a New York state trooper sitting on the ground, screwing red bulbs into a long string of Christmas tree lights.

"I asked him what he was doing and he said, 'I'm making a heliport.' I said, 'Can I help you?' He said, 'Sure.' So the trooper and I sat there and screwed in dozens of red bulbs, then we strung the lines on top of a fence. Instant heliport. Later at night, it really looked nice."

By Friday morning, Alexander's group realized the enormity of the event—looking out across the bowl to the rising hill of people in front of the stage—and recognized how their planning had paid off. During breaks in the music, they could return to Camp Richie.

"We were actually getting a kick out of it because we had a great spot," she said. "We didn't care how many people showed up for the weekend—it was all cool to us."

For Alexander and her friends, Woodstock was all about the music; they stayed until the end.

"I was *very* happy up there," she recalled. "I was so into the music that nothing was bothering me. We ran into some friends, and when we started sharing, our food began to run out. So we had to go to the food tents after a while. I remember that was the first time I ever ate granola—it was great. I thought, 'Maybe it will be more fun eating at the food tents.'"

With their campground haven for a retreat, Alexander and her friends were not selective about where they sat in the bowl, eventually watching the concert from many locations on Saturday and Sunday. By Sunday evening, as the crowd shrank, Alexander wound up sleeping near the stage and being awakened to the loudest wake-up call ever: Jimi Hendrix playing "The Star-Spangled Banner." She had slept through the first 45 minutes of Hendrix's set.

"I love Jimi's music," Alexander said. "But I was so tired at that point, I wanted to take that guitar and wrap it around his neck."

And then it was over. Alexander and her friends packed up Richie's U-Haul and headed back to New Jersey Monday afternoon, thus avoiding the traffic jams in both directions. Her first crisis of the trip came when she got home and had to face the music of a different kind.

"I got yelled at by my mom," she recalled—the advance planning had not included telling her mother where she was going that weekend.

For Alexander, her focus for the weekend was the music. But not long after, her look back at Woodstock began.

"I was so focused on the music—I could just feel it," she recalled. "I didn't think a lot about anything else. But it did hit me that there was a lot of people who were truly affected by what was going on—there was a certain mindset of peace and love that we could feel.

"I'm not sure if I could call Woodstock a life changer for me, but it certainly opened my eyes to how many people thought about the world the way I did—about peace and happiness and love and let's stop the war," she said.

The little things at Woodstock made a lasting impression for Alexander; the alternatives to the conventions of 1960s life that Woodstock demonstrated would later shape her life.

"One thing that still stands out for me is when I was walking near the woods and I saw a woman sitting under a tree openly breastfeeding her baby. Of course, now breastfeeding is preferred, but it wasn't as common then, and I remember thinking to myself: why would anybody want to feed their baby any other way?

"At that point I was only 18, and not married or even involved with anyone. But that image stuck with me the whole time until I had children in the late 1970s. And I thought, I don't care if it's accepted or not, and I breastfed my children, and didn't care what anyone thought. So just that one simple thing I saw at Woodstock—that's one thing that really stuck in my mind from Woodstock is that woman sitting under the tree. And I think maybe if I hadn't seen that, I wouldn't even have thought about nursing my children. But yeah, I realized, 'that's the way to do it.'"

Alexander soon began to find focus in her life. She married at 22 and raised a family. When she divorced, she went back to school and became a nurse, ultimately also serving in the army reserve. When American hostages came home from Iran in 1981 after 444 days in captivity, Alexander served on the medical team that provided their care.

During her army service, Alexander went back to Woodstock for the 25th anniversary reunion concert—another three-day event, and this time with more than 550,000 in attendance—working in the medical tents and providing care to a new generation of marathon concert-goers. But the reunion concert was not at the original site, but in Saugerties, New York, at Winston Farm. And while the concert was a success—including many of the same bands from 1969—for Alexander it didn't feel the same.

"It was a great experience being able to support the kids, and it felt like I was giving back after having it so easy at the first concert," she said, "but the vibe just wasn't like the first time."

"I think that how much we all cooperated made it a great experience for everyone," she said. "I've never seen so many people in one place acting so similarly; it really was an eye-opener that so many people could get together in one place, and be hot, and then wet, and then out of food, and still act so civilly."

⚬≫⚬

At the top of the hill on Friday, Glenn Wooddell stood in his food booth, throwing ice cream bars to hungry kids.

Wooddell was a rarity at the event—a local who worked at the concert and a teacher at what was then known as Jeffersonville Youngsville Central School. He was new to the Catskills and to the East Coast when he arrived the year before—a transplanted Kansan studying in the graduate school at the University of North Texas. Wooddell saw a job notice in his department office for a position at Jeffersonville; a conference call with the school board secured his future as a teacher in rural New York.

"I packed up my Volvo with everything I had," Wooddell said, "and headed out."

Wooddell, then 21, taught music, media, and film, and during the summer followed the news about a big outdoor concert that would be held somewhere—location still uncertain—in the Catskills. Sitting on his porch with his friend Helen on an evening in late July, he read in the local paper that a final site had been chosen—12 minutes from his home.

"We were already starting to hear the buzz about Woodstock," Wooddell remembered. "There was just a kind of nervous energy among the people in the villages. Some people were excited about the business it would bring to the communities. But the wise old dairy farmers knew that a big event could be a problem, because the cows have to be milked no matter what. Later, when the big stainless steel tankers couldn't get through, they had to dump thousands of gallons of milk."

But that was two weeks away. Sitting on the porch, Wooddell wanted to join the party.

"I told Helen, 'I think this is going to be historic—I don't want to read about it in the paper, I'm going to go over and be part of it.'"

With the concert site chosen, the organizers began hiring. Wooddell landed two jobs: first to interview other job candidates, and then later to manage three of the food booths that would be built in tents at the top of the bowl. On the Thursday before the event officially opened, all went well; food was available, and the crowds were manageable. On his way home, however, he knew things would be different the next day.

"To walk down the road, I had to step over sleeping kids who were lining the highway," Wooddell said. "They were in no danger, because everything had just stopped; traffic wasn't moving."

"This was all new to me—not only just the concept of the festival, but just seeing those masses of people," he said. "Everything in the Catskills is always so quiet and calm and tranquil. I had never experienced anything like this before."

But the crowds and the traffic changed all the plans for the food booths.

"Nothing could get in," Wooddell said. "So now I'm managing three food booths, and we can't get any kind of supplies other than what we started with."

On Friday, however, things were different; to the west, driving was easier, and Wooddell had arranged for a ride to drop him off at a dairy a mile from the site. As he walked toward his food booths, Wooddell realized they were in trouble.

"The music was great, and the kids were fantastic," Wooddell said. "It really was a tremendous social experience—we could see that even from our booths. But our food was running out fast, and we knew there was no way that we could get more supplies in because of the traffic. So we sold what we could, and when the food ran out, all we had left was ice cream bars. We didn't bother selling them—we just threw them out to the crowd."

That was Friday.

"I went home to sleep for a few hours, and when I came back on Saturday morning, I knew there was nothing we could do," Wooddell said. "So we closed up."

Eventually, emergency food was provided by local volunteers—who prepared thousands of sandwiches—and the Hog Farm collective, the group directed by Hugh Romney (better known as Wavy Gravy), which had originally been hired to help with gently administered security. Romney's group served brown rice and vegetables as well as the granola that Alexander — along with thousands of others—tried for the first time.

"The Hog Farm seemed to be able to make food out of nothing," as Wooddell described their efforts.

But by Saturday afternoon, Wooddell's involvement in Woodstock was over; even for a local, the rain and the growing traffic made a return to the site impossible. His last memory of the concert itself was before heading home Saturday afternoon, as he watched the events unfold from his position at the top of the bowl.

"There was no way I could return," said Wooddell. "I wound up hearing about the end of the concert like everyone else—watching at home."

"I was exhausted. It had been a pleasant enough struggle for three days and nights, but I must confess that I was relieved that I didn't have to come back."

Wooddell later got his paycheck from the administration trailer—warned by his friends to get the money quickly before management went bankrupt. Wooddell raced to the Jeff Bank in Jeffersonville, deposited his check, and waited, but no bounce ever came; his check cleared.

The next Monday morning, preparing for the school year, Wooddell saw no anger or upset in town, more just "a general relief among the locals that it was over," he recalled.

"I think there were a few people close in proximity that were nervous and maybe were not happy about the crowds and the fuss," he said, "but collectively I just didn't sense any great resentment."

Wooddell's appreciation for Woodstock would take years to develop.

"I grew up in Kansas, and was then sheltered in the Catskills, so for a long while I didn't think back about the impact of Woodstock," said Wooddell. "I'm not proud of that, but I didn't.

"I was not a 'child of the '60s'—I didn't have to serve in Vietnam. I never had encounters with social activism. The issues of the era didn't confront me every day—they were just not directly connected to my world.

"But then I finally began to appreciate that I had dropped into the world of Woodstock by choice and it was wonderful," Wooddell said. "The experience of being with all of those people acting so well together made me more aware of what was going on, and have more sympathy for the causes—especially about the other causes of the era, like the protests over the Vietnam War.

"It was because of Woodstock that I began to truly recognize the importance of human values—I think individuality and the rights of an individual became more important. And I think a lot of those ideals just became second nature. I don't want to say people took their compassion for granted before that, but we've all become more sensitive and wiser about that. So, we slowly just turned that around—with empathy and caring and kindness and helping our fellow humans. There was a sensitivity that maybe hadn't been pre-Woodstock."

Now, when Wooddell goes back to Bethel to show young visitors the event grounds, he sees a greater tolerance than when he first arrived in the region in 1968.

"I can see just by the reception to what I'm saying at the Woodstock site itself, that they're much more receptive and understanding than I was at that stage in life," he said.

His lingering memory of Woodstock was, and still is, the feeling of optimism that was shared at the concert.

"I had to extend beyond my own little world," he said. "And I encountered just in my short time there an optimism and a feeling and I knew—I don't want to get spooky here—but I knew that down the road, it was going to change things in a good way."

Wooddell still lives only 12 minutes away from the concert site. "Sometimes I take that road home from Bethel, and it feels like one of the days of Woodstock," he said. "I think to myself, 'I'm going back home just to sleep for a few hours.'"

❧

Beth Henry described her life in the summer of 1969 as "nowheresville."

Henry would go on to graduate from college and became a social worker, and later an alcohol abuse counselor, a parole officer, and a probation supervisor; after retirement, she continued to write reports on serious offenders for the public defender's office. But in 1969, Henry was, like many others, aimless.

"I don't even remember if I had a job that summer," Henry said. "How did I ever become a responsible adult?"

But that summer was also a time that allowed Henry to be a free spirit, so when the invitation came to go to Woodstock, she took it. She tagged along with Elizabeth Alexander and Richie in the U-Haul group, but she had no idea of the enormity of the event until she stepped out of the truck in Bethel to witness the flood of spectators.

"I can remember that my mouth fell open and I said, 'Oh my God— *look at all these people,*'" Henry recalled.

The time before the concert began became a long expedition for Henry and Alexander to explore the grounds—"I remember I kept saying to Lizzie: 'Oh, let's go look at the stage. Let's check out this. Let's check out that.' I must have driven her crazy."

One of their excursions led to the fence that bordered the field—a fence that soon would be crushed down when the tidal wave of the crowd made barriers useless. There Henry and Alexander found a sheriff's patrol car; they hopped on the hood and sat for their portrait; the sheriff was unconcerned (see plate 16).

For Henry, food at her campsite was plentiful, but out in the bowl in the August sun, she was parched.

"I was happy but then sometimes not happy," she recalled. "The music was great, but there were a couple of times during the concert where the weather got a little overwhelming," she said. "We didn't have water with us, and we were getting very thirsty."

It was then Henry began to notice the spur-of-the-moment group self-help that was building all around her—a phenomenon she had never experienced before.

"Everyone really was sharing," she said. "For instance, a canteen would get passed around. We'd only take a little sip because we wanted to make sure everyone got a little. You know, that 'sharing attitude' was growing all around us."

That perspective was enough to inspire Henry to want to give back to the community after the concert; when she saw news coverage of the sea of garbage that the festival had left behind, she drove back to the concert site, taking her sister Linda and a few friends in the family Volkswagen bus to help clean up.

"I think that when I went to the concert, it opened up some parts of me that I didn't even know existed—I wanted to be a helping person," Henry said. "When we heard about the trash that we left behind, I knew I had to go back and help clean it up."

Henry's group was not alone. Dozens had lingered at the concert site to clean the 37 acres' worth of litter; and others like Henry had returned.

"It almost seemed overwhelming," Henry said. "But we made a dent in the garbage."

That involvement led to her growing awareness of being part of social support—a path that would guide the rest of her life.

"I think my future came out of what I experienced at Woodstock," Henry said. "I don't know if I ever would have become a counselor or a social worker if I hadn't experienced at Woodstock what people could be. That weekend tapped into a part of me that I didn't realize was there; I absolutely got caught up in the Woodstock mentality—I began to believe in people."

◦◯◦

At the top edge of the bowl, Patricia Tempel and her friends were walking the fringe of the crowd, trying to stay dry and out of the mud.

Active in political causes, Tempel was typical of the activist college student of the 1960s.

"I had spent a lot of time in my college years doing what people did in the '60s: a lot of political protesting—the Sheep Meadows antiwar rallies in Central Park, the Pentagon—all of them," said Tempel.

But Tempel had taken time off from the protests that summer to celebrate her college graduation, touring Europe before returning to the realities of graduate school. She returned to the United States just in time for the Woodstock Festival.

"I came back from Spain where three weeks earlier in Seville, I had watched the walk on the moon with a group of elderly Spanish gentlemen who thought the whole thing was a fake," she recalled.

After a cheap student flight from Madrid to New York, Tempel was on her way to Woodstock with her brother and two friends.

"In a way, it felt like the end of my childhood," she said.

Tempel's group left Connecticut for Woodstock in the early morning hours on Saturday—"it was actually more like very, very late Friday night," she recalled. They had heard nothing on the news about the crush of the crowds on Friday; to Tempel and her friends, it seemed like a normal trip to a folk festival.

"I must have been the only one at Woodstock in a dress and high heels," she said.

The drive took six hours—on a normal day it would have required less than a third of that time. The walk from the closest parking required another three hours. By the time they reached the concert grounds, it was late afternoon on Saturday.

As she neared Woodstock, one of her first impressions was that not all of the spectators were acting in the spirit of community.

"What struck me when I arrived was that it was the first time in my life that I saw tap water being sold," Tempel said. "It wasn't the locals who were selling it—it was a few kids who had been clever about bringing some big bottles and paper cups for 25 cents apiece. I was shocked and horrified."

(Yasgur noticed the same vendors. He posted a sign on his barn that read "Free Water." Later, he angrily told a reporter, "How can anyone ask for money for water?")

Tempel's group turned up Hurd Road and reached the concert at the peak moment, when more than 400,000 people were in the bowl.

"It was incredible," said Tempel. "All we could see was an ocean of people. It was so crowded that from my view there was nothing discernible—just bodies and bodies and bodies.

"Just being there was immediately thought provoking—more thought provoking than entertaining. But it was endlessly amazing to me what so many people were doing there," she said. "It all had a very earthy feel to it, because at that point everything was damp, yet everyone seemed completely oblivious to the discomfort. Even with the mud, and the lack of sanitation, and no food at that point, people were having a wonderful time. It had an almost mystical feel.

"I was dressed wrong, I got rid of my high heels, and I wasn't comfortable, but it was my first experience—my only experience—in my whole life of being in a situation like that, where there was rain and where there was mud and most people were unprepared. But it was overall so pleasant to be there. It was considerably wilder than my experience of other big concerts, but somehow more mellow at the same time."

For about 12 hours, Tempel and her friends stood, never sitting, but watching and listening as they walked along the top edge of the bowl. At some point early on Sunday morning, when it was still dark, Tempel had to leave; her flight for graduate school was that week. Between the long walk to the car and the even longer drive on the clogged roads, they did not reach home in Connecticut until Sunday night.

"When we got home," Tempel remembered, "we jumped into the Atlantic and then had martinis."

Tempel had heard none of the news coverage, but her parents had been watching the story unfold on TV, the Tate-LaBianca murders in Los Angeles the weekend before putting them on edge.

"They were concerned," Tempel remembered. "I had just spent three months hitchhiking through Europe, but there I was, one state away, and they were nervous because they heard reports of traffic and lack of food."

Tempel's Woodstock experience was brief, and the rush to graduate school put it out of her mind for the moment.

"Woodstock was a fun coda to my summer," she said. "For several years before I had been politically active, and at the time I didn't see the festival as having that kind of stature. And then I went off to graduate school in Chicago, buckled down, and grew up."

But Tempel later realized that Woodstock seemed like a declaration about her generation.

"For many of us who had gone to protest marches and got increasingly involved, it felt like counterculture was kind of our secret," she said. "And then the shock of Woodstock was 'oh my god, I'm not alone in this—there are at least a half-million other kids like me.' That was an amazing revelation, that countercultural ideas, which I had always associated with the music of our era, had become mainstream all at once.

"There were reflections then over the years that led to other reflections," she said. "Woodstock certainly means a lot more to me as time goes by. That group spirit of cooperation and good feeling made a huge impression that has grown ever since.

"It's odd—I participated in so many things in my youth that had historic significance because I grew up during the Vietnam War protest era and the struggle for civil rights. But who would have ever imagined that we would become known as the Woodstock Generation?"

Tempel went on to a career in education and journalism in Chicago and on the East Coast. She met her husband-to-be while they were both working in Connecticut, and they married in 1983. By sheer coincidence, he was from Sullivan County; they later returned there and bought a house a few minutes from Bethel.

"When I'm at the concert site, the significance of the festival is a topic of conversation all the time," she said. "It was the beginning of this incredible period for young people and bringing counterculture values—music, clothes, values—into the mainstream.

"Some people assume that Woodstock was all 'hippies,'" Tempel said. "It wasn't anything like that—it was mostly students and soldiers and all kinds of people. But we all learned something about a counterculture experience—belief in a more antimaterialistic, peaceful way of living—that we took with us for the rest of our lives. The ideas that represent Woodstock may be even more important than what actually happened there."

⚭

On Saturday, in the center of the crowd on the hillside, Jim Shelley and his friend Tony Tufano sat sweating in the August sun, reinforcing Shelley's own later explanation of who was attending the concert: "We seemed," Shelley remembered, "like a lot of white kids getting sunburned."

Shelley and Tufano were two typical middle-class kids—Shelley described the pair of them as "short-haired rock-and-roll no-drinks beardless buddies living in pre-Springsteen Jersey and on our way to engineering degrees that I would never get and he would barely use."

Shelley was a student at Notre Dame, home from Indiana after his freshman year. He had started college as an engineering student but then quickly realized his error.

"I was completely unsuited to be an engineer—I just didn't get it," Shelley said. "And then my second semester, I took an introduction to sociology class and it fit into the background hum of my entire life—the idea that stuff is going on in the world that is worth exploring out there that I don't understand yet, but I'm going to try to get behind the scenes to learn about it."

For Shelley, the music was everything. Since he was seven years old, he had been buying 45s ("the little records with the big holes, as we called them") and then graduated to stereo albums ("the big records with the little holes").

Shelley's primary connection to the music scene of the 1960s came from being a regular listener to WNEW-FM, the legendary New York radio station that by 1969 was one of the focal points of the rock world. WNEW, a progressive rock music station, was born from the 1967 split between co-owned AM and FM stations mandated by the Federal Communications Commission, a move intended to encourage the growth of FM. The split limited the number of hours that co-owned stations could "simulcast" during a broadcast day; as a result, many new FM station formats were born, including WNEW as a voice for the music world.

"It's easy to forget now, in a world with the Internet, how hard it was 50 years ago to get information about anything outside the mainstream," Shelley said. "There weren't many sources on radio for information about underground rock music or concerts or anything youth-oriented, and WNEW was one of them."

It was through advertisements on WNEW that Shelley and others first heard about the Woodstock Festival. He bought his tickets at the Village Oldies Store in Greenwich Village—a New York institution for record enthusiasts now gone—and looked forward to the festival weekend.

Shelley's story of the journey to Woodstock began like many others': he and Tufano left home in Cliffside, New Jersey, on Friday evening, and hours later and miles from the concert were inching their way through the countryside.

"And at a point when the traffic was basically at a standstill, we pulled off the road, got out of the car, and asked people what's going on," Shelley recalled.

At 6:00 a.m., the scene on Route 17B was four lanes of parked cars pointing toward the venue.

"We gathered our stuff, stared a moment, and started walking. We didn't know where we were going," he said. "We just followed the crowd."

Shelley remembered that there were many people walking away from the site, all asking the same questions and getting the same answers:

"How far is it?" "Just ahead."

"How was it?" "Wet."

"Is it still on?" "It's canceled."

Shelley and Tufano took a chance and started walking—eight miles.

Hours later, they got to the bowl, which was already packed with more than 250,000 people and more arriving by the minute.

"Tony and I stood in the middle of the field, which sloped down to the stage a couple hundred yards away," Shelley wrote years later. "The smell of wet hay, the sounds of thousands of people, and the sight of tents surrounded us. Nappers rested under the warm sun. We had arrived."

The pair managed to wiggle their way into a spot about 400 feet from the stage—"we staked out our eight-foot square"—and baked while they were immersed in the music.

"It seemed that everyone in the world who should be there was and everyone else was at home hearing about it," said Shelley. "All was fine."

The crowd was huge, but the true magnitude of its size hit Shelley and Tufano at 2:30 Saturday afternoon, when Santana played "Soul Sacrifice," an early signature piece for the Latin rock band that became one of the highlights of the event.

"When Santana finished, the 400,000 in the crowd stood and cheered and screamed," Shelley remembered. "When I say I felt the whole atmosphere moving—that is my very distinct memory. The roar was overwhelming, but not in a scary way; it was just—'oh my god, I've never felt anything like that before or since.' It was a physical moment."

Shelley turned to his right and snapped a photo, and then to his left—forever capturing the moment when, for him, Woodstock reached its peak.

The music played all night; Shelley and Tufano alternately listened, talked with their many neighbors, and napped. But Shelley was awake as the Sunday sun came up.

"The vision I will take to the grave," he recalled, "will be Jefferson Airplane's 'Plastic Fantastic Lover' accompanying the sun's rise."

For Shelley and Tufano, Woodstock was magical musically, but they personally experienced none of the counterculture that stereotyped the concert weekend.

"Tony and I never saw *Life* magazine's Woodstock, like the smoke shops, the little children playing in the mud, the free food, or the nude bathing—those were all stories we heard later on. Instead we stretched out, watched others, listened to people reading the *New York Times'* account of our party, and began to realize how big and amazing the event had become."

Later on Sunday, Shelley and Tufano persevered through the alternating rain and sun, but then they realized—still drenched and two days without food—they had reached their limit.

"Everything we had was soaking wet," Shelley said. "We hadn't brought spare clothes, or plastic in case it rained. We had planned our weekend like a couple of dumb 19-year-olds."

So after Joe Cocker performed, they started out for home; their last memory of Bethel that summer was riding on the back of an already-packed sedan as they headed back to their car.

"We just laid down on the roof and hung on," said Shelley. "When we got near our car, we just knocked on the side and they stopped to let us off."

Woodstock came to mean more to Shelley than a weekend of music in the sun; he has always cherished the energy of the people around him on that weekend, especially that moment when they all stood for Santana.

"The impact of so many people there has never left me," he said. "I felt such a strong impression that we were all brothers and sisters.

"I definitely had the strong sense that many of us felt the same about a lot of things—the music, of course, but about the country too—about civil rights, about Vietnam, and about making a better world. Woodstock wasn't a protest, but there was a consciousness there about changing the world that we all shared."

Shelley became a social science teacher, working at his hometown's high school in Cliffside Park; his son teaches at the same school. Nearly a half-century later, Shelley still feels the pull of Woodstock; he owns a second home not far away and is a frequent tour guide.

But his friend Tony never felt the draw.

"For years, I would bug Tony about Woodstock," Shelley said. "I'd tell him, 'You've got to come up with me sometime so I can pick your brain about the concert.' But he would always say that he didn't remember much about it.

"But finally, a few years ago, I convinced him to come back to Bethel with me. We walked out onto the bowl, and I asked him, 'Do you remember where we sat?' And he pointed out the exact spot where we had been that weekend. And then it all started to come back to him."

Shelley was not engaged politically in the 1960s, but to him Woodstock is nevertheless a reminder of the unceasing care required for the fragile victories won in that era.

"Because of Woodstock, I'm constantly aware that the issues we thought had been taken care of in the '60s will always need attention," he said. "Like when the Civil Rights Act was signed in 1964, we thought the right of everyone to vote was taken care of, but that issue needs attention now more than ever. We made a lot of progress on the environment, but now the issues about global warming and new forms of pollution are growing. There was a level of shared consciousness that occurred that weekend—that we need to stay involved and be sure that the next generation knows that it's their turn to be involved."

17

COMING FROM A DREAM

"This weekend says a lot about the youth of America. More than 350,000 people came looking for peace and music. Many said they learned a lot about themselves, and learned a lot about getting along together, and priorities. And for most, that alone makes it all worthwhile."

—Lem Tucker, *NBC News*

Three days that could have been chaos instead became harmony. On the Woodstock weekend, it seemed that potential disasters were somehow being transformed into serendipitous miracles.

When the cars stopped moving, people walked, and then walked some more. Many—like Jim Shelley and Patricia Tempel—remembered walking to the concert, farther than they had ever walked before in their lives. When food dwindled, everyone gave a little of what they brought, and Hugh Romney's Hog Farm group with their rice and granola took care of many more.

When medical services were overwhelmed, volunteer emergency physicians came together in New York and were helicoptered to Bethel. Even the U.S. Army came—not as troops to enforce, but as medical teams with aid. When rides were needed, people like Shelley piled onto the outsides of cars—a stunt they would have considered folly anywhere else; one sedan was spotted on Hurd Road, full to capacity with 11 people hanging on to the outside.

And when young passersby came through Monticello or Jeffersonville, the local residents let go of their concerns about the concert and their resentment about counterculture and provided food, water, and good cheer.

The open-air community that had become one of the largest cities in the state had become an homage to the essence of humanity.

"When the town saw who these people were, their concerns broke down; they all became a community and a family," event promoter Michael Lang said. "It changed everybody."

Among those who witnessed the transformation was Mike Kaufman, a reporter who had walked six miles to reach the festival. As he experienced Woodstock over the next two days, Kaufman, who had covered everything from wars to the Dalai Lama, was awed by the spectators and the well-being that prevailed.

"I was completely overwhelmed," Kaufman recalled 40 years later. Comparing the weekend to the only other event in his life with the same impact—Martin Luther King Jr.'s march on Washington in 1963—Kaufman realized that at Woodstock, "I was watching consciousness change in an afternoon."

And the police—the authorities who the youth of the era usually defied the most—were the first to defend the young visitors.

"I was very, very much surprised and I'm very happy to say we think the people of this country should be proud of these kids," said the local police chief. "Notwithstanding the way they dress or the way they wear their hair—that's their own personal business—but their inner workings, their inner selves, their self-demeanor cannot be questioned; they can't be questioned as good American citizens."

The feeling of enthusiasm and inclusiveness was shared by all involved, from the musicians to the security team of Hog Farm members and their graceful application of "please force" security ("please don't do this—instead do that") to the steadying presence of production manager John Morris and lighting designer Chip Monck, both recruited at the last minute to serve as stage announcers, whose articulate, hip commentary instantly connected with the crowd.

"Now, let's face the situation," said Morris. "We've had thousands and thousands of people come here today—many, many more than we knew or even dreamt or thought would be possible. We're going to need each other to help each other to work this out because we're taxing the systems that we have set up. We're going to be bringing the food in.

"But, the one major thing you have to remember tonight," Morris said on Friday, "when you go back up to the woods to go to sleep or if you stay here, is that the man next to you is your brother. And you damn well better treat each other that way because if you don't, then we blow the whole thing. But we've got it, right there."

Monck issued his own unique brand of drug alert: "You might take it with however many grains of salt you wish, that the brown acid that is circulating around us is not specifically too good. It's suggested that you do stay away from that. Of course it's your own trip, so be my guest. But please be advised that there's a warning on that one, okay?"

No one will ever know for certain how many people actually attended Woodstock. Estimates range from 250,000 by local officials to 500,000 by some attendees, with most observers willing to compromise at about 400,000 for the weekend.

But whatever the actual number was, everyone agreed that the measures by local residents and volunteers to support the young spectators had stretched resources to the absolute limit. Any additional attendees would have created a crisis—which is what almost happened.

By the second day of the concert, the area around Bethel was an impassable 10-mile circle of choked roads and abandoned cars. Yet when news of the first day of the extraordinary event began to reach New York and other East Coast cities, thousands still came, hoping to drive as close as they could and then walk the rest of the way. The New York state police estimated that as many as 1 million people were turned away along nearby freeways, thus avoiding the unmanageable influx that no doubt would have resulted in a major emergency.

Event promoter Michael Lang, ever enthusiastic about the popularity of Woodstock, acknowledged the probable calamity that 1 million more spectators would have caused.

"*That* would have been a disaster," he said.

⠶⠶⠶

By Monday morning, August 18, the event was winding down, running hours late because of the rain. Jimi Hendrix did not start his closing act until 8:30 on Monday morning; although Lang tried to persuade Hendrix to perform the night before, his manager had insisted that Hendrix be the closing act no matter what time he performed. Hendrix played for nearly two hours—the longest concert set of his career.

Forty-five minutes into his performance, Hendrix broke into his own rendition of "The Star Spangled Banner"; it was the national anthem with new meaning for a new generation.

"The guitarist performed his most famous solo, channeling the atmosphere of beauty and love amid anger and aggression that defined the culturally tumultuous era," said music writer Andrew O'Brien. "You can hear the air force dive bombers staking their lives for the country in Vietnam through Jimi's whammy bar dives. You can feel the mourning of American mothers and fathers in the fragments of military funeral hymnal 'Taps' he added near the song's end. You can hear the nation's chaos in the atonal distortion. And you can hear the hope shine through as Hendrix hits the anthem's final notes with optimistic purpose."

Hendrix's performance of the anthem also remains an iconic visual moment—not just of Woodstock but also of the 1960s.

"I looked out with one eye," said director Michael Wadleigh, who was filming Hendrix from the stage, "and I saw people grabbing their heads, so ecstatic, so stunned and moved, a lot of people holding their breath, including me."

By the time Hendrix performed "Hey Joe" to end the show, "only" about 40,000 people were there. The rest were on their way home to jobs, school, and the real world.

The concert officially closed with comments by stage announcer Chip Monck as he implored the stragglers to grab a plastic bag and help clean up—to do "anything you can do to give us a hand to leave this area somewhat the way we found it. I don't think it will ever be quite the same."

Monck was right; it was never quite the same.

For Michael Lang, the end of the festival was a return to the real world.

"My most vivid memory was leaving in a helicopter," Lang said. "John and Joel had left, and I had to meet them at the bank. As we came up over the field we saw this huge peace symbol (made of trash), and kids were dragging garbage into this. So that was the image I left with, and the next thing I remember is landing on Wall Street! And it was a rude awakening, you know, coming from a dream."

At the offices of the *New York Times*, the staff and editors were divided by the same types of conflicts concerning Woodstock that the generations of Americans were experiencing about counterculture across the country.

Over the weekend, most of the nation's newspapers—drawing on news articles written by national wire services—had covered Woodstock by focusing on the disaster angle, with sprinklings of drug overdoses and mud thrown in. Typical of the headlines was the banner across the top of the *New York Daily News* on Saturday morning: "Traffic Uptight at Hippiefest." A caption for a photo that showed a choked road began "Go-Go Is a No-No."

An example of the least representative coverage was the story distributed across the country by United Press International (UPI), which ran with the headline "Drugs and Mud Plague 300,000 at N.Y. Music Fair."

"More than 300,000 persons wandered about in a sea of mud, sickness, and drugs Saturday at the hippie-style Woodstock Music and Art Fair," UPI reported. "Officials asked Gov. Nelson A. Rockefeller to declare the festival site a disaster area." (Rockefeller had called promoter John Roberts to see if the National Guard should be called out, but Roberts, whose family was prominent in New York pharmaceuticals, persuaded him that intervention was unnecessary.)

Covering the story entirely in a negative light by focusing on the muck, rain, and "thousands of drug overdoses," UPI quoted "one far-out music lover" as saying, "I don't know, man—this thing is just one bad trip."

Writers from the *New York Times* who were on site at Woodstock knew better, and writer Barney Collier fought by phone with the news desk to cover the event as the social milestone that Woodstock was becoming.

In the Saturday paper, Collier's first story, filed before the concert got underway, was a straightforward news account of traffic jams and some of the arrests. But on Saturday morning, when newspapers began to arrive at the concert site, announcer Chip Monck read some of the headlines to the crowd in between acts, including the "Hippiefest" coverage in the *Daily News*; Collier realized he would have to press his case with his editors for more responsible coverage of the event.

"To me, it looked like an amazingly well-behaved bunch of folks," Collier recalled in 2009. "Every major *Times* editor up to and including executive editor James Reston insisted that the tenor of the story must be a social catastrophe in the making—that it was a bunch of drugged-up freaks that were causing a terrible problem—all of the things you'd expect. It was difficult to persuade them that the relative lack of serious mischief and the fascinating cooperation, caring, and politeness among so many people was the significant point.

"I had to resort to refusing to write the story unless it reflected to a great extent my on-the-scene conviction that 'peace' and 'love' was the actual emphasis, not the preconceived opinions of Manhattan-bound editors.

"This caused a big furor at the *Times* in New York," Collier recalled. "And this eventually went up to Reston, who said, 'If that's the way Barney sees it, that's the way we'll write it.'

"After many acrimonious telephone exchanges, the editors agreed to publish the story as I saw it, and although the nuts-and-bolts matters of gridlock and minor lawbreaking were put close to the lead of the stories, the real flavor of the gathering was permitted to get across."

Collier's article ran as the lead story on page one of the Sunday *Times* and was picked up by other papers across the country.

"Despite massive traffic jams, drenching rain storms, and shortages of food, water, and medical facilities, about 300,000 young people swarmed over this rural area today for the Woodstock Music and Art Fair," Collier wrote.

"Drawn by such performers as Joan Baez, Ravi Shankar, Jimi Hendrix, and Jefferson Airplane, the prospect of drugs and excitement of 'making the scene,' the young people came in droves, camping in the woods, romping in the mud, talking, smoking and listening to the wailing music."

Collier's article went on to describe how police and organizers agreed that the crowd was "well-behaved" the attendees were "hip, swinging young-sters," and included a quote from Lang, who described the audience as "about the quietest, most well-behaved people in one place that can be imagined."

To Collier, "That was probably the most important thing I did—to get it to be seen as it was, rather than the preconceptions of a lot of editors back on the desks. After the first day's *Times* story appeared on page one, the event was widely recognized for the amazing and beautiful accident it was."

But Collier, Michael Kaufman, and other *New York Times* writers who had been at the event had no control over the editorials that appeared in the paper, and the reaction of the editors demonstrated the broader rift in the nation about America as it had been, compared to the new culture that was coming. On Monday, August 18, in a staff editorial titled "Nightmare in the Catskills," the *Times* editors—none of whom had firsthand knowledge of what had occurred in Bethel—blistered the Woodstock Festival.

"The dreams of marijuana and rock music that drew 300,000 fans and hippies to the Catskills had little more sanity than the impulses that drive the lemmings to march to their deaths in the sea," the *Times'* editors pon-tificated. "What kind of culture is it that can produce so colossal a mess?"

Later, the editorial described the event as "this outrageous episode" and the promoters as showing "a complete lack of responsibility."

Reporters at the *Times* rebelled against the editorial, some supposedly threatening to quit if the paper did not revise its view. And incredibly, the *Times* did something rare for the paper: it recanted—reluctantly.

On Tuesday, August 19, the editors ran a new editorial, this one entitled "Morning After at Bethel," which toned down the volatile rhetoric from the day before with a somewhat more thoughtful post-event appraisal.

"Now that Bethel has shrunk back to the dimensions of a Catskill village," the editorial began, "and most of the 300,000 young people who made it a 'scene' have returned to their homes, the rock festival begins to take on the quality of a social phenomenon."

The attendees endured the discomforts, the *Times* wrote, "to enjoy their own society, free to exult in a life style that is its own declaration of independence."

To Ken Paulson—at the time a 15-year-old fledgling music writer who four decades later would become editor of *USA Today* and then president of the First Amendment Center—the *Times* coverage of Woodstock and the internal strife it produced were an example of the disconnection at many media outlets about how they covered the music scene, and by extension the lack of understanding about other major issues of youth culture in America.

"The news media didn't know how to cover a cultural event like Woodstock, and they had no appreciation of the art involved," Paulson said. "This was no surprise. Newspapers across the country were staffed with people who grew up on Elvis, and it is a giant leap from Elvis to The Who."

This lack of current-day awareness shapes not only media coverage but also the perceptions of the people who read it.

"It's not unusual for mainstream news organizations to be clueless about emerging cultural developments," Paulson said, "especially when it involves the art of young people. Woodstock inspired a reexamination among the nation's news media about how they cover these events—and without appearing to be totally out of touch."

These reappraisals say much about thoughtful discussions of news coverage but also speak even louder about the financial needs of the media. In the 1960s, news organizations needed to court the emerging baby boomers—a generation strong in numbers and in buying power.

"Media slowly began to realize that they needed younger readers to buy their publications and buy from their advertisers," said Paulson. "In the late '60s and '70s, there was a shift in fashion and there was certainly a shift in music. But most aspects of counterculture just didn't lend themselves to advertising revenue or support for general-interest publications.

"So music coverage was the most visible form reflecting the culture at the time. As a result, in the early '70s, major publications hired young people who could write about young people's music as well as film."

And that cultural gap never closes.

"I think the gap has intensified now—it's just taken different forms today," Paulson said. "For instance, it's very difficult for mainstream news organizations to understand rap or to truly appreciate hip-hop.

"But I think it's fair to describe Woodstock as a turning point," said Paulson. "Rock music was no longer an oddity. It was clear that the future had arrived—that for three days, 400,000 people were part of an instant city that defined its own culture."

Said Collier, "Suddenly we began to realize that we were coming into a different world."

The conflict at the *Times* over Woodstock only began to scratch the surface of questions about the media coverage of many divisive issues of the late 1960s. Woodstock was a lightning rod that would draw commentary both positive and negative about the state of America's youth; to some, Woodstock became the ultimate demonstration of new social accord on a mass scale, while to others the concert weekend was yet another excuse to avoid conventional adult responsibilities and the demands of a middle-class lifestyle. The debate about Woodstock and many other issues involving the counterculture of the 1960s would continue for decades.

While newspapers across the country continued to focus on the messages of a disaster area and "hippiefest" in their coverage during the Woodstock weekend, it was perhaps surprising that the network television news—often the most benign of mainstream media—began to enlighten America about the broader relevance of the events that occurred at Woodstock on the night the concert ended.

In the days before cable TV, CNN, and digital content, the medium with the broadest reach was the nightly evening news provided by the three broadcast television networks: ABC, CBS, and NBC. At a time when every home had a favorite network for news, more than 20 million households saw their first glimpses of Woodstock that Monday night.

With Hendrix's last notes still echoing across the pastures, all three networks had crews at the site on August 18 to wrap up coverage of the concert. While all of them touched on the problems over the weekend, the reporters—each with experience covering youth and the issues of the 1960s—focused their coverage on the message of Woodstock.

"This weekend says a lot about the youth of America," said Lem Tucker from NBC, standing near the stage and surrounded by a sea of refuse. "More than 350,000 people came looking for peace and music. Many said they learned a lot about themselves, and learned a lot about getting along together, and priorities. And for most, that alone makes it all worthwhile."

ABC's Gregory Jackson's coverage focused on the townspeople in nearby Monticello, and Jackson also criticized the negative print articles across the country from the weekend.

"Unfortunately, because much of the press news coverage was so jaundiced in its reports of what happened here, not many people in the country will have learned what the people of Monticello learned," Jackson said. "Suffice it to say that it was not a disaster area. But before it was over, something happened in Monticello. Residents and resorts freely emptied their cupboards to the kids. Merchants and police praised the kids.

"It's true one may not ask for the tailors of these youngsters," Jackson concluded. "But would anyone care to venture a guess what would have happened if 450,000 well-dressed businessmen were thrown together for three days under similar circumstances?"

Richard O'Brien from CBS did a straightforward job of covering the aftermath, mentioning both the problems and the positive experiences. And then CBS reporter John Laurence—still the network's lead reporter dealing with the issues of the young since his Generations Apart project from two months earlier—delivered a commentary that looked past the drugs and the traffic.

"What happened this weekend may have been more than an uncontrolled outpouring of hip young people," said Laurence. "What happened was that hundreds of thousands of kids invaded a rural resort area totally unprepared to accommodate them, among adults who reject their youthful style of life. And that somehow, by nature of old-fashioned kindness and caring, both groups came together, in harmony and good humor, and all of them learned from the experience."

Laurence described Woodstock as "a revelation in human understanding." The local—and older—eyewitnesses, Laurence explained, "had not been aware, as the kids are, of the gentle nature of kids to one another. These long-haired, mostly white kids in their blue jeans and sandals were no wide-eyed anarchists looking for trouble.

"So what was learned was not that hundreds of thousands of people can paralyze an area . . . but that in an emergency at least, people of all ages are capable of compassion," concluded Laurence. "And while such a spectacle may never happen again, it has recorded the growing proportions of this youthful culture in the mind of adult America."

ABC's broadcast agreed. "Over the last few days we've had a glimpse of our future," said veteran journalist Howard K. Smith, "and this is what it looked like."

Later on Monday, late-night talk show host Dick Cavett devoted his whole program to a celebration of counterculture. Cavett, who in a tailored khaki shirt and slacks looked uncomfortably dressed for a safari rather than a discussion of Woodstock and America's youth, hosted Joni Mitchell and Jefferson Airplane.

Halfway through the show, Stephen Stills and David Crosby stopped in to chat.

"It was incredible," said Crosby about Woodstock, "probably the strangest thing that's ever happened in the world." Stephen Stills—still wearing the same clothes he wore during his performance at Woodstock—showed off the mud from Yasgur's farm still on his jeans. Many in Cavett's audience had attended Woodstock, coming directly to the studio from Bethel.

Cavett tried hard, and he was almost of the same generation as most of the performers—only three years older than Grace Slick from Jefferson

Airplane. But the culture gap between them was obvious, and the conversation was often stilted. In the end, Cavett tried to keep the conversation going by cheerfully asking the group if there was "anything you always wanted to say on television but nobody ever gave you the chance?"

Crosby raised his hand like a fifth-grader in class. "I got one," he said. "The air that we are breathing is not clean . . . consider this: the only way to solve it seems to be to convince GM, Ford, Chrysler, 76 Union, Shell, and Standard to go out of business. Which is merely a setup for the punchline, which is 'fat chance.'" Cavett replied, "Yeah, especially because four of them are my sponsors"—which did draw a laugh from the guests. Easing the mood, Stills and Mitchell each performed a solo, and Jefferson Airplane closed the show with two numbers. Not a perfect program, but it was, at least, an opportunity to showcase the participants of Woodstock for a broader national audience.

⌒∞⌒

Even with the breaking-news notoriety of the event and the memories of 400,000 attendees, Woodstock might have lingered as just a pleasant shared experience rather than a milestone for a generation if not for the March 1970 release of Michael Wadleigh's documentary about the event. Titled simply *Woodstock*, and directed in a frank, intimate study that focused as much on the experiences of those who attended as it did on the magic of the music, the film elevated the concert into an icon of its age.

Woodstock was a tremendous hit, becoming one of the most popular films of the year and in March 1971 winner of the Academy Award for Best Documentary Feature.

"The remarkable thing about Wadleigh's film," wrote critic Roger Ebert, "is that it succeeds so completely in making us feel how it must have been to be there."

In the process, *Woodstock* the film became the link between the significance of the concert for those who attended and how the rest of the world would begin to respond to it.

"The notoriety of the festival really started with the film a year later," said attendee Patricia Tempel. "I chalked up my appreciation of the festival to my enjoyment in attending. But when the movie was released, all of a sudden Woodstock became significant—it just exploded onto the culture."

The documentary also clearly demonstrated that the hundreds of thousands of attendees represented only a fraction of the young Americans who were bringing new attitudes and ideas to the nation.

"The movie began to open some eyes up to what was really going on at Woodstock," said Paulson, "that the music and attitudes of an entire generation was bringing change to America."

❧

Two weeks after the Woodstock Festival ended, CBS News sent a crew back to Bethel to follow up. At the bowl—with volunteers still piling up garbage bags while damp stacks of burning paper smoldered—reporter John Laurence found the last seven campers, who were packing up for their trip back to Buffalo; they had been living nearby for almost a month.

"The first night we got here, we didn't have much money," said Terry, one of the campers. "The police took me and the people in my car out to dinner and offered to let us stay in his house."

In the same segment, Yasgur continued to defend the concert and champion the people who attended—even as he talked with Laurence near his now-stripped field.

"This concert was contracted for no more than 45,000 people," Yasgur said. "When I realized Friday night and Saturday morning that we were getting up close to the half-million mark, and there was a sea of people here, I became quite apprehensive.

"These young people made me feel guilty," Yasgur said, "because there were no problems. They proved to me and proved to the whole world that they didn't come up here for any problems. They came up here for exactly what they said they were coming up for—three days of music and peace."

❧

It was back to reality. But it was a new reality—a recognition that for many of the 400,000 people who attended, and millions around the world who watched what happened, that their world had changed.

"On Max Yasgur's 600 acres," said Michael Lang, "everyone dropped their defenses and became a huge extended family. Joining together, getting into the music and each other, being part of so many people when calamity struck—the traffic jams, the rainstorms—was a life-changing experience. None of the problems damaged our spirit. In fact, they drew us closer. We recognized one another for what we were at the core, as brothers and sisters, and we embraced one another in that knowledge."

Richard Harris, a participant in Woodstock—one of the people who led the opening prayer—described Woodstock as the type of sharing experience that can become part of a broader worldview.

"For me, Woodstock was more than a concert," Harris said. "As you walked through the farmland, you were able to come across different pockets of people who were open and accepting to anybody that came, and you were able to eat with them and talk with them.

"That's what the Woodstock Nation was about—about sharing and loving and helping," said Harris. "You saw people just being kind with each other. It showed the world that people could live together in peace under the guise of music. But it was such a strong social statement that we did not have any external political agenda. This was just about being together."

In the months that followed Woodstock, such thoughtful views would be a welcome contrast to the dark vision that soon would be revealed with the arrest of Charles Manson and his "family" and the message of hate that he would expound about America.

Only weeks after the event, writer Ellen Sander perceived the far-flung implications of the event that looked past the mud, drugs, and music and saw how the legacy of Woodstock would begin to shape the broader American experience.

"No longer can the magical multicolored phenomenon of pop culture be overlooked or underrated," Sander wrote in *Saturday Review*. "It's happening everywhere, but now it has happened in one place at one time so hugely that it was indeed historic.

"The audience was a much bigger story than the groups—these were the least significant events of what happened over the Woodstock weekend," Sander said. "What happened was that the largest number of people ever assembled for any event other than a war lived together, intimately and meaningfully and with such natural good cheer that they turned on not only everyone surrounding them but the mass media, and, by extension, millions of others, young and old, particularly many elements hostile to the manifestations and ignorant of the substance of pop culture."

America would begin to learn that the message of Woodstock had little to do with LSD or swimming naked in Filippini Pond; what truly mattered was the experience of spontaneous group cooperation on an unprecedented scale, the first and possibly the only time that most of the participants experienced life without traditional boundaries. And incredibly, those involved found earnest respect, kindness in the face of potential calamity, and unconditional acceptance of others. When eyewitnesses recall their memories of Woodstock, they seldom, if ever, linger on the drugs or the sex; what they do cherish are the three days of unity—stringing Christmas lights with a local cop, or sharing oranges with strangers, or standing on a street corner handing out lollipops—the simple human dignity of sharing and caring.

Woodstock vividly represented the intangible best qualities of the American experience. A month earlier, Apollo 11 demonstrated the most tangible expression of U.S. achievement; Woodstock symbolized the possibilities and dreams for a new generation—whether they could be achieved or not.

That sentiment was expressed often at Woodstock; said one idealistic young vendor at the event selling *Rat Subterranean News*, an underground newspaper, "The power to the people is just starting to be imagined—the things we never could have *believed*!"

For Lang, Woodstock also represented the challenges faced by a new generation in confronting issues—challenges that are just as relevant today as they were in 1969.

"Woodstock declared that a young generation could take on the issues of personal freedoms, stopping an unjust war, creating respect for the planet, and work for human rights," said Lang.

"Woodstock showed that the world can be a better and more peaceful place, and that view keeps resonating," said Lang. "That message continues to this day."

Woodstock did not solve the nation's ills in the late 1960s, but after the concert, for many there was a renewed appreciation for their fellow human beings. Woodstock came to represent the earnest expectation that America can be as open, inclusive, and free-spirited every day as three days of peace and music had been in 1969 at Bethel, New York.

"What Woodstock represented, and what it still represents today, is hope," said Barry Levine, who photographed the entire weekend for the documentary team. "Woodstock gave the hope that things could be different."

While broad definitions are often used to describe the generations since 1969—such as "baby boomers," "millennials," and "xennials," among others—the term "Woodstock generation" has taken on a special meaning as a description that applies to a group of any age or orientation still committed to the ideals of the 1960s. And the term "Woodstock" has become part of the American vernacular, not just as the name of an event in 1969 but also as a no-explanation-needed term that is synonymous with uplift and inspiration. When Barack Obama was inaugurated almost 40 years after the concert, the *Wall Street Journal* called the event attended by more than 1 million people "Washington's Woodstock."

"Woodstock showed that people can take care of each other," said concert promoter Artie Kornfeld. "For that reason alone, it reaffirmed my faith in people."

IV

INTERNET

October 29, 1969: An experiment at UCLA and Stanford
Research Institute signals the birth of the Internet

29 OCT 67	2100	LOADED oP PROGRAM	CSK	
		FoR BEN BARKER		
		BBN		
	22:30	Talked to SRI	CSK	
		Host to Host		
		Left op. imp. program	CSK	
		running after sending		
		a host dead message		
		to imp.		

The birth of the Internet. On October 29, 1969, at 22:30 (10:30 p.m.), UCLA
graduate student Charley Kline recorded a connection between the computer in the
university's Network Measurement Laboratory and a computer staffed by Bill Duvall
at the Stanford Research Institute. As much as any moment would be, this was the
first cry of the newborn Internet. LEONARD KLEINROCK.

18

COLOR AND FLASH

"Did you ever think back then that it would all turn out like *this?*"

—Question to Professor Leonard Kleinrock at the thirtieth anniversary of the birth of the Internet

Atherton, California
September 24, 1999

The town of Atherton was founded in 1866 and grew into a lush, exclusive community in the heart of Silicon Valley decades before the concept of a "Silicon Valley" ever existed. The town—and in spite of its location surrounded by the high-density communities south of San Francisco, residents gently remind visitors that Atherton is a "town"—with its wooded landscape and country-lane-like curbless streets, is a haven for the supremely successful.

"If you live in Atherton," said one former resident, "it means you've made it."

By the 1990s, the recent arrivals to Atherton who had "made it" were the new elite of the computer world—especially the executives and entrepreneurs at the growing number of companies in Silicon Valley that were creating enterprises on the Internet. Just as Beverly Hills is a symbol of status in the movie industry, Atherton had reached the same prominence for the tech realm.

And like Beverly Hills, on occasion Atherton becomes a setting for glitz and glamour. This night, on a particularly private lane, the elite of technology were gathering at the home of one of technology's "angel" investors to celebrate a special event: the 30th anniversary of the Internet. The scene had all the color and flash of a Hollywood premiere: the convoy of limousines, a red-carpet entrance, jostling paparazzi, and frantic publicists nudging clients toward interview opportunities in a brightly lit staging area.

But it was at the back of the grounds in the pool house, sheltered from the chatter and the music, where the royalty of the evening were taken for their moment in front of the cameras—dot-com CEOs chatting with network reporters, offering up sound bites of commentary about how online companies were reshaping the nation.

Yet one of the reporters' favorites was not an executive but a quiet, good-natured college professor named Leonard Kleinrock, who sat patiently waiting for his moment in the spotlight.

A visitor caught Kleinrock's eye.

"Did you ever think back then," the visitor asked Kleinrock, "that it would all turn out like *this*?"

Kleinrock looked around at the lights, and the cameras, and then through the window at the celebration. He stood as a production assistant arrived to guide him to an interview with CNN.

"Like this?" Kleinrock grinned. "Never—not a chance."

19

"LO"

"Here is a question: how many revolutions do you know that you can tell the exact minute when the revolution began?"

—Leonard Kleinrock, UCLA

UCLA
October 29, 1969
9:30 p.m.

Boelter Hall on the UCLA campus is a nondescript but pleasant enough brick building, framed by California olive trees and bordered by the grass-lined walkway known as the Court of Sciences in the south section of the university. Built for the UCLA engineering school in 1959 and named for the university's first engineering dean, Boelter from the front appears as a relatively modest four-story structure. However, constructed in a long cut carved into what was once a gentle slope in the Westwood hills, the structure's back side shows its true size: extending downward, Boelter is a beast of a building, with 10 floors and more than 1,000 rooms, arranged in that maddening, unfriendly confusion of floors, exits, and numbering that in the 1950s marked college structures everywhere.

During the day, Boelter Hall teems with engineering students. But in the evening, with most student housing far across the campus, the building descends into quiet solitude—an ideal setting for work that requires time and focus.

It was a perfect night to change the world.

Charley Kline, a graduate student in the engineering school's computer science department, viewed the late hours as a time to work in Boelter free of distractions. At 21, Kline was the personification of a computer geek before the phrase became a cliché, habitually wearing button-down shirts and plastic pocket protectors for his pens. His one concession to 1960s counterculture was hair that could be generously described as slightly longish—but with cheek-length sideburns.

"I was a tech guy who liked to program at all hours," Kline said, "and it was much easier for me to stay focused in the middle of the night."

But "to program" in 1969 was vastly different from what today's UCLA engineering student would describe as time in a Westwood coffee shop a few blocks from campus, pecking on a two-pound laptop that is linked by Wi-Fi to files housed in the cloud. For Kline, and a generation of students studying in the relatively young field of computer science, a personal computer of any size or price was almost a decade away; "to program" meant going to an on-campus laboratory, "computers" were room-filling systems, and "keyboards" usually meant cumbersome stand-alone terminals shrouded in sheet steel.

That night, Kline's project would be relatively simple—if it worked—and involved the test of a new system that had been at UCLA for almost two months. The project was funded by the federal government to establish the feasibility of creating links between computers in locations across the country.

For Kline, such assignments were departures from the traditional education that most computer science students pursued in the 1960s. Although some opportunities in computing involved government or academic systems that were used for scientific research and calculation, in that era, jobs in computer science generally meant support for large systems that served as giant calculators and billing machines for banking and other industries.

But Kline sought different types of opportunities.

"I was interested in exploring the problems that were emerging in a world where computers worked independently with some success, but had a great deal of trouble communicating with each other," Kline recalled. "Our goal was to determine how to make them talk."

Kline found an opportunity for that mission in the laboratory of Leonard Kleinrock, who at 35 was already recognized for developing a mathematical theory of the methods to create communication pathways between computers at different locations. A slim, curly-headed New Yorker who had joined the UCLA faculty after receiving his PhD at MIT, Kleinrock was considered a supportive mentor to a legion of graduate students who—although they did not know it at the time—were preparing for a new era in computer science.

"Kleinrock . . . gave his graduate students remarkable freedom," said Vint Cerf, at the time a UCLA graduate student who would soon have a role of his own in creating advances in computing. "We had free rein to pursue our ideas."

In 1969, Kleinrock's principal project to validate his theoretical discoveries was to help build an experimental network, a system that would, according to the July 3 press release, "for the first time, link together computers of different makes and using different machine languages.

"As of now, computer networks are still in their infancy," Kleinrock explained in the release, "but as they grow up and become more sophisticated, we will probably see the spread of 'computer utilities,' which like present electric and telephone utilities, will service individual homes and offices across the country."

Creation of the network, reported the release, "represents a major forward step in computer technology and may serve as the forerunner of large computer networks of the future."

Almost 50 years later, Kleinrock recalled, "In simplest terms, we were trying to shift the thinking from everyone using a large stand-alone computer, to a linked network that could exchange information."

The project was funded by the Advanced Research Projects Agency— much better known as ARPA—that seemingly omniscient government agency created during the Eisenhower administration with a finger on the pulse of progress on many technological fronts; the new system had already been dubbed the "ARPANET."

A year earlier, when UCLA had been named the first site on the ARPANET, graduate student Steve Crocker headed a team in Kleinrock's group that developed the procedures for communicating between computers.

In what history would later recall as an "Internet all-star team," Kleinrock and the members of his group, including Crocker, Kline, Cerf, and Jon Postel, would each have a place in creating the underpinnings of the Internet as we know it today. But for the moment functional networks were still in the future; first came learning how to create practical connections between computers, with a goal of linking systems at universities, government agencies, and scientific institutions so they could communicate and exchange information. To start, four computers would serve as the foundation of the system: machines at UCLA, the Stanford Research Institute, UC Santa Barbara, and the University of Utah.

In 1967 at UCLA, just accepting delivery of the computer became a logistical headache; the machine, a Sigma 7 built by Scientific Data Systems of Santa Monica, at eight feet wide and almost six feet tall, was so cumbersome that no elevator in Boelter could accommodate it. To move the Sigma

7 into the building required a forklift on the loading dock at the back side of the building to raise the plastic-wrapped computer to the third floor, where a section of railing had been ripped out to allow the equipment to slide through.

In the lab, the Sigma 7 was later connected to a smaller computer—this one merely the size of a refrigerator. The Honeywell DDP-516, a "mini-computer," was chosen not only for its price and performance but also for its rugged structure built to military specifications; to demonstrate the computer's strength for visitors, Kleinrock would often pound on the cabinet with his fist.

The Honeywell was equipped with extra technology created by the consulting firm of Bolt, Beranek, and Newman, a company in Cambridge, Massachusetts, that added the additional parts necessary to transform the computer into an "Interface Message Processor," better known as an IMP (this was the first device now called a "router"). When attached to the Sigma 7, the IMP would—everyone hoped—serve as an all-purpose gateway that would link computers in many locations, built by separate manufacturers, created for a range of purposes, and all using different types of programming languages. It would be an ambitious project.

The first IMP—node number one in the ARPANET—had been delivered to UCLA on August 30; three days later, Kleinrock's team successfully linked the IMP to the Sigma 7. With each IMP requiring a month to construct, the second was ready late in September; on October 1, 1969, it was delivered to the Stanford Research Institute in Menlo Park, 350 miles north of UCLA. There the IMP was connected to a Scientific Data Systems model 940, a rugged computing workhorse of its era. Later, the third and fourth IMPs would be sent to UC Santa Barbara and the University of Utah, completing the equipment for the quartet of various types of computers that would be the start of the new network.

The next step was to encourage the machines to talk, listen, and respond.

Around 9:00 p.m., Kline walked across the Court of Sciences to the upper entrance of Boelter and then downstairs to room 3420, the home of the UCLA Network Measurement Laboratory, where the new computers had been shoehorned through the door.

Kline sat down at the industrial-metal desk next to his terminal, picked up the phone, and dialed a number in Menlo Park.

At the Stanford Research Institute, Bill Duvall was waiting for Kline's call. A nonprofit research institute in Menlo Park spun off from Stanford University in 1946, the institute (now known as SRI) had been established to serve as a "center of innovation"—an organization-for-hire that conducted research, designed products, and developed plans for government agencies, private industry, and nonprofit organizations.

SRI was involved in projects as diverse as studying plants that could be tapped for rubber and creating the magnetic ink for bank checks. Outside of industry and government circles, the work of SRI may have been best known to the public—especially to eager children in southern California—when the institute was hired by Walt Disney to choose the site of the original Disneyland: Anaheim, California was selected. Sixty years later, SRI would develop—with a name that in spite of many other supposed explanations was surely no coincidence—the original project from which came the "Siri" virtual assistant for Apple systems.

Duvall, at 25, a few years older than Kline, was already working full time in a lab at SRI. Duvall had assumed some of the trappings of 1960s fashion, northern California style: plaid flannel shirts, jeans, and a chest-length beard.

For Kline and Duvall, the task that night was clear.

"Our goal was to test the capability of the UCLA machine to log in to the computer at SRI," said Kline.

The original plan was to allow computers at UCLA and SRI to log in to each other, but limited access to the UCLA computer made it impossible for SRI to log in. That meant the initial trial would have to be from UCLA going to SRI.

It would have seemed a simple experiment, but in practice, the process was much more complicated. That night they would try it.

At 9:30 p.m., Kline and Duvall, each on a telephone headset, powered up their equipment and activated their experimental operating systems that would allow Kline to connect.

Just after 9:30, Kline typed a letter.

"The first letter I typed was an L," Kline said. On Duvall's terminal, the "L" appeared.

Kline tried again; he typed the "O."

"I got the 'O,'" Duvall reported.

But that was all; the computer at SRI overloaded and the connection crashed. Two letters was as far as they got.

But two letters were enough. For at least a moment, the connection had worked. The first communication between the computers was "LO"—an inadvertent, almost biblical declaration of the beginning of a new age.

"We couldn't have planned a more powerful, more succinct, more prophetic message," Kleinrock remembered.

Duvall was able to quickly fix the problem, and an hour later the two machines were again connected, with Kline successfully logging in. At 10:30 p.m., Kline duly recorded the moment by writing the result in the laboratory's logbook (see page 191) and then went home to bed.

Duvall did not see the need for festivities, either. He stopped by a local hangout for a burger and a beer.

"It was no celebration," Duvall said. "I was hungry."

Kline and Duvall did not mark the moment because they did not realize they had a reason to celebrate. The pair viewed their work that night as simply another step in what they knew would become a long and complex series of technological events.

But leading to what? The link between computers at UCLA and SRI was never intended to become the indispensable technology used every day by billions. For most involved in computer science in 1969, that future was not even the remotest practical consideration and was being pondered in theory by only a handful of visionaries. At a time when the first personal computers were still many years away, there was no realistic method of communication that could affect the entire world.

The birth of the Internet—if one technological link in a long chain can be described as a "birth"—had no emotion associated with it; there were no ticker-tape parades, no drama of Thomas Edison watching the first light bulb burn while he contemplated the enormity of what he had done. But the connection achieved on October 29 was, if nothing else, the starting point of a journey that would lead to technology that not only succeeded in its original objective but would also evolve at breakneck speed into a phenomenon for communication beyond anyone's most outrageous expectations.

If there was a single moment that would define the start of the technology that would become the Internet, this was it: the future was born.

Like all great technological achievements, the Internet as we know it exists thanks to a serendipitous intersection of events, people, and inspiration. Over decades, some of those combinations would thrive and change the most fundamental activities of work, play, and human interaction; others would fail spectacularly, including a series of colossal misjudgments that resulted in economic catastrophe with deep and lasting effects across the nation.

From a modest beginning, the Internet would become the most pervasive communications tool of its age—possibly of any age—affecting everything we do, say, and achieve. It serves as an instrument for soaring to creative heights, and it spotlights troubling questions about the lowest forms of human depravity. It produces unprecedented opportunities for social interaction while raising deep questions about personal privacy and national security. Because of the Internet, perhaps more than any other technology, the world is now a much different place, and the world continues to be reshaped as the Internet changes.

But as a starting point of this journey, in the years before the first connection between UCLA and SRI, it could also be said without too much overstatement that the Internet was born out of frustration and one man's need to find more space on his desk.

20

HOW TO MOVE THE WORLD
FROM THE RIGHT PLACE

"The obvious idea came to me: why not just have one terminal, and it connects to anything you want it to be connected
to? It was kind of an 'Aha' idea."

—Robert Taylor, ARPA

In 1966, Robert Taylor looked at his office in the Pentagon and did not like what he saw.

Taylor, a senior administrator managing technology projects at ARPA since the previous year, was not trained in computer science; his background was in aerospace. Taylor had worked in ballistic missile development for Martin Marietta before joining NASA in the early days of the Apollo program as a program manager in the Office of Advanced Research and Technology.

Taylor's strength was in his vision, his insight into the possibilities for innovation that sprang from what others developed, and his understanding of how those talented people could be nurtured in their work. Taylor, wrote historian Leslie Berlin, "could hear a faint melody in the distance, but he could not play it himself. He knew whether to move up or down the scale to approximate the sound, he could recognize when a note was wrong, but he needed someone else to make the music."

Taylor left NASA in 1965 to join ARPA, when the agency was directed by Charles Herzfeld. The job positioned Taylor in a lead role in funding research on computing that promised to shape industry, government, and academics.

One of those ARPA-funded projects was support for timesharing—the concept of linking many individuals to a single central computer to share the costs of processing.

The key technological breakthrough of networking technology, said Kleinrock, was resource sharing; it was the sharing of communication resources that made networking so powerful.

"Time-sharing was really resource-sharing," said Kleinrock. "At a point when computers were incredibly expensive, the idea that users could share access to processing made computing practical."

Timesharing put computing power in the hands of users who could never afford it otherwise; in the late 1960s, IBM featured the concept in its business advertising, showing a happy timeshare user and the caption, "This man is sharing a $2 million computer."

But in 1966, timesharing also meant connecting each user to a central computer through an independent terminal. And that was precisely why Taylor was unhappy: he was buried in computer terminals.

"In my office in the Pentagon," Taylor recalled, "I had one terminal that connected to a time-sharing system at MIT. I had another one that connected to a time-sharing system at UC Berkeley. I had one that connected to time-sharing at the System Development Corporation in Santa Monica. There was another terminal that connected to the Rand Corporation. And for me to use any of these systems, I would have to move from one terminal to the other.

"So the obvious idea came to me: Why not just have one terminal, and it connects to anything you want it to be connected to? It was kind of an 'Aha' idea. I went over to Charlie Herzfeld's office and told him about it."

Such spontaneous suggestions—including projects with daunting price tags—were routine at the anything-is-possible ARPA.

"To get something going," Taylor recalled of his ARPA days, "was very easy."

It was a philosophy that would govern ARPA for years.

"No one in government has more constructive power," ARPA declared in an employment brochure to recruit program managers. "You can move the world, if you stand in the right place."

Eight years before, only a few months after Explorer 1 was launched, ARPA had indeed moved the world by funding a bold, ultra-top-secret gamble in space. Code-named Project SCORE—a conveniently constructed acronym for Signal Communications by Orbiting Relay Equipment—and planned in the panicky early days of the American space program when no launch was a sure bet, SCORE reached orbit on December 18, 1958.

With nerves on edge because of the limited success of the American program—the explosion of Vanguard on national television was only a year before—SCORE's mission was kept so secret that only 35 people knew its true purpose until it was flying overhead.

SCORE was the first communications satellite.

America's new mission in space broadcast a recorded holiday greeting from President Eisenhower to the world and also captured messages sent from Earth stations and transmitted them back to listeners. The broadcasts were faint, but they foreshadowed the orbiting network of communications satellites to come.

So when Taylor proposed to Herzfeld that ARPA fund a network of computers, the idea resonated immediately.

"He pretty much instantly made a budget change, and took a million dollars away from one of his other offices and gave it to me to get started," Taylor said. "It took about 20 minutes."

Networking computers may have been an "aha" idea to Taylor as a practical solution to a real-world problem, but as a theoretical issue, plenty of groundwork had already been laid.

In the early 1960s, J. C. R. "Lick" Licklider, the first director of the Information Processing Techniques Office in ARPA, had suggested the idea of a global computer network.

"Licklider was a strong, driving visionary, and he set the stage," said Kleinrock. "His early work—he was a psychologist by training—was in what he called man-computer symbiosis. When you put a computer in the hands of a human, the interaction between them becomes much greater than the individual parts. And he also foresaw a great change in the way activity would take place: education, creativity, commerce, just general information access—a connected world of information."

In April 1963, Licklider wrote a 3,300-word memo to colleagues, outlining many of his views about computer networks.

"Consider the situation in which several different centers are netted together," Licklider wrote, "each center being highly individualistic and having its own special language and its own special way of doing things. Is it not desirable, or even necessary, for all the centers to agree upon some language?

"It seems to me to be interesting and important," Licklider concluded, "to develop a capability for . . . network operation."

Kleinrock, too, was already looking at the idea of networks and how they would function; his doctoral thesis, proposed in May 1961, was titled "Information Flow in Large Computer Networks."

Kleinrock proposed "to investigate the problems associated with information flow in large communication nets.

"These problems appear to have wide application," he pointed out, "and yet little serious research had been conducted in this field."

Kleinrock would expand on his original idea in a related book titled *Communication Nets* two years later.

But how best to send the information on this network-to-be? One approach had been developed by Paul Baran, an electrical engineer working at the RAND Corporation in Santa Monica who had already been studying the grim prospect of maintaining "survivable" communications after a nuclear attack. (Later, Baran's early work led some to incorrectly assume that the funding for the ARPANET was intended to develop a war-proof computer network, which it was not.)

Baran's projects, which included theories about storing data and moving it from place to place, would later develop into the notion that information did not have to be sent in one long stream (like a telephone call) but could be broken up into pieces for easier transmission, a concept Baran called "message blocks." Independently, British computer scientist Donald Davies developed the same concept, describing it as "packet switching" (a term Davies and Baran agreed to use because it could be translated conveniently into other languages).

"Packet switching is the way your messages, your videos, your voice, your pictures, your data are transmitted—in little chunks called packets," said Kleinrock.

"In the 1960s," said Kleinrock, "Baran's theory was that it was useful to break up long messages into smaller packets. Each packet is addressed and sent through the network—like a bunch of postcards each carrying a section of a long letter. The packets independently make their way through the network, arriving at the other end, and are put back together as a longer entity."

The beauty of the packet-switching theory was that since each packet contains code to reach a final destination (similar to an email address), the individual packets could travel any route in a network of many computers, following whatever path was fastest or available, and then reassemble at their end point.

With fresh funds authorized by Herzfeld, Taylor proceeded with developing a plan for his network. Wesley A. Clark, physicist and co-designer of the original personal computer, suggested an intermediary in the process: a smaller computer at each end of the connection that would serve as an all-purpose transition in the communication; that idea took form as the IMP.

In retrospect, as explained by Charley Kline to a lay audience, the process seemed remarkably simple.

"I would type a character," said Kline, "and it would go into my computer. My software would take it, wrap around it all of the software needed to send it to the IMP. The IMP would take it and say, 'Oh, this is supposed to go up to SRI.'"

If it worked.

In 1968, Taylor and Larry Roberts (the program manager for the ARPANET) were ready to fund the project, but willing bidders were hard to find.

"None of the big computer companies like IBM or AT&T were interested in the idea," said Kline. "They not only thought that networking couldn't be done, but they considered it useless even if it worked. They believed that the future of computing was in creating bigger and bigger mainframes."

Bolt, Beranek, and Newman (BBN), a small but dynamic company that was moving into computing projects after more than two decades of consulting in acoustics for such projects as the construction of the United Nations General Assembly Building, had no such concerns; BBN built the IMPs.

Politicians would have much to learn about the budding technology: when the seven-figure deal was announced, Senator Edward Kennedy, who represented Massachusetts, wrote to BBN with congratulations for building an "Interfaith" Message Processor and acknowledging the company for its ecumenical work.

Before the end of 1969, the first four nodes of the ARPANET at UCLA, SRI, UC Santa Barbara, and Utah were alive and chattering. Testing included not only the effectiveness of the network but also its reliability, with gleeful graduate students creating test software to see if they could bust the system.

"I remember thinking we should paint a sort of network symbol on the side of the UCLA computer for each time we crashed the network, as fighter pilots used to do with 'kills' in the Second World War," recalled Cerf.

And the ARPANET began to grow—slowly at first. In 1970, the first four nodes, or "hosts," were joined by five others. By the end of 1972, the host count had increased to 31; by 1974, it had doubled, and it reached 100 in 1977. Then the upsurge began: the number was 1,000 in 1984, 100,000 in 1989, and 1 million in 1992.

At that point, the ARPANET was entirely a tool for academic communication and research, and communicating between computers was cumbersome.

"Between 1969 and 1974 the first thing we had to do was develop a method of communications that all the sites could implement," said Kline.

The result was the development of "protocols"—the procedures—that added steady improvements to the process of computers talking with each other, and the first was Network Control Protocol.

Creating new technology so *people* could connect with each other took a major step forward in 1971, when Ray Tomlinson, then working at BBN on the ARPANET, was developing what he considered "a neat idea."

The product of Tomlinson's work would be viewed by generations to come as major progress in instantaneous global communication or a daily misery for time-strapped computer users everywhere: Tomlinson merged a program he had written to transfer files with another application that sent messages through timeshare systems; Tomlinson had invented the first practical email.

"I'm often asked, did I know what I was doing? And the answer is, yes, I knew exactly what I was doing," Tomlinson said. "I just had no notion whatsoever of what the ultimate impact would be. What I was doing was providing a way for people to communicate with other people."

Tomlinson's achievement would also bring prominence to a symbol on the keyboard that, until his invention, was ignored by nearly everyone: the "@" sign. The @ symbol, which had emerged out of billing methods to mean "at the price of," was one of the least-used keys for nonaccountants until Tomlinson chose to use it as a separator between the user's name and the email service.

"The @ sign just makes sense," said Tomlinson. "I used the @ sign to indicate that the user was 'at' some other host rather than being local."

Tomlinson saw his achievement as even less of a milestone than Kline and Bill Duvall saw theirs in 1969; years later, Tomlinson could not remember the first messages delivered with his breakthrough system.

"I sent a number of test messages to myself from one machine to the other," he recalled. "The test messages were entirely forgettable and I have, therefore, forgotten them."

A few years after the emergence of email came the arrival of *unwanted* email: on May 1, 1978, the first reported unsolicited email message to a group was sent by computer marketer Gary Thuerk, who invited several hundred of his contacts to the demonstration of new computers manufactured by Digital Equipment Corporation. At the time, email was a one-to-one proposition; sending an unsolicited email to a large group of users was forbidden by network administrators everywhere.

"This was a flagrant violation of the use of the ARPANET," wrote Major Raymond Czahor, chief of the ARPANET management branch, to users after Thuerk's message was delivered—and complaints ensued.

At the time, such violations had no specific name. But it wasn't long before British email users recalled a sketch by the Monty Python comedy troupe in which patrons of a restaurant are continuously interrupted by an invading hoard of Vikings chanting "spam, spam, spam." The sketch was an inspiration, and—to the horror of meat processor Hormel, which makes Spam—would spawn a new term in the computer glossary. By the 1980s, long before many computer users had even heard of email, unwanted messages would become known as "spam." *The New Oxford Dictionary of English* would forever legitimize the term in 1998, when "spam" was first included in the dictionary, defined as "irrelevant or inappropriate messages sent on the internet to a large number of newsgroups or users."

By 2003, spam accounted for almost half of all email.

In the early 1970s, as the ARPANET continued to expand to universities and research organizations across the country, one issue was becoming clear: the original Network Control Protocol that was used to operate it did not suit the system as it grew.

"We were getting concerned because Network Control Protocol just didn't scale up well as the network grew," said Kline.

To fix the problem would take a new leap of technology.

Of the many "fathers" of the Internet, two in particular—Vint Cerf and Robert Kahn—could claim a right to their titles for creating a way that the toddler system of computers talking to each other could be made practical and efficient.

In 1973, Cerf met with Kahn, who was working on the networking project at DARPA (the new name for ARPA as of 1972) to see if they could develop a method that would address the growing problem of how a diverse range of computers—separate manufacturers, different systems, incompatible configurations—could stay connected in the growing world of networks.

"Kahn foresaw the need to link together networks with different designs," said Cerf, "so that any computers could communicate freely, no matter what the communication path. Kahn started a research program focused on this problem."

Said Kahn, "At the time, we saw this as an exciting technology challenge and research project. You have to realize that there wasn't anything known as the personal computer. We didn't know where things would lead."

Where their work did lead was to creating the protocol that would set a worldwide standard that is still used today.

In only a few months in early 1973, Cerf and Kahn developed their theories into the ideas that would become known as Transmission Control

Protocol and Internet Protocol—better known as TCP/IP—the structure of the Internet.

"After we built the ARPANET, lots of people built networks. Everybody was competing," said Roberts. "Everyone had their own thing that they wanted to do. So it became very important that the world have one protocol, so they could all talk to each other."

In the early 1970s, TCP/IP solidified the communication between large computers; it was work that would earn Cert and Kahn, among countless honors, the Presidential Medal of Freedom in 2005 "for designing the architecture and communication protocol that gave rise to the modern Internet."

᪥

In the late 1960s and early 1970s, communicating through computers was tedious, typically accomplished by sending lines of unformatted type or data. But even before the first connection between UCLA and SRI, the prospects for the potential of computing as an engaging and inspiring experience had been demonstrated, and with an impact that would soon transform how technology was designed and used.

By 1968, Douglas Engelbart had been exploring technology with the hopes that he could create a better world.

Engelbart, trained as an engineer, had worked at the Ames Research Center in wind tunnel research but then detoured back to school to earn a PhD in electrical engineering before joining SRI in 1957. Years earlier, in the waning days of World War II, while serving on a remote island in the Philippines, Engelbart stumbled across Vannevar Bush's article "As We May Think," which opened a door to the realm of what imaginative use of technology makes possible. Engelbart was particularly fascinated by Bush's idea for the "memex"—a theory Engelbart would remember when he started to develop his office at SRI.

Engelbart was convinced that the world could be improved and that complex problems could be solved by using computers to enhance human capabilities—a revolutionary idea at a time long before the personal computer and well before most people had any contact with a computer or even considered the idea of using a computer at home or work.

"Consider an augmented architect at work," Engelbart wrote in 1962. "He sits at a working station that has a visual display screen some three feet on a side; this is his working surface, and is controlled by a computer (his 'clerk') with which he can communicate by means of a small keyboard and various other devices."

Engelbart formed his own lab at SRI and was awarded more than a dozen patents, some for projects that focused on the physical interaction between people and computers. (In October 1969, it was in Engelbart's lab where Duvall was working when he connected with Kline at UCLA.)

Engelbart's "Augmentation Research Center" at SRI would be involved, either directly or indirectly, in the evolution of a number of devices that are today familiar to every computer user, such as the practical use of hypertext, video monitors, and multiple windows. And perhaps most notably, Engelbart developed a computer accessory that looked like a small shell that encased two metal wheels. In Engelbart's patent application, the device was called an "X-Y position indicator for a display system." But because the cord of the palm-sized device looked like a tail, Engelbart called it a mouse.

Much of Engelbart's work had been funded, of course, by Taylor, first through his office at NASA and later when he moved to ARPA. It was Engelbart's philosophy of how people interacted with computers that attracted Taylor to the work.

"A proposal from Doug came across my desk proposing to work with computers in the development of information—not numbers, not arithmetic, but information," Taylor recalled. "Engelbart's proposal was the first manifestation of this idea that I had seen."

Eventually, Engelbart's early work came into focus with a presentation given on December 9, 1968, at a conference in San Francisco sponsored by the Association for Computing Machinery and the Institute for Electrical and Electronic Engineers. The official name of Engelbart's talk was "A Research Center for Augmenting Human Intellect," but years later, it would be dubbed with the name that will forever describe the magnitude of the event: "The Mother of All Demos."

In his 90-minute talk, Engelbart appeared on a giant screen, describing many of the developments that were percolating in his lab, including, among others, graphics, word processing, spell checking, windows, and video conferencing—all concepts that are commonplace today but in 1968 were revolutionary. As part of the presentation, Engelbart showed how he could remotely manipulate a computer at his lab 35 miles away by using his mouse. (Engelbart's presentation is still viewable; see page 280.)

Before the presentation, many in the often-staid world of 1960s computing had viewed Engelbart's work at best as a folksy aside that distracted researchers from more important endeavors and at worst as the delusional product of a crackpot.

"It's hard to believe now," recalled Bill Paxton, Engelbart's colleague, 40 years later, "but at the time even *we* had trouble understanding what he was doing. Think of everyone else out there."

But by the time Engelbart concluded his talk, for much of the audience the presentation had been transformational. Engelbart had made an impressive case for the creation of computers not only as personal devices that anyone could use, but also as tools that would challenge, entertain, and inspire.

Charles Thacker, who would go on to work on such revolutionary technology as the Xerox Alto (the first computer to use a graphical user interface that would lead to the first Apple Macintosh) and the Microsoft Tablet PC, described the presentation as "dealing lightning with both hands."

Many computer developers would remember Engelbart's work as a turning point in their own careers, as they first began to understand the computer, and the evolving Internet, as a powerful machine for the individual. Learning where to go next would take almost 10 years.

⚬✖⚬

From the mid-1970s and through the 1980s, the personal computer became available to general-interest users. It was small, affordable, and with more limited processing power compared to larger machines but enough computing ability to be useful for home programming or games. The first Apple computers were sold in 1976, and the IBM PC arrived in 1981. The Commodore 64, which entered the market in August 1982 for $595, today remains the most popular single computer model of all time. Although the exact number produced is uncertain—company-announced numbers vary considerably—at least 13 million Commodore 64s were sold between 1982 and 1994.

By 1989, with such computer brands as Radio Shack, Atari, and Commodore competing with Apple and IBM, Americans had bought more than 54 million personal computers; a product that did not exist 15 years earlier was by the beginning of the 1990s a feature in more than half of American households.

Email use would also explode: in 1995, 10 percent of Americans used email; that number tripled in three years. By 1996, the number of emails sent by computer would surpass the number of letters mailed through the post office.

But for most of these new computer users, the Internet was an unknown quantity. From home, communication between individual computers was possible but only through snail-slow modems that could send a short document in a tolerable amount of time; anything else would require hours. The websites of today were years away.

By 1990, for most computer owners, going online for anything other than email was impractical and unappealing; to transform the communication between computers from a plain-vanilla device used by academics, government agencies, and companies to an engaging method of communication available to everyone would occur after four developments that changed the nature of the Internet. They would transform online technology into the most powerful vehicle for information access and personal interaction since the invention of the printed page.

21

FOUR STEPS IN
GAINING MOMENTUM

"I don't feel like a father of anything. It's not how I think of
myself. Every now and again, I think, 'you know what? I
invented the search engine.'"

— Alan Emtage, developer of "Archie,"
the first search engine

In the early days of computers and networks, when the management of
online systems was primarily a partnership between the federal government and academia, suggestions of new ideas about online technology could
be proposed through a publication called a "Request for Comment." Now
a project coordinated by the Internet Engineering Task Force, a Request
for Comment—better known as an RFC—describes a suggestion about the
Internet or a proposed change that can be reviewed by anyone and, after
enough comments, is eventually accepted or rejected.

The Requests for Comments Series was developed by Steve Crocker,
one of the graduate students from Kleinrock's team at UCLA. Jon Postel,
another bruin from Kleinrock's group, would serve as editor of the series
from 1969 until his death in 1998. RFC 1, written by Crocker in April
1969, described the software and methods that would be used by Charley
Kline and Bill Duvall to operate the IMP.

The Request for Comments Series remains a productive yet sometimes informal venue for communicating about all things Internet—including fake projects delivered on April Fool's Day with clearly ridiculous
propositions to "improve" the Internet. For instance, RFC 2549, submitted
April 1, 1999, suggested the delivery of Internet packets by birds.

Many Requests for Comments are routine, but some are revolutionary,
including the proposal outlined in several RFCs beginning in March 1983

by Paul Mockapetris, a computer engineer then at the Information Sciences Institute at the University of Southern California. Mockapetris described a new system for managing online content that would eliminate the confusion of how websites were identified: he proposed associating information about online content to a word that he called a "domain name"; his plan was called the Domain Name System, or DNS.

Each name chosen for a domain (or a website) would be followed by an "extension" that described the type of organization: for instance, ".com" for companies (as in nytimes.com for the *New York Times*), or ".gov" for government organizations (nasa.gov), or ".edu" for schools (harvard.edu). Many other extensions would develop in the next three decades, and they continue to be developed.

By using domain names, identifying a website became much clearer, vastly simplifying how the Internet could be understood and accessed. The first domain name for a company, symbolics.com, was established in March 1985; the site still exists today.

Like many other Internet innovators, Mockapetris chose to develop his innovation for the online world without charge; he earned nothing from a development that would affect every one of the billions of websites worldwide. Later, Mockapetris would joke about his decision.

"A friend of mine said I was smart enough to invent the DNS," he said, "but not smart enough to own it."

⸏⸎⸏

In the hallway of Building 1 where Tim Berners-Lee worked at the European Organization for Nuclear Research, better known as CERN, the plaque on the wall begins with large black engraved letters: "Where the Web Was Born."

In 1991, Berners-Lee was at CERN as a software consultant, and he felt stymied by the limited abilities of computers to share information. He described his annoyance with late 1980s technology in tones that recalled the concerns expressed by Robert Taylor about an office cluttered by terminals in the mid-1960s.

"I found it frustrating that in those days, there was different information on different computers, but you had to log on to different computers to get at it," Berners-Lee recalled. "Also, sometimes you had to learn a different program on each computer."

Berners-Lee noted that in the late 1980s, CERN hosted guest scientists and consultants from institutions worldwide, who came with a variety of computing systems—from personal computers to mainframes—many of them incompatible.

"I actually wrote some programs to take information from one system and convert it so it could be inserted into another system," he said.

"Can't we convert every information system," Berners-Lee proposed, "so that it looks like part of some imaginary information system which everyone can read?"

From that frustration grew Berners-Lee's interest in developing a method that would standardize how information could be identified and accessed online.

In March 1989, Berners-Lee collaborated with Robert Cailliau on a project that merged elements of hypertext, domain names, and TCP/IP protocol, bringing together the work of visionaries like Cerf, Kahn, Mockapetris, hypertext pioneer Ted Nelson—even theories expounded decades before by Vannevar Bush.

"Most of the technology involved in the web, like hypertext, like the internet, had all been designed already," Berners-Lee said. "I just had to put them together. It was a step of generalizing, going to a higher level of abstraction, thinking about all the documentation systems out there as being possibly part of a larger imaginary documentation system."

What Berners-Lee described as "a higher level of abstraction" was an inspired innovation that would transform how information could be stored and accessed online. Berners-Lee, working with Cailliau, had invented the World Wide Web.

Cailliau named their innovation during discussions in the CERN cafeteria.

"Tim and I [tried] to find a catching name for the system," Cailliau recalled. "I was determined that the name should not be taken from Greek mythology. Tim proposed "World Wide Web." I liked this very much, except that it is difficult to pronounce in French."

By May 1991, the software for the World Wide Web was released on the CERN central computers. Berners-Lee created the first-ever "website" at CERN; unveiled in August 1991, the site, in plain text with no formatting or design, provides basic information about the World Wide Web project. (A duplicate of the original website is still posted; see page 280.) The World Wide Web was opened to everyone.

In April 1993, CERN released the software into the public domain, solidifying the ability of the World Wide Web to proliferate.

"At one point CERN was toying with patenting the World Wide Web," recalled Cailliau. "I was talking about that with Tim, and I could see that he wasn't enthusiastic. He said, 'Robert, do you want to be rich?' I thought, Well, it helps . . . no? He apparently didn't care about that. What he cared about was to make sure that the thing would work, that it would just be there for everybody. He convinced me of that."

Recalled Berners-Lee, "CERN's decision to make the Web foundations and protocols available . . . royalty free, and without additional impediments, was crucial to the Web's existence. Without this commitment, the enormous individual and corporate investment in Web technology simply would never have happened, and we wouldn't have the Web today."

Discussion of Berners-Lee's work often leads to confusion about how the "Internet" differs from the "World Wide Web." The "Internet" is the physical network of computers; the "World Wide Web" is the broad collection of web pages that follow the protocol that Berners-Lee developed that can be accessed through the Internet from anywhere.

However, in spite of the clear differences, over the years the public perception of the terms has melded, with World Wide Web dropping away in common usage in favor of "Internet" becoming the all-purpose word that describes the global entity of online technology—hardware, content, and all.

Before the World Wide Web transformed the Internet into a functional global system for all to use, progress was underway on a development that would make going online a simple, productive experience—for general users, perhaps the single most important step in the transformation of the Internet into a powerful, near-instant source of information and access.

Even with the addition of domain names, the Internet was still a massive and confusing jumble of information—hard to explore and difficult to sort through. In the late 1980s, when the *total* number of web hosts was less than 1 million—let alone the billions of addresses of websites and pages that exist today—finding information without knowing a specific address was nearly impossible, akin to going to the Library of Congress and trying to find a specific sentence just by going through the books. Before the Internet had any hope of being a practical tool, users—especially the general public—needed tools that would help.

In retrospect, the solution was so important that it is impossible to imagine the Internet without it. But computer networks existed for almost 20 years before anyone developed a practical way to look for information contained anywhere on the network and quickly identify it. What was needed was a tool that would cut through the detritus and find the treasure; it would be called a search engine.

⤳

Alan Emtage would later state with pride that he was the first person from Barbados, and also the first from the Caribbean, to be elected to the Internet Hall of Fame—an honor he received in 2017. Emtage choose a frostier climate for his college studies, heading north to McGill University in Montreal to study computer science. While training for his graduate degree, in 1989, Emtage created a collection of software that he called "resource discovery tools"—services that the average user could employ to regularly connect to computers around the world and automatically download listings of files available to the public.

"It happened organically," Emtage would say of his work. "I didn't have to ford rivers or climb mountains."

These tools, which Emtage called "Archie" (short for "Archive") would combine to serve as the world's first Internet search engine, pioneering many of the techniques still used by search engines today. (For an example of the original Archie, see page 280.)

Emtage was yet another Internet innovator who deliberately chose to not patent his discovery—a decision that would have earned him millions as other search engines were developed that contained his fundamental processes.

"I'm not a billionaire; that's okay with me," Emtage told an audience when he was inducted into the Internet Hall of Fame in 2017. "We thought about [licensing] it long and hard; to do so would strangle the baby in the crib—it would restrict the ability of people to use what we had learned and expand on it.

"The Internet as we know it today would not exist were it not for the fact that a lot of the organizations and individuals allowed the fruit of their work to be used for free."

Emtage is also a rare technology groundbreaker who routinely declines recognition as being a "father" of the Internet (although he graciously passes along credit to Archie for being "the great great grandfather of Google and all of those other search engines").

"I don't feel like a father of anything," Emtage told a reporter in 2013. "It's not how I think of myself. Every now and again, I think, 'you know what? I invented the search engine.'"

Archie was a useful first step toward practical searching online. However, it was rudimentary and, for general-interest Internet users, unwieldy to use—as was Gopher, a set of tools for searching and web browsing created by staff at the University of Minnesota's microcomputer center led by Mark McCahill, who named their program after the institution's mascot.

But Gopher, which was released in 1991, arrived at an opportune moment. Gopher emerged as Internet access was becoming more commonplace for use at universities beyond the halls of computer science departments. For millions of college students and nonscience faculty in the early 1990s, Gopher would become their first introduction to the World Wide Web and a catalyst to encourage them to go online.

"I remember learning at freshman orientation that we would 'get to use Gopher'—none of us in the arts had any idea what it was," said Cynthia Thompson, who was a freshman at the University of Iowa in 1994. "But Gopher opened a door for me to the Web that I never knew was possible."

Gopher led to the creation of two supplemental search engines called Veronica and Jughead. Although Archie had not been named for the teenage character of comic book fame, Veronica and Jughead were dubbed deliberately not only to honor Emtage's creation but also to serve as tributes to the characters. Such an objective required imaginative retrofitting of a full name to match each acronym: Veronica stood for "Very Easy Rodent-Oriented Net-wide Index to Computerized Archives," while Jughead was from "Jonzy's Universal Gopher Hierarchy Excavation And Display."

Many more tools for accessing the Internet would follow—Infoseek, Aliweb, and WebCrawler were among many names that came and went. But one tool in particular for accessing the Internet that debuted in 1993 would outshine most others, primarily because of what it represented for both the form and function of how users would go online.

∾⊗∾

For the 20-year-old Marc Andreessen in 1991, the Internet seemed like a giant opportunity waiting to happen.

"The whole internet phenomenon had been gaining momentum for the past decade," said Andreessen years later, "but it was still very much limited to a small audience of people. And its full potential was not being tapped. At the time, the internet worked fine as infrastructural device, but wasn't friendly enough for people who wanted to do interesting things."

Andreessen, while still an undergraduate at the University of Illinois at Urbana–Champaign, and programmer Eric Bina, found a way to help millions do those interesting things. Andreessen and Bina developed a web browser that was both useful and engaging: released in late 1993, they called their software Mosaic.

Where other browsers were gray and required multiple steps by users, Mosaic was alive with opportunity—a pleasant user-friendly screen, icons for choices, and, a particularly handy new innovation, bookmarks that would store the address of a chosen website for later use.

In other words, recalled Andreessen, "it was appealing to non-geeks."

"One idea was that multi-media should be a key part of the internet," Andreessen said. "Everyone knew desktop computers and the network were perfectly capable of handling images. The new part was simply combining this idea with the ability to link together resources across the globe. I figured out that this was something that we should do and it was the right time and place to do it.

"We targeted the users. We wanted to make Mosaic friendly for people to use."

Mosaic cut to the core of what users wanted when they went online: software that was practical but also appealing and intuitive.

"When it comes to smashing a paradigm, pleasure is not the most important thing—it is the only thing," wrote Gary Wolfe in *Wired* in 1994. "If this sounds wrong, consider Mosaic. Mosaic is the celebrated graphical 'browser' that allows users to travel through the world of electronic information using a point-and-click interface. You can travel through the online world along paths of whim and intuition.

"In the 18 months since it was released," Wolfe said, "Mosaic has incited a rush of excitement and commercial energy unprecedented in the history of the Net."

Mosaic was the jump-start that the Internet needed to capture the public's interest—by mid-1994, more than 50,000 users a month were downloading the browser—and Mosaic is remembered as one of the prime catalysts for igniting the Internet.

"No matter who really gets the credit for being the very first web browser, no one can argue Mosaic was the first popular web browser," wrote Steven J. Vaughn-Nichols of ZDNet on the browser's 25th birthday. "Mosaic changed everything."

Andreessen and Bina developed Mosaic together, but Andreessen gladly gives Bina credit for creating all the coding for the software.

"A lot of people don't realize that Eric did all the hard programming on Mosaic. As far as I know, the entire time he only ate Skittles and Mountain Dew."

Andreessen, at 22, joined entrepreneur and computer scientist James Clark in Silicon Valley, creating the company that (after haggling with the University of Illinois over the term "Mosaic") would be known as Netscape.

Netscape would dominate as a web browser; four months after the company released Mosaic Netscape 0.9, it accounted for 75 percent of all browsers. In the mid-1990s, Andreessen was portrayed as one of the young darlings in the emergence of Silicon Valley—an unconventional, anything-goes, financial adventurer. When he appeared on the cover of *Time* magazine in February 1996, Andreessen, in jeans and with bare feet, sat in an ornate chair next to the headline "The Golden Geeks." Netscape would be acquired in March 1999 for $4.2 billion—making Andreessen one of the world's richest computer scientists four months before his 27th birthday.

The creation of the World Wide Web, domain names, search engines, and web browsers were four essential milestones in the evolution of the Internet from a technical tool to a functional, practical, appealing device that could be used by everyone. The transformation had begun; how users communicate and find information would never be the same.

Given the dramatic growth in personal computer use by the last decade of the millennium—more than 20 percent of American homes already had a computer by 1990—it was clear that there was a huge untapped audience who could be enticed to use their computer for something besides word processing, spreadsheets, and occasionally loading software from disks. Next would come the expansion of Internet service providers, including one that not only opened the door to online access for millions but also demonstrated both the best and the worst ways to accomplish it.

22

ON HOLD

"One of my earliest memories of technology was being five
years old and having an America Online start-up CD fall out
of the Sunday comics."

—Andy Buchanan, historian

In the early 1990s, the personal computer was becoming comfortably
fixed as part of the American home. By early 1994, nearly one in three
households had a personal computer, and more than 20 million adults said
they used a personal computer every day.

But using those computers to access the Internet was a different story.

A study conducted in 1995 by the Times Mirror Center for the People
and the Press showed that while 12 percent of households had a modem-
equipped computer, only 6 percent of Americans went online; in 8 million
homes, the modem installed on the household computer went unused.

"The number of Americans going online to an information service or
directly to the internet has more than doubled in the past year, but most
consumers are still feeling their way through cyberspace," read the first line
of the study. "Few see online activities as essential to them."

The survey title summed up the era: "Americans Going Online . . .
Explosive Growth, Uncertain Destinations."

"The World Wide Web, which offers a whole new dimension of the
internet, is still unchartered waters to most users," concluded the study.

While the findings may have painted a picture of a still-unconnected
nation, they did find hints of the emerging role of home computers and
going online: almost two-thirds of computer users said they would miss
their PC a lot if they no longer had it—more than would miss their cable

TV subscriptions. And while the percentage of users in America was low, the real number of Internet users in 1994 was impressively high—some 11 million Americans went online from home.

But there were more significant indications to come: in 1997, only 18 percent of American homes had Internet access; by 2000, that number would more than double to 41 percent. That same year, more than two-thirds of Americans were online, either at home, at work, or at school.

But before 1994, with the freshly minted World Wide Web widely available for less than two years, most Internet "browsing" was more of a "stroll"—as in a stroll through a garden. To many American Internet users, going online meant logging into a commercial provider known as a "walled garden," a closed system that offered its own email and proprietary services—including many features that were provided by outside companies for a fee.

Two of most popular providers, CompuServe and Prodigy, dominated the online services in the early 1990s, offering everything from email to news to games to chat rooms to cooking hints, each directly accessible through its own proprietary menu; for most users, there was no incentive to poke around the Web unattended.

But it was another provider, America Online, that became the steamroller that crushed much of its competition, outpacing the larger ones and buying some of them—including, in 1999, the astonishing price tag of $4.4 billion it would pay for Netscape. By then, almost half of U.S. homes with Internet access received it through America Online (AOL).

AOL evolved in a journey that began in 1983 as a small company called PlayNET that was used to host an online video game for Atari game consoles. Not long after, the company hired Steve Case, a marketing executive at Pizza Hut, first as a consultant and later as full-time employee. The company's strategy evolved into other dedicated online services for specific computers, including Apple and IBM PCs. In 1989, with Case as executive vice-president, the company became America Online, selling itself primarily to new computer users or those who had limited experience being online—or little desire to learn much about it.

"In those days, America Online was the internet with training wheels," said Jeffrey I. Cole, director of the Center for the Digital Future at USC Annenberg. "AOL made it easy for anyone to capitalize on the power of the internet."

When Case became CEO, he expanded the company's features with a range of services that surpassed the competition, including an attractive user interface, free trial memberships, and innovations such as some of the first games with graphics (instead of just text) that could be accessed online by several players competing together—a concept now known as massively multiplayer online games.

AOL also offered increased ability for users to communicate with each other through chat rooms, instant messaging, and forums on every conceivable subject, setting an early standard for social media.

"We always believed that people talking to each other was the killer app," said Case. "And so whether it was instant messaging or chat rooms, which we launched in 1985, or message boards, it was always the community that was front and center. Everything else—commerce and entertainment and financial services—was secondary. We thought community trumped content."

But AOL became legendary—some would say notorious—for an entirely different type of presence in the community, through an eight-year sales philosophy that so thoroughly saturated every market it touched that its manager would call the plan "carpet bombing."

Jan Brandt came to AOL as vice-president of marketing in 1993 with a primary mandate to build the subscriber base. While other companies focused on television and print advertising to recruit new subscriptions and charged new users for start-up software, Brandt created a plan that distributed trial AOL start-up diskettes and CDs that new customers could use for free.

"The reason I started sending live software out there was because it was very difficult to describe to someone who had not actually seen it," Brandt said. "Chat room? Email? Conversing on computers in real time? It's like trying to describe swimming to someone who has never seen water."

When Brandt's plan reached full flower, AOL start-up diskettes and CDs were distributed in every conceivable location—among many methods, glued into magazines, attached to popcorn boxes in movie theaters, mailers sent to millions, or stack upon stack in tech shops and record stores.

"One of my earliest memories of technology," said historian Andy Buchanan, "was being five years old and having an AOL start-up CD fall out of the Sunday comics."

Brandt's work paid off: AOL's subscriber base of 250,000 rocketed, at its peak reaching 30 million.

But AOL faced fierce backlash to the marketing campaign. The environmental cost was staggering: for several years, the company was distributing tens of thousands of start-up kits *every day*; at the peak of the marketing, half of all CDs produced worldwide were made for AOL, the vast majority winding up in landfills. Brandt later estimated that AOL produced at least 1 billion start-up CDs. The assault of AOL disks was ceaseless; *PC World* magazine named the CDs the most annoying tech product.

The marketing campaign inspired a protest group that aggressively pressured AOL to stop the distribution by creating an organization called NoMoreAOLCDs.com, its goal to collect 1 million disks that would be sent back to the company. The project had collected more than 410,000 CDs before AOL discontinued sending unsolicited kits in 2007.

AOL's marketing had produced success beyond any expectations, but it would be the first drip in what would become a flood of problems. At the same time that AOL was earning praise for providing low-cost service to a new generation of Internet users, launching cooperative programs with education organizations, and developing parental controls and teaching aids, the company received even more notoriety for its customer service foibles and questionable business practices.

The issues were endless, and some were a direct result of the company's rapid growth. The number of members quickly surpassed AOL's ability to serve them. In an age of Internet service primarily through dial-up modem, the company became notorious for busy signals; angry customers began referring to the company as "America On Hold." In print advertisements and on the company's websites, Steve Case tried to assure customers that the capacity would be increased. But improvements to service took years.

Other problems were more serious: charges of labor law violations, class-action suits, improper billing practices, inaccurate calculation of service connection time, software that inhibited use of other Internet service providers, and perhaps most aggravating of all, charges that AOL ignored demands to cancel service while billing continued—a problem that was later revealed to be caused in part by a company policy to pressure customer service representatives to "retain" subscribers.

AOL was the biggest target for media scrutiny of problems among the major Internet service providers; given the company's high profile, the issues would stifle interest in going online, or staying online, for millions of users, creating a new category in the study of Americans' relationship with technology: "Internet dropouts"—nonusers who had been online but were no longer. Subscriber numbers began to sink.

"By then, AOL was already synonymous with 'stodgy' and 'obsolete,'" said Cole. "Many users with AOL email addresses changed to other providers just to avoid looking like they were out of touch."

In 2000, AOL merged with Time Warner in a stupefying $164 billion deal, the largest in the history of communications. The AOL–Time Warner merger was supposed to build on the combined strengths of united companies but quickly demonstrated that it did little. In 2002, when Time Warner reported a net loss of $98.7 billion—primarily to write down the value of AOL—it marked the largest annual corporate loss in history.

In 2006, "America Online" as a name ceased to exist; the company was formally rebranded solely as "AOL" (in stand-alone use, as a company logo the name is inexplicably spelled with upper- and lowercase letters *and* with a period, as in "Aol."). A year later, AOL's subscriber base was one-third of its peak. In 2015, AOL was purchased by Verizon for $4.4 billion—almost the same price for the entire company that AOL paid for just Netscape 16 years before.

Yet AOL had opened the door to the Internet for millions of new users, and before its decline helped to firmly establish the permanent role of online technology in U.S. households. But as the turn of the millennium approached, two new developments would shape the Internet, the second of which would transform online technology and the daily lives of everyone who used it. But the first development would nearly kill it all.

23

PUMPKINS AND MICE

"When will the Internet Bubble burst?" For scores of 'Net upstarts, that unpleasant popping sound is likely to be heard before the end of this year."

—Jack Willoughby, *Barron's*, March 2000

It was too good to last.

By the late 1990s, the Internet had evolved beyond anything that its pioneers ever thought it could be, and was blossoming into a dynamic and extremely popular technology for a rapidly growing public audience. As a result, the Internet represented a river of investment opportunity and potential profits for dot-com developers and entrepreneurs.

As the new millennium approached, the business of creating online organizations was brisk; with almost-daily news of new dot-com companies, multimillion-dollar investment deals, and even bigger stock offerings, the prospects for a new era of Internet-based business never looked brighter. From the mid-1990s until 2000, investing in budding dot-coms was the wildest of rides, expanding with an aura of wealth, power, and optimism that had become the hallmarks of the go-go Internet world.

Lavish spending on marketing reached a high-profile peak on January 30, 2000, when 14 dot-com companies each paid more than $2 million to advertise during Super Bowl XXXIV—inspiring the game to be called the "Dot.com Super Bowl."

But behind lucrative deals festered a problem—a simple, disaster-provoking problem: for the most part, neither the new dot-com companies nor the investors who bought into them had the slightest idea what they were doing.

Much of the growth of new Internet companies was a façade, an industry fed by its novelty and its perceived investment potential—but in most cases without planning or financial evidence to back up the talk. Hard-boiled financiers threw common sense out the window, investing in companies that, with even a moment of consideration, would have been viewed as the most absurd folly.

In retrospect, investment mistakes are always crystal-clear, but even so, the depth of the miscalculations in the late 1990s now seems almost unfathomable.

"Investors desperately, *desperately* wanted the dot-coms to succeed," said Jeffrey I. Cole, director of the Center for the Digital Future at USC Annenberg. "Company management offered only promises about the potential for their startups, and backers had expectations that had nothing to do with reality.

"The dot-com bubble," Cole went on, "was business plans written on the backs of napkins."

For many of the start-up companies, the problem was demonstrated in a single question from editor Rich Karlgaard to a young vice-president of "business development" at a start-up. When Karlgaard asked if his dot-com was profitable, the executive said, "We're a pre-revenue company."

And then in 2000, the bubble burst.

What pin had pricked the surface? Some warnings had been coming from calmer voices, but the reckless types viewed them as unwelcome noise. With legions of companies operating with no rational business plans for short-term survival—let alone long-term success—and most roaring ahead with a "grow big, grow fast" mentality, the end was inevitable.

On March 10, the prices of dot-com stocks peaked, and the slide began.

An indisputable alert came on March 20, 2000, when *Barron's*, the weekly financial magazine, splashed its cover with drawings of mounds of cash on fire behind the headline "Burning Fast." The issue featured a study of more than 200 Internet firms with the publication's analysis of "which ones could go up in flames, and when."

"When will the Internet Bubble burst?" asked columnist Jack Willoughby in his column titled "Burning Up" that preceded the study. "For scores of 'Net upstarts, that unpleasant popping sound is likely to be heard before the end of this year."

By April 6, dot-com stocks had lost nearly $1 trillion in stock value.

Barron's followed up the original story three months later, this time with "burn rates" for Internet companies that were blazing through their cash at the end of 1999; by the time the list appeared in *Barron's* six months later, the problems were much worse. At the top of the list of companies draining their reserves were such now-forgotten names as Netzee, CDnow, Boo, Beenz, eToys, Flooz, Kozmo, and Netivation; none would survive. For many other dot-coms as well, the cash from investors began to run out.

The bubble "burst" dragged on for several years—the worst of it in 2000 and 2001—as a growing list of dot-com companies floundered under the weight of too-high expectations and too-low revenue.

Two companies in particular tell much of the story of the business misjudgments and the misplaced investor enthusiasm that created the dot-com collapse. Perhaps the most high-visibility example of the peak and downfall was Pets.com, which called itself "a new breed of pet store."

Pets.com debuted in February 1999, with financing from some of the premiere venture capital companies, selling a full line of supplies for America's pet owners. Marketing for Pets.com was backed by plenty of traditional print advertisements, but it was the company's mascot, a ragged-eared dog sock puppet, that appeared in dozens of television commercials and became the company's high-profile face to the public (see plate 20). The puppet (voiced by comedian Michael Ian Black) became instantly popular with a celebrity role that extended far beyond advertising: the puppet was "interviewed" on talk shows and had its own giant helium balloon in the 1999 Macy's Thanksgiving Day parade.

But within months, the puppet would also become the poster child for the entire meltdown.

Even with such a prominent position in retailing, Pets.com was never a sustainable enterprise. The company lost money almost every time a purchase was made, as it sold millions of dollars' worth of products for as little as one-third of their cost in the hopes that customers could be converted to high-margin buying. In spring 2000, Pets.com spent $17 million on sales and marketing, at the same time bringing in half that much in revenue. By autumn, the company was spending $158 for each customer it acquired.

Later, many would ask: What could explain the reasons that investors sank money (literally) into the company?

"In light of the company's many challenges, it begs the question of why initial backers would support Pets.com," wrote tech columnist Mike Tarsala. "Perhaps venture capitalists should have been leery of Pets, since even off-line retailers barely make any margin on pet food—the company's staple seller. The money came rolling in anyway."

The company's "plan" could not last; less than a year after the puppet balloon floated through Manhattan, on November 9, 2000, Pets.com stopped taking orders, and the company laid off most of its 320 employees.

In June 2008, CNET named Pets.com as one of history's greatest dot-com disasters.

The demise of Pets.com may have been a high-profile debacle, but other meltdowns were even more costly, including some that showed just how unaware dot-com investors could be—even when alerted to problems.

Possibly the worst of all was Webvan.com, the grocery delivery service, which opened in 1996 operated by a team of executives—not one of whom had management experience in the supermarket industry. When Webvan stock went on sale in November 1999—and in spite of public notices that the company had already lost more than $65 million for the year and warned of losses for "the foreseeable future"—the stock sold for 65 percent over its initial offering price.

With huge expenses—at one point committing more than $1 billion for construction of distribution centers and delivery trucks—Webvan expanded too quickly, its costs far outstripping its revenue by millions, then hundreds of millions. The prospects for attracting customers were unrealistic and the returns were low; on July 8, 2001, the company website carried the notice, "We're sorry. Our store is temporarily unavailable while it is being updated. It will be available again soon." The next morning, 2,000 employees were laid off and Webvan closed—eight months after the initial stock offering. Overall, the company lost $830 million—reportedly the largest of the dot-com disasters.

But many of the more responsible dot-coms survived the bubble relatively unscathed, including eBay, Priceline, Craigslist, Monster, WebMD, and others that still thrive today. All were companies that had not overpromised and did not overexpand, and each had something that almost all the failed dot-coms had lacked: a thoughtful business model based on solid financial planning and realistic projections.

After the bubble, there were some well-earned opportunities for "I told you sos." In 1999, superstar investor Warren Buffett had warned early investors—those whose stock had risen based on unreasonable expectations—to get out before the end came. (Buffett had the effrontery to suggest that investors enjoying large stock gains in the bubble should consider the wisdom of investing in companies that were not showing a profit.)

"After a heady experience of that kind," Buffett said of the gains in previous years, "normally sensible people drift into behavior akin to that of Cinderella at the ball. They know that overstaying the festivities . . . will eventually bring on pumpkins and mice."

Buffett—whose purchases of more than a half-dozen companies in 2000 did not include a single technology firm—was pummeled by critics for his seeming lack of vision. But in 2001, with his investments intact, he looked back on the fallout, saying, "The fact is that a bubble market has allowed the creation of bubble companies—entities designed more with an eye to making money *off* investors rather than *for* them."

When the dot-com dust had cleared, the results were gruesome: by 2004, more than half of new dot-coms—hundreds of companies—had failed. About $5 trillion in stock value was lost. Hundreds of cocky start-up executives who had been made instant millionaires—on paper at least—in initial stock offerings found themselves penniless. And thousands of employees—some estimates as high as 85,000—confident that they had joined exciting and viable ventures, were suddenly on the street. The ripple effects also damaged the value of other successful dot-coms and computer and software companies as well.

Perhaps worse—but understandable given the financial debacle—investors temporarily lost faith in new companies, whether they were viable or not: in 1999, 107 start-ups doubled their stock value on the first day; in 2000, the number dropped to 67; by 2001, the number was 0.

Of the 14 dot-coms that advertised on the 2000 Super Bowl, in less than a year, five were gone. For the 2001 Super Bowl, E-Trade, a survivor of the bubble, ran an ad showing a chimp riding a horse through a ghost town of defunct dot-coms. The ad ended with the single line: "Invest Wisely."

⚬✖⚬

As a cautionary tale and a business school lesson about irrational investor expectations, no modern example proved better than the dot-com bubble. But beyond the hysteria came a message that was even more telling about the perception—a hope to some—that the Internet was going to have a limited, perhaps-shrinking role in the American experience.

"After the bubble burst, it was amazing to see how many people in industry just assumed that the collapse meant the end of the internet itself," said Cole.

"We had been studying the internet since the early '90s," Cole remembered, "and I would be asked, 'now that this internet thing is over, what are you going to do now?' And I wasn't just hearing from leadership in retail—it was journalists, advertising executives, and people in other fields as well. But we knew that even after the bubble burst, a failure of the internet could not be farther from the truth."

Those who watched the online world could see that in spite of the bubble, not only was "the Internet thing" still viable; it was more popular than ever. Internet use declined not a bit between 1999 and 2002, in fact going online continued to increase; by 2001, more than 70 percent of Americans were users, and were spending more time online at home every day and at work as well. Even after the collapse of many dot-com retailers, the number of Americans who bought online grew as well; by 2001, half of Internet users had also become Internet buyers.

America had no intention of giving up on the Internet.

And something innovative was emerging that would have significant benefits for users. While the dot-com bust was raging out of control, a new technology had evolved that so profoundly changed the experience of going online at home that it would become almost as influential as the creation of the Internet itself.

✿

In the dictionary, the many services that transmit data are described by a jumble of acronyms, specifications, and standards: among them ADSL, DSL, VDSL, G.993.2, IEEE Std 1901-2010, and countless others. But in the early 2000s, to home Internet users who were fed up with the fussiness and snail pace of going online through a dial-up connection, the jumble was irrelevant; the service they wanted was generally known as "broadband," and to users it meant one thing: "high speed."

With the spread of broadband in the early years of the millennium—usually piggybacked onto a cable TV subscription—Internet users could forget about their outdated dial-up service and its busy signals, screeching link noise, and oh-so-slow access. With broadband, Internet at home was fast—much faster. Even looking beyond exaggerated marketing hype, in actual use broadband was at least 25 to 100 times faster in accessing pages and downloading information than the best dial-up service.

"Once you used a computer with a broadband connection," said engineer and entrepreneur Henry Samueli, "you knew you would never go back to the old modem connection, even if it was free."

The dramatically increased speed that broadband added to going online was welcomed by millions—and with rapid acceptance. In 2000, less than 10 percent of Internet users went online with broadband; in only five years, more than half of users had broadband. By 2009, that figure had jumped to 83 percent.

The additional speed was welcome, but the deeper implication came in how the constant access to broadband transformed the role of the Internet in the lives of everyone who used it.

It was the "always on" feature that made all the difference for how users went online—and stayed online. The slow speed and unreliability of dial-up meant that the average user logged in—turned on a modem, dialed, waited (often enduring busy signals), connected, and only then started working online—two to five times a day for 20 to 40 minutes at a time. Even with the most efficient dial-up services, getting online was a time-consuming annoyance, and at a time when most services charged for time online, a pricey activity.

As a result, going online became a back-of-the-house pursuit—something users would deliberately go and do, usually outside of the mainstream of the household.

But with the arrival of broadband, all of that changed. Simply, modem use had been disruptive; broadband use became integrative. Going online was no longer an occasional ritual; it was an ongoing element of the daily routine.

For those unaccustomed to a high-speed connection at an office or university, the convenience of always-on was a revelation. Instead of saving up digital chores for the occasional online session, users quickly grew accustomed to stopping at the computer many times a day for a quick check of email, a look at the news, or a fast purchase. Even better, the computer could be left on all the time and checked at leisure. The task-stacking required of using a modem was a thing of the past.

For most, broadband was billed not by the minute or the hour but at a single monthly rate. So even though online access was faster with broadband, when users replaced slow modems with fast broadband, they stayed online *longer* as they explored the wonders of the online world. In 2000, the typical Internet user was online about three hours a week at home; by 2010, that time had increased to more than 12 hours.

For the first time, going online created a significant dent in other daily activities, such as reading, but most of all, in watching conventional television. Viewership of the mainstream broadcast networks, ABC, CBS, and NBC, already on the downswing, sank even lower; in 1980, the top-rated show, *Dallas*, was viewed in one-third of American homes; by 2010, the top-rated show, *American Idol*, was viewed in half that number of homes.

And in part because broadband access created more and better opportunities for users to find information online, the usefulness of the Internet grew as well. By 2006, the Internet was viewed as an important source of information by 80 percent of adult users—more than newspapers, television, or radio.

As a result, the home computer—at a point in tech history when many homes still only had one—started to become more of a focal point of the household and was moved to more central locations such as living rooms or, especially, the kitchen. Broadband brought the Internet full force into American lives.

To the corporate world, broadband at home would soon become the sharpest of two-edged swords. High-speed access was making possible the success of businesses that had been impossible (or unbearable) at slower speeds, including some of the fastest-growing companies to come in the first and second decades of the 21st century: audio and video streaming.

For instance, Netflix, founded in 1997 by Reed Hastings and Marc Randolph, had started out as a DVD-by-mail rental service and at first struggled to survive, picking up the cost of postage in both directions—including for customers who paid a fixed monthly fee for unlimited service that allowed them to watch and return as many discs as they wanted (one or two DVDs at a time, depending on the service level). Netflix did not show a profit until 2003; two years later, it was shipping 1 million DVDs every day.

But after noting the success of streaming services such as YouTube, Netflix developed online video delivery in 2007. The success of Netflix's streaming of productions owned by others opened the door to the company creating its own video content. By 2019, Netflix was producing hundreds of new series each year, for a total of more than seven hundred; the one thousand series mark is just around the corner.

In 2013, when Netflix began releasing entire series of its products all at once, the new offerings—reinforced by full series of existing programs that were already available from the company—inspired a phenomenon in marathon TV watching, leading to a new term in the modern lexicon: "binge viewing." The concept of binge viewing, rather than the traditional method of watching one new episode a week that had dominated television since its inception, created an entirely new trend in television viewing; within a year, Netflix reported that more than half of Americans were binge watchers. In 2015, *Collins English Dictionary* chose "binge-watch" as its word of the year.

House of Cards, the Netflix-produced series, earned the company its first Primetime Emmy Award nomination in 2013—the first nominee ever for web-based television. In 2018, Netflix alone won 23 Emmys; that year, all of the traditional television networks combined won 19.

Netflix still delivers DVDs by mail, but it has grown into a major tech power because of streaming video that was made possible by broadband at home—success not possible in a dial-up world. (Hulu, Sling, and others also reap the same benefits.) In November 2018, Netflix announced it had added more than 27 million new subscribers for the year—more than HBO added in almost 40 years.

But for many traditional industries, broadband became a demon; video stores by the thousands shuttered because of Netflix and other online streaming services, the primary victim being the Blockbuster Video chain of 4,500 U.S. outlets—and 58,500 employees.

But even worse was the fate of the recorded music industry—a textbook example of companies denying reality in the face of change. For decades, the music industry had profited by selling albums (and later tapes and compact discs) with 10 to 15 songs when customers often wanted to buy only two or three of them. As home broadband use grew, methods of digitally recording individual songs multiplied, and the size of music files shrunk, the result was devastating: sharing a single song illegally through a dial-up link had once required 40 minutes to download—too long for even the most patient music pirates; through broadband, the same download required only a few seconds.

The recorded music industry—which should have seen the handwriting on the wall when broadband was being developed—for years did little to change, refusing to adapt to new methods for selling individual songs while legal download services such as iTunes were booming in the early 2000s. The record industry still flounders along selling CDs, but after existing happily and profitably for nearly 100 years, its decay was quick, the math simple and brutal; in 2000, sales of compact discs were at $13.3 billion; by 2017, total sales had plummeted to much less than one-tenth of the previous decade, while iTunes alone earned $8.5 billion. And revenue from subscriptions to streaming services far outpaced both CDs and downloading combined.

By the early 2010s, the majority of retail record stores in the United States had closed—yet more victims of broadband and the services available through high-speed access. Best Buy, which for years was a principal seller of CDs, in July 2018 finally gave up on the record business.

But whether industries boomed or busted because of the arrival of high-speed access, in large measure customers were the beneficiaries. Because of broadband, users gained access to a new array of companies and services that were faster, cheaper, and offered more.

"Just as the arrival of the internet created a flood of social change, the proliferation of broadband technology as a method of accessing the internet is beginning to cause its own revolution," reported the Center for Digital Future in its 2004 study of the impact of the Internet on American users. "Broadband is changing entirely our relationship with the internet."

24

ALL THE HEAVY LIFTING

"It is considered illegal to use the ARPANET for anything
which is not in direct support of Government business."

—1982 MIT Artificial Intelligence Lab handbook
about going online

Creating new technology inevitably leads to a discussion of money;
buying and selling has been a part of the online experience practically
since the Internet was created.

In either 1971 or 1972—no one remembers for certain—students
at Stanford and MIT made history of sorts by connecting through the
ARPANET to orchestrate a sale of marijuana, which *New York Times* reporter John Markoff described as "the seminal act of e-commerce."

Later, what no one involved in the transaction could explain was why
they arranged an interstate sale of an illegal substance—a federal crime—
through an online connection that left a electronic trail when they could
have just picked up a phone.

Many other private transactions in America in the early years of the
Internet no doubt occurred, thanks to email on the ARPANET, but much
of the early progress in e-commerce was developing outside of the United
States. In 1979, British inventor Michael Aldrich took a first step toward
making online buying possible by linking a television with a computer that
processed sales over a telephone line. Aldrich called it a "new, universally
applicable, participative communication medium—the first since the invention of the telephone."

Aldrich's device became the first rudimentary step in how users could
go online, connect with businesses, and buy. By 1981, British travel company Thomson Holidays UK was using the first business-to-business online

shopping system, and two years later, France Telecom unveiled Minitel, an online service that included features for purchases.

Progress in the United States was slower—primarily because of rules enforced by the National Science Foundation (NSF), which had assumed management of the nation's computing backbone when the ARPANET was decommissioned in 1990. The NSF had maintained a policy of using the Internet for government and education purposes only—no commercial enterprises or sales. Eventually the National Science Foundation faced the inevitable; in 1991, it released its restrictions on using the Internet for businesses, which not long after would pave the way for commerce across the Internet.

Earlier, however, when CompuServe created its proprietary Electronic Mall in April 1984, the service became the first comprehensive online shopping system; CompuServe called it "a shopping mall in your living room" and linked users to such products and services as software, books, magazines, and gardening products.

"Let your fingers do the shopping in the Electronic Mall," read an ad in CompuServe's magazine, *Online Today*.

The Electronic Mall at first involved only 60 retailers, and shoppers could not venture outside of the mall. But it was a start.

Other e-commerce followed (primarily through the walled gardens at CompuServe, Prodigy, and America Online). But in 1992, Charles Stack created Book Stacks Unlimited, first selling books on dial-up bulletin boards and then going online with the name books.com in 1994—becoming possibly the first person to sell books directly from the Internet. At about the same time, a hedge fund manager named Jeff Bezos read what he called a "startling statistic"—that Web use was increasing by 2,300 percent each year.

"I decided I would try to find a business plan," said Bezos, "that made sense in the context of that growth."

Bezos left his job in New York to create, as he called it, "this crazy thing": to start an online store.

Bezos headed west. On the plane to Seattle, he began to write the business plan for his soon-to-be organization, which he named Cadabra. As the dot-com bubble began to swell around him, his detailed planning while airborne would be one of many steps that would separate Bezos from the start-up pack.

Over the next 20 years, Bezos would take his company—which after a false start with Cadabra, he renamed Amazon—from a small online bookseller to a company that, when measured by revenue, is now the world's largest Internet retailer. Bezos, who walked away from a lucrative career in fund management, would become—at least until his 2019 divorce—the richest person on earth.

Not surprisingly, given his pinnacle status in the online world, Bezos has become a lightning rod for commentary about his company and the role of e-commerce in the life of every Internet user. Bezos is assessed endlessly by journalists, pundits, and academics—a human cottage industry of business case studies and psychological dissection explored in enough media coverage, books, and case studies to fill shelves in an MBA school library. Bezos's comments on subjects ranging from business management to personal improvement to moving humanity to other planets are cited as the gospel of e-commerce; in 2019, a Google search of "Jeff Bezos" and "quotes" produced more than 5 million results.

Bezos would lead Amazon beyond books and into selling practically every product on earth. He would then create Amazon's own products, such as the Kindle line of e-readers and tablets, before turning to emerging forms of artificial intelligence technology for Alexa and other interactive products that would expand retailing beyond a computer or smartphone and into the canopy of the entire home, and then into a user's larger world as well.

But three issues in particular would speak loudest about how Bezos and Amazon have shifted views of e-commerce and its effects on the American experience: every mistake Bezos did *not* make while most of his competition was drowning, his near-obsession about dealing with his customers, and how one product in particular would fundamentally change how millions of Americans shop and perceive the role of e-commerce in their lives.

⌒∞⌒

In the earliest days of Amazon, Bezos sought $1 million to start his company, but he made the fund-raising effort even tougher for himself by informing prospects—mostly family and friends—that the company had only a 30 percent chance of survival. Bezos was able to convince 22 of them to take the risk, and they had enough faith in him to invest an average of $50,000 each to support his vision. The return on those investments would eventually exceed the craziest expectations of the go-go dot-com start-ups emerging at the same time: each of the investments by Bezos's original backers, which bought 1 percent of Amazon, was in 2018 worth $7 billion—a return of 14 million percent.

Talking face to face with friends and family and asking them to fund a venture that even the entrepreneur thought would most likely fail was the beginning of a philosophy about frank dealings with investors and setting his own rules for those relationships that would remain constant for Bezos from the uncertain early days to his broad success in the 2010s.

Working out of his garage—following in the tradition of Steve Jobs, Steve Wozniak, and Bill Gates as yet another Internet entrepreneur with a garage-based start-up—Bezos opened his e-doors in July 1995. His first sale was a book about artificial intelligence with a mouthful of a name, *Fluid Concepts and Creative Analogies: Computer Models of the Fundamental Mechanisms of Thought* by Douglas Hofstadter, which was ordered by computer scientist John Wainwright (the record of the sale is still listed in Wainwright's Amazon order history).

For Amazon, the early years were demanding; the day's book sales were packed and taken by Bezos to the post office in the back of his 10-year-old SUV. "I was dreaming one day," he remembered, "that we might have a forklift." When staff needed desks, Bezos did not buy them, he built them, using stout lumber for the legs and a door for the top that he purchased at the Home Depot across the street from the office (see page 280). But unlike many dot-coms that had to build a support structure around them, Bezos never viewed his company as a start-up in a solo struggle in the Internet world; he saw Amazon as an integral element that fit into the online landscape, drawing on a broad assemblage of existing resources.

"If you think about ecommerce, all of the heavy lifting was already done," he recalled of the early days of Amazon. "We had all of these big pieces of infrastructure in place. We didn't have to roll out a national transportation network to deliver parcel packages—the Postal Service was already there, UPS was already there. That would have been billions of dollars in assets and taken many decades to deploy. We could do the internet in the early days standing on top of another huge piece of infrastructure, which was the local and long distance telephone network; it wasn't designed for ecommerce. Same thing with remote payments: you had credit cards. So there were a bunch of pieces already existing."

Bezos further distanced himself from other dot-com retailers with his view of the purpose of his company—that Amazon was *not* in business to be a retailer of products; instead, he reinforced Amazon's role as a business to simplify online transactions for consumers.

From the start, Amazon's sales growth was astounding: revenue of $16 million in 1996 jumped to $148 million in 1997 and $610 million in 1998. However, Amazon would not show a profit—not even in one financial quarter—for four years after the company went public in 1997, during which time Bezos faced wrath from investors and analysts looking for typical short-term solutions. In 1997, Amazon found itself going head to head with Barnes and Noble's new website: Amazon had 125 employees; Barnes and Noble had 30,000. One headline describing the head-to-head competition read simply: "Amazon. Toast."

But the company expanded; in 1997, Amazon became the first dot-com retailer to attract 1 million customers.

Midway through the dot-com bubble, Bezos was doing what most other start-ups were not: unlike soon-to-be failures like Webvan, in the early years Bezos ignored perishable products and identified books as his primary market because of the millions of titles for buyers to choose from.

"When you have that many items," he said in 1997, "building a store online couldn't exist any other way."

Like other dot-coms, Amazon adopted a "get big fast" philosophy—a plan that would prove disastrous for many. However, while start-ups like Pets.com and others required millions for huge distribution centers and products from the start, Bezos built his company with the sale of books he acquired as orders arrived, at first maintaining stock of only 2,000 of the best-selling titles while offering more than 2.5 million other volumes that he could acquire quickly from suppliers.

In the fourth quarter of 2001, Amazon showed its first profit, but the fallout from the dot-com bubble burst made the year overall a financial disaster. While dot-coms were failing all around him and without a hint of an apology, Bezos reported a $567 million loss for the year. Nevertheless, he told shareholders, "by almost any measure, Amazon.com . . . is in a stronger position now than at any time in its past."

The optimism wasn't misplaced. In the depths of his early red ink, Bezos maintained his original vision, telling stockholders and analysts that an investment with Amazon was an investment for the long term—a philosophy of financial relations that runs counter to the short-term performance goals that drive most companies that are focused more on quarterly profits and not long-range stability.

And in an age when CEO time is often dominated by constant show-and-tell for financial analysts and investors to reinforce perceptions about stock value, Bezos says he dedicates about six hours a year to investor relations.

"Bezos prefers to meet with the investors with the lowest churn, the ones who have held Amazon's stock the longest," wrote *Fortune* in 2014.

"We don't meet with our biggest investors—we meet with our investors who have the lowest portfolio turns," Bezos told *Business Insider* in 2014. "Many investment portfolios have very high portfolio turns—they turn their portfolios multiple times per year. They're not really investors, they're traders. There's nothing wrong with that, it's just a different thing. So if we're going to spend time explaining the company, you should do it with people who are long-term investors—that's our point of view."

Instead, Bezos relies on communicating with frank commentary blended with his own personal philosophy in to-the-point communication about the company's performance.

"I believe we are in the best place in the world to fail (we have plenty of practice!)," he told shareholders in one annual letter. "Failure and invention are inseparable."

Every year, along with the current annual letter to shareholders, Bezos sends a copy of his original 1997 letter to, as he wrote in 2001, "help investors decide if Amazon.com is the right kind of investment for them, and to help us determine if we have remained true to our original goals and values. I think we have."

Prominently featured in that 1997 shareholder letter is the headline, "It's all about the long term."

For patient investors in Amazon, the wait was worth it: in 2003, Amazon showed its first annual profit; by 2010, net profits passed $1 billion. In May 1997, a share of Amazon stock sold for $1.50; by 2000, the price reached $106. In 2016, a share was worth $1,250. By then, Amazon accounted for more than half of all growth in online selling.

Amazon focuses so intensely on customer service that Bezos describes the policies as a near-manic focus that drives every element of the company's work. The 2018 annual report did not lead off with buoyant announcements of record income, which at $3 billion was truly remarkable; instead, Bezos proudly described the news that the American Customer Satisfaction Index recently announced the results of its annual survey, and for the eighth year in a row customers ranked Amazon number one.

"We continue to aspire to be Earth's most customer-centric company," he said.

In an era when other large and industry-dominant companies routinely top lists of "worst customer service" (AT&T, the world's largest telecommunications company, and Walmart, America's largest retailer, come to mind as leading companies that are regulars among leaders of the worst list), Amazon touts its customer policies, such as its quick exchange procedures, an extensive system of customer product reviews that is now copied by most other retailers, and easy returns (often free home pickup). When personal contact about an order is needed, buyers don't call customer service; customer service calls them—within seconds after a customer requests a call through a help screen, the phone rings.

Bezos defines his relationship with customers through his understanding that they are "divinely discontented," including, as usual, his own philosophy of the human experience as part of the mix.

"Their expectations are never static—they go up," Bezos said of his customers in 2017. "It's human nature. We didn't ascend from our hunter-gatherer days by being satisfied. People have a voracious appetite for a better way, and yesterday's 'wow' quickly becomes today's 'ordinary.' I see that cycle happening at a faster rate. You cannot rest on your laurels in this world. Customers won't have it."

But of the many changes that Amazon has brought to how Internet users perceive and use e-commerce, the most impactful has been Amazon Prime.

First offered in the United States in 2005, Amazon Prime provides a range of services to customers for a single annual fee, including music, video, and Kindle e-books, among others. But it was Prime's shipping policies that were transformational for the e-commerce experience: free two-day shipping, reduced fees for next-day shipping, and for some products, same-day delivery.

Prime's free shipping is not only a feature of convenience; it substantively shifts how and when people buy. Amazon Prime has changed e-commerce as much as broadband changed how Americans use the Internet at home. Before Prime, when online shoppers placed orders, they would tally up a list of items to buy and condense their purchases into occasional orders. But the Prime feature completely redefined buying online. Without shipping charges to consider, Prime shoppers can buy as much or as little as they want, sometimes placing multiple orders in a day.

And with Prime items delivered in one or two days guaranteed, product interests change; Amazon customers who previously bought only books, CDs, and other occasional purchases started to buy toothpaste, batteries, and other routine items that they formerly would run out to buy at a local store. As a result, customers started to integrate Amazon into their lives; instead of waiting to purchase several items in one big order, customers can use Prime to buy one item at a time, anytime—sometimes more than once a day.

Prime is not a giveaway; it debuted with an annual fee of $79.99, and the price has increased several times since. Amazon sees the service not only as a benefit for customers but also as an incentive to ensure that shoppers drill down into the company's product lines.

"Once you become a Prime member, your human nature takes over," said former Amazon executive Robbie Schwietzer in 2013. "You want to leverage your annual fee as much as possible. Not only do you buy more, but you buy in a broader set of categories. You discover all the selections we have that you otherwise wouldn't have thought to look to Amazon for."

For Amazon, Prime comes with a cost: the company loses money on shipping for nearly every Prime customer. "But the company makes up for that loss," said Brad Berens, principal at Big Digital Ideas Consulting. "Prime members buy nearly twice as much annually as non-Prime customers."

As of 2019, more than half of U.S. households have Amazon Prime subscriptions.

⚬◈⚬

Amazon has its critics, and when the company falters, the fallout is thoroughly documented on a global scale. Amazon is, most agree, a demanding, high-pressure employer, viewed by some as "not work for the faint-hearted" and by others as "brutally aggressive." The company has also been subject to a series of lawsuits by employees—some would say encouraged by union activists—who accuse the company of unrealistic work targets, razor-thin break times, and a domineering atmosphere. The company consistently refutes the charges. But Bezos's own work ethic and how it reflects on the corporate culture cannot be denied—"Bezos," said one former employee, "makes ordinary control freaks look like stoned hippies."

And for Amazon, with its high profile and almost-daily media coverage, mistakes can be whoppers. For example, in 2009, when Amazon learned it had accidentally distributed unlicensed e-copies of George Orwell's *1984* and *Animal Farm*, instead of explaining the problem to customers, the company arbitrarily deleted the books from Kindle e-readers before telling their owners. Amazon refunded the cost of the books, but the personal intrusion of the company into users' private realms produced outrage among customers. And because of the Orwell titles involved, the problem could not have been a more delicious media delight, with characterizations of "Big Brother" and "Amazon" used side by side. A canned response from the company did not help.

Then Bezos offered his own regrets.

"This is an apology for the way we previously handled illegally sold copies of *1984* and other novels on Kindle," Bezos wrote to customers. "Our solution to the problem was stupid, thoughtless, and painfully out of line with our principles. It is wholly self-inflicted, and we deserve the criticism we've received. We will use the scar tissue from this painful mistake to help make better decisions, ones that match our mission."

⚬◈⚬

Of course, Amazon is not the only retailer to thrive in the postbubble era, and many others have succeeded with vastly different strategies from

Bezos's. In San Jose, for instance, computer scientist Pierre Omidyar developed a website that featured direct person-to-person auctions; the first item sold in 1995 was a broken laser pointer. Omidyar expanded the website into a service he called AuctionWeb; in 1997, the company's name was changed to eBay. Five years later, eBay reported that 638 million items had been offered for sale that year. By 2005, annual revenue on eBay passed $4.5 billion; by 2012, revenue reached $14 billion.

At about the same time that Omidyar was tinkering with the start-up of eBay, 50 miles north in San Francisco, Craig Newmark was distributing an email to family and friends that featured items of local interest. In 1996, Newmark expanded the email into a website that featured other categories, including items for sale; the site would become known as Craigslist. Now available in 70 countries with local listings for 700 cities or regions, each month Craigslist offers more than 50 million new classified ads while receiving some 30 billion page views.

All of the traditional brick-and-mortar retailers, including Target, Walmart, Kroger, and Costco—have expanded their once-minimal online sales opportunities into broad commitments to e-commerce. However, perhaps most significant about Amazon's competition is how much time passed before most of them even started to try to catch up.

Walmart, for example, by far America's largest brick-and-mortar retailer and theoretically Amazon's principal competitor, struggled to establish an effective online presence throughout the 2010s. Walmart had experimented with ShippingPass, its own version of Prime, which the company rolled out in 2016—11 years after Amazon began its service. Walmart then upped the stakes when it canceled ShippingPass a year later and began offering free two-day shipping on some products in 2017 without a membership fee.

However, as late as 2018, Walmart was still hampered in its attempts to develop its Internet capabilities with the impact and customer service focus of Amazon. In March 2018, Walmart U.S. CEO Greg Foran tried to explain away his company's lack of online prowess to a national gathering of financial analysts. Foran described how his company, late in the e-commerce game, had been trying to work out the kinks in its overall structure for several years, pushing a retail model that advocated "customers should be able to shop when they want, where they want, and how they want." The explanation was hardly a confidence-builder about Walmart's role in the online world.

"For the last three years, we have been focused on 'fixing,'" Foran said. "And I think that's been appropriate.

"First and foremost," Foran itemized, Walmart has to "fix the basics in the store. Secondly, develop the skills to be able to pick items from the store and make them available for pickup. Third thing, as you develop that muscle, work out how we can deliver those to customers."

But by 2019, when Walmart and several other companies (including Home Depot, America's largest home improvement retailer) were offering free two-day shipping without a membership fee, that benefit came only with a minimum order—typically $35 or $45—leaving it to customers to balance the value of that offer against the Amazon approach of annual membership equals free shipping for many orders of any value. In either case, the outlook for online retailing in America continues to evolve.

But opportunities for e-commerce come with consequences—some apocalyptic—for many traditional brick-and-mortar retailers, from local merchants to national chains. One of the most prominent victims is Sears, which was founded in 1886 and for decades was America's largest retailer. Sears had been in decline even before being surpassed by Walmart in 1989, and the growth of e-commerce accelerated the fall. In 2005, Sears had 2,300 stores; as of 2019, more than 85 percent have closed, and the company is hanging on by a thread—not even among the top 30 largest retailers. As e-commerce continues to grow as a staple of American purchasing habits, there will be many more Sears, both large and small.

As with the arrival of broadband, the primary beneficiaries of changes in retailing and the growth of e-commerce has been users, who now have myriad opportunities for shopping—both online purchasing and in traditional brick-and-mortar retail stores.

"These days, taking into account all of the services offered by Amazon and traditional retailers like Target and Walmart, buyers can have products shipped to their front door, the trunk of their cars, or a drop-off at a 7-11, or even delivered directly into our locked homes—all of this in addition to just running out to a good old-fashioned store," said Berens. "Even though ecommerce has existed since the 1990s, we are only beginning to scratch the surface of opportunities."

⚬❀⚬

The particularly noteworthy lesson learned about the effect of e-commerce on the American experience is that the issue once considered the single most important barrier to online retailing never materialized.

From the earliest days of Internet use by the public, Americans have expressed strong concerns about their personal privacy while online. The concerns became magnified when those initial worries were compounded by questions about the security of credit card information when buying over the Internet.

By 2001, national studies reported sky-high concerns about privacy while purchasing online: one study showed that 96 percent of Internet users reported some level of concern about their privacy while involved in e-commerce, and nearly as many users—84 percent—were worried about the security of their credit card information when making Internet purchases.

"For many in retailing, concerns about privacy and security of credit card information were viewed as deal-killers for the long-term success of online shopping—a notion that produced great relief among traditional re-tailers," said Berens. "The general assumption was that those concerns about privacy and security had to be eliminated *before* ecommerce would succeed."

However, the persistent worries had no effect on Internet users and their buying online: concerns decreased slightly, but they remained generally high even while online buying continued to grow. In 2018, when at least 90 percent of online users reported some level of concern about their privacy when buying online, more than 80 percent of Internet users bought online.

"As it turned out, most people remain concerned about their on-line privacy and security, but their worries don't stop them from buying," Berens said. "Today, many people continue to be troubled about their online security when they buy online—and the issues have been magnified by seemingly endless reports about hacking and corporate security breaches. But those concerns are not getting in the way of the continuing growth of ecommerce."

25

DISSOLVING CONTAINERS

"We will be able to eliminate mundane tasks, live more complete lives, be more productive, and do more creative things
because machines will assist humans, as they always have, by
taking over the dull and the drab and the ordinary and repetitive tasks that humans are not good at. I think that's a very
interesting new reality to hope for—human beings perfectly
assisted and augmented by machines."

—Marcus Weldon, Bell Labs

There is a story about the Internet—actually a true incident—that vividly illustrates how swiftly events can change in the online world.

The story goes like this: in 2003, two historians who studied the dot-
com industry in the wake of the bubble burst decided to write a book about
the future of the Internet. They talked to a publisher, who told them, "If you
can make a case for major changes to come in the Internet, I'll buy your idea."

But the historians could see nothing on the near horizon that seemed
like a major transformation to come, so they gave up their idea for a book,
thinking that the Internet, as far as they could see, would thrive without
major changes for the foreseeable future.

In the next five years came Facebook (2004), YouTube (2005), Twitter
(2006), the iPhone (2007), and the Android operating system (2008)—five
developments among many that would, yet again, profoundly reshape the
Internet in the American experience.

Facebook, YouTube, Twitter, iPhone, and Android would open new
opportunities for online interaction—how users communicate and present
themselves to the world. Each of these applications found its own path into
the American mainstream. Facebook, for instance, developed in 2003 by a

group of Harvard students led by Mark Zuckerberg, was created as a social networking service for their fellow students on campus. That mandate later expanded to include many colleges and some cities and was eventually eliminated by the time the service became accessible by the public in 2004. By the beginning of 2019, Facebook had more than 2.3 billion monthly active users worldwide and 1.5 billion people logging on daily. Even while others such as Instagram, Snapchat, and WhatsApp are gaining wider usage, Facebook is still the primary platform for global social media.

YouTube was produced by Chad Hurley, Steve Chen, and Jawed Karim, who developed the video-streaming service when they were frustrated by the lack of opportunities to find clips of events on the Internet. YouTube quickly evolved into a social platform for users to upload, view, and rate video content—at first for individuals and later for corporate productions as part of a partner program.

The success of YouTube ranks as one of the fastest rags-to-riches stories in the history of technology. The site debuted on Valentine's Day 2005; the first posted video (still viewable) is "Me at the Zoo," a video taken of elephants at the San Diego Zoo that was posted by cofounder Jawed Karim. Seventeen months later, the company was purchased by Google for $1.65 billion.

By 2019, almost a half-million hours of video were being uploaded to YouTube every day, while 5 billion hours are viewed. With the exception of its parent company's search engine homepage, YouTube is the world's most popular website.

Twitter took the basic functions of email and texting and refined them into a service for broader content posting and social interaction. Developed in 2006 by Jack Dorsey, Noah Glass, Biz Stone, and Evan Williams and launched in July of that year, Twitter created a new method of reaching out to communicate with groups.

But unlike other online services, Twitter did not fit a previously defined pattern.

"There are certain businesses that you know what they are when they're born," said Williams in 2013. "Google, for example, was always a search engine.

"With Twitter, it wasn't clear what it was. They called it a social network, they called it micro blogging, but it was hard to define, because it didn't replace anything. There was this path of discovery with something like that, where over time you figure out what it is."

Twitter became not only an all-purpose delivery system for individual communication but also a source for breaking news and political coverage.

By the beginning of 2019, some 340 million monthly active users were posting more than 500 million tweets a day.

Twitter debuted with a restriction of 140 characters, which was increased to 280 characters in most countries in November 2017. But during the 140-character era, users found interesting challenges in posting content that fit the space limitation, not the least of which was creating complete cooking recipes that fit into a single tweet. For example, a cookie recipe that easily fits within the limit is: "Chocolate Chip Cookies: Combine 2 bananas & 1¾ c quick oats. Add ¼ c chocolate chips (optional). Bake at 350 for 15 minutes."

Facebook, YouTube, and Twitter have been responsible for opening new gateways to socialization and expression for billions of users worldwide. However, the three services have also become lightning rods for controversies that say much about the changing nature of privacy, personal intrusion, and political confrontation in the online American experience of the 21st century.

Facebook has been the subject of intense scrutiny for its role in spreading fake news and in Russian interference in the 2016 presidential election, and its policies for marketing user data—including the "harvesting" of personal information from more than 80 million Facebook users by the now-defunct political analysis firm Cambridge Analytica, which had consulted during Donald Trump's 2016 presidential campaign.

YouTube reportedly worked to increase viewership by giving search priority to videos that showcase fringe content. The results, reported the *Wall Street Journal*, included "channels that feature conspiracy theories, partisan viewpoints and misleading videos, even when users haven't shown interest in such content"—this despite assurances from YouTube that the company had modified its service to avoid delivering unwanted radical viewpoints.

Twitter has been used to organize political protests and civil disobedience against a range of political persuasions worldwide. However, the site has also become a focal point in the increasingly contentious debate about fake news, with Twitter as the primary outreach platform for outrage and denunciations by Trump, even amid rebuttals—with actual facts to back them up—about Trump's own distribution of distortions in his tweets. The even broader issue of tweets with fraudulent political content on Twitter became so heated that in 2018 the company partnered with nonpartisan Ballotpedia to add labels to legitimate political content that would verify the authenticity of tweets distributed by U.S. political candidates running in the midterm elections.

∽✕∾

Facebook, YouTube, and Twitter each had potential as broad services for communication and social contact, but their value was amplified by the development of the principal personal tool of the 2000s.

It would be difficult to overestimate the impact of the smartphone, with its touchscreen keyboard, storage for thousands of pictures and songs, built-in camera, Internet connection, and ability to use millions of add-on applications. Because of the smartphone—first the Apple iPhone in 2007 and then its competition devices powered by the more-popular Android operating system in 2008—Internet use, and social communication in particular, were no longer limited to a computer at home or a laptop to be lugged around.

One can imagine, 50 years ago, just how magical the prediction of a smartphone would have seemed: a replacement for a conventional telephone, computer, flashlight, wallet photo insert, credit cards, calendar, books, audio and video players, magazines—all in a device that also has Internet access and fits in a pocket.

In large parts of the underresourced world—especially in Africa and Asia—the smartphone is not just a convenience; for the billions for whom the personal computer is an unaffordable luxury or office space is at a premium, the smartphone is the only link to online communication.

"More people have access to the smartphone," said Marc Andreessen, "than have access to running water."

In 2019, an estimated 2.5 billion smartphones were in use worldwide, seemingly as a permanent fixture in the Internet landscape. The smartphone has become the current physical manifestation of the power and influence of the Internet in the lives of users, but its future represents how much digital technology will change.

∽✕∾

Where is the Internet going? First, perhaps, comes recognizing that the questions are no longer about the Internet as a single entity. The Internet's evolution will be defined by the broad and evolving range of hardware and software that encompass "digital technology," as the online realm continues to grow, change, and then change again.

For example, new directions to come in digital technology are foreshadowed by shifts that have already occurred, such as the decline of "containers"—a physical item such as a DVD—for content that is now often distributed by digital files or devices.

"The vinyl record album became the CD, which became the mp3 file," said Berens. "Photographs shot with film and printed on paper became jpgs that are stored in the cloud. For some, ownership of a car is dissolving into get-a-ride services like Uber or Lyft.

"The desktop computer shrank into the laptop, which became a tablet, and now many people increasingly use their smartphone as a regular alternative to a larger computer. But if the trend continues for physical objects to become absorbed into other devices, then there is no reason to think that the object we currently call 'a smartphone' represents the final evolution of how we communicate.

"Most of us now consider the smartphone to be a primary tool in our lives, but the smartphone as we know it may soon 'dissolve,' in the not-too-distant future, into a different kind of device that is even more comprehensive in function than our current phones.

"For example, we've already seen the smartwatch replace some functions of the smartphone," Berens said. "The smartphone may continue to dissolve until it is merely a tiny processor in your pocket that controls several sensors for communication that we carry or wear. By then, the physical form of the 'phone' will no longer be relevant."

As the smartphone changes, that evolution will be typical of the broader progress to come in how communication and information gathering will expand around individuals, by some predictions filling a person's physical environment.

"Why do we need to have a physical device we hold in our hand to communicate with other people just because they aren't physically near us?" said Marcus Weldon, president of Bell Labs and chief technology officer of Nokia. "It won't be long before we will not just connect people more intuitively, but we will actually connect everything—your environment, buildings, cities—so that we can actually optimize you in your world. The future won't be about Fitbits or smartwatches, but in fact about adding, embedding, or even ingesting sensors on—or in—everything. That will require new sensor technologies and new devices, and also new Augmented Intelligence systems and new massively distributed mission and 'life critical' networks to connect them.

"Biological sensors will measure your physiology and let you know whether you're well at every moment in time," Weldon said. "Your home will sense you and be able to pick up your movement and your vitality—maybe even measure your heart rate. So the infrastructure will measure you.

As a result, said Weldon, "We will be able to eliminate mundane tasks, live more complete lives, be more productive, and do more creative things because machines will assist humans, as they always have, by taking over the dull and the drab and the ordinary and repetitive tasks that humans are not good at. I think that's a very interesting new reality to hope for—human beings perfectly assisted and augmented by machines."

That type of monitoring, believes Leonard Kleinrock, could also include voice recognition that would identify individuals at any location.

"Computing and digital technology should be useful to me wherever I go," said Kleinrock. "I should be able to reach out to any computer without a privacy breakdown, so it recognizes me and allows me to use it."

But if continuous monitoring seems like a troubling specter of "Big Brother," developers emphasize that the control of information is key.

"It won't be a creepy, 'Big Brother' way of gathering information," said Weldon, "but rather done in a way that users are in control of their own information.

"If, for example, you're carrying a sensor that detects your metabolism, that information would only be shared with people you choose, like your doctor or your family. So it's not 'creepy Big Brother,' but 'friendly Little Brother or sister'—a supportive personal assistant. That's the world we're moving towards."

If the idea of continuous monitoring seems unlikely, note that the technology has already arrived: for instance, auto insurance companies such as Allstate, Progressive, State Farm, and others have developed software and a monitor that are embedded in a car or activated with a smartphone app that transfers data to the company to judge driving performance. The reward for participating—and driving safely—is lower insurance rates. The opposite, of course, also applies: rates go up when a predetermined number of rules about speeding or other infractions are broken.

"It's easy to see the extremes of continuous monitoring," said Berens. "As a positive, for example, a sensor that monitors diabetes that sends information to your doctor and activates the release of insulin in your body is part of a benevolent network of support that keeps track of you, takes care of you, and gives you objective choices about your life. However, the dark perspective is that continuous monitoring seems like a constant observation of your behavior, violating your privacy at every moment, as larger forces beyond your knowledge are monitoring everything you do."

But some people already view monitoring with digital technology as a positive. An early example occurred in July 2017, when employees at Three Square Market, a technology company in Wisconsin, were given the opportunity to have a tiny chip the size of a grain of rice implanted between their thumb and index finger, with the benefit being that they no longer needed a staff ID or keys at work, and they could buy lunch from the company cafeteria without cash or credit cards. Fifty of the company's 80 employees agreed to the implant.

However, not everyone is so enthusiastic: a 2018 national survey asked Americans, "If a digital chip could be put into your finger that is painless, invisible, and removable, and that allows you to eliminate all keys, IDs, boarding passes, credit cards, passports, and all possibilities of fraud, would you consider it?" More than half said they would probably or definitely not. However, 19 percent said they would probably or definitely consider an implant.

Exploring the future of the Internet—or rather digital technology— also requires new definitions for long-standing ideas. For instance, in 1969, when a parent asked a 13-year-old in the next room what he was doing and the reply was "I'm watching television," that response likely meant he was watching a weekly program on one of the three television networks or perhaps a local channel. Ask the same question in 1990, and the "I'm watching television" response meant not only the television networks but also dozens of cable channels accessed through a set-top box.

But by 2010, the definition of that reply changed dramatically: "I'm watching television" could describe television networks, or cable, or of subscription services such as Netflix, or billions of programs on YouTube, or any of the countless other opportunities available online.

The changing definitions in many aspects of the American experience in a digital world take on even deeper importance when exploring how they affect individuals and the relationships in their lives.

"The internet is changing the fabric of our social relationships," said anthropologist Genevieve Bell. "We connect with each other differently because of social media, but we also define those connections differently."

For instance, how do we define a friend?

"Social media has dramatically expanded our connections to other people, but they have also redefined how we perceive friendship," said Berens. "In terms of how we develop our relationships, our definition of 'friend' is vitally important."

How people view their friendships, and the perceived roles of those "friends" in their lives, can have deep emotional effects. Several studies have shown that merely viewing Facebook can lead to depression, because when users see the momentary peaks posted by others—parties, trips, family events—those highlights lead viewers to amplify the less-exciting routines in their own lives.

"On Facebook," said Cole, "everybody appears to be having a better life than we are."

Even more important, definitions of "friend" in the online world can have deep effects on children and how they view their relationships.

Parents can focus so closely on ensuring that their children are not exploited by online sexual predators that they can miss the larger picture: how children interact online with others of their own ages. Parents who would not hesitate to intercede in an unhealthy association by their child in the "real world" often fail to see the depth of problems with children's relationships while online; for every bully in the schoolyard there are a thousand potential bullies in cyberspace. And too often, parents ignore the problem and take no responsibility for children's online "friendships"; surveys since the early 2010s show that about one-third of parents never monitor their children in their online social networking.

Such issues about the Internet and technology in the American experience will continue to emerge, and there will continue to be wide pendulum swings between the unlimited possibilities and the dark corners in the digital realm. The online tools that connect families across the world or would-be bakers to links for chocolate cake recipes can also deliver plans for 3D-printable guns or messages of hate.

"We need to be mindful," said futurist Rishad Tobaccowala, "that the same technology that was a key part of Barack Obama's election strategy also helped the Russians influence the next campaign that elected Trump."

The Internet has long been on a path of constant reinvention, with flux being the only constant. The biggest question of all is: Where will digital technology go next?

"Nobody saw the Internet coming as we know it today," Kleinrock said almost a half-century after the events in his lab that sparked online technology. "Fifty years ago, no one considered the idea of search engines, or websites. And when they came, they were surprises, and explosive. We created this tool called the internet that is constantly shocking us with surprises. It will continue to surprise us."

EPILOGUE

MOON

In spite of the risks, the unknowns, and the seemingly impossible deadline that challenged the 400,000 people who created the Apollo program, the Saturn V was launched successfully in all 13 attempts: 12 for the Apollo program plus one to launch the Skylab Orbital Workshop in May 1973.

Each Apollo mission was more sophisticated and productive than the one before it; by the time Apollo 17 concluded the final lunar mission on December 19, 1972, American astronauts were driving a rover across the lunar surface for the third time, venturing almost five miles away from the landing site.

The six successful moon landing missions returned almost 900 pounds of lunar samples to Earth and produced a trove of scientific findings in fields as diverse as soil mechanics, meteorites, seismic studies, magnetic fields, and solar wind. Rocks and soil from the lunar surface, and the findings produced by the experiments, continue to be studied today by a new generation of geologists and space scientists—many of whom were not born when the Apollo missions landed on the moon.

Although the mission of Apollo 13 ended prematurely with an explosion in its service module, the creation of a rescue strategy that called on the talents of all in Mission Control and brought the crew home safely was itself a shining moment for the space program.

⚬⧖⚬

Thanks in large measure to the vision of Vannevar Bush and the plan he outlined for the nation's future in "Science: The Endless Frontier," the nation's system of higher education and teaching new generations of American research scientists continued to expand long after the Apollo program ended.

Every state in America has universities with comprehensive research programs in not only the sciences but also in the humanities and in schools of law, medicine, and other professional studies as well. The postwar years also saw the growth of hundreds of private colleges and comprehensive non-PhD–granting public universities across the country. In 1940, 186,500 Americans graduated with a bachelor's degree. In 2000, 1.2 million earned a degree.

By the first decade of the 21st century, 17 of the world's 25 best universities were in the United States.

The scoreboard of accomplishments that earned Nobel Prizes in science and medicine shifted dramatically toward the United States after World War II: between 1901 and 1945, the 18 medals won by American scientists paled in comparison to achievement over the next 40 years: between 1946 and 1985, Americans won 119 science and medicine Nobel Prizes. American dominance of the Nobel Prizes continues today.

⤷∞⤶

The costs of developing and building spacecraft are much larger than the costs of operating the missions themselves; in 1966, NASA's funding needed to create the Saturn V rockets and Apollo spacecraft had peaked, and by the time Apollo 11 was launched in 1969, engineering and manufacturing across the country had already scaled back dramatically, and layoffs numbered in the tens of thousands.

With the space race "won," missions to the moon were no longer a strategic political objective; other priorities, such as the Vietnam War and social programs at home, took precedence. As a result, Apollo missions 18, 19, and 20 were canceled. Since Apollo 17 returned from the moon in December 1972, no humans have left Earth's orbit.

However, the scaled-back American space program continued after Apollo—with an agenda of basic science, one could argue, that was more noble than the original goal of proving U.S. superiority over the Soviets. The Skylab space station was occupied by three crews over 171 days in 1973 and 1974; von Braun's 1950s vision for an American platform in orbit was finally realized—although on a much more limited scale.

Then in July 1975, Kennedy's goal of a joint United States–Soviet project in space was finally achieved with the rendezvous of an Apollo command module with a Soyuz spacecraft. That project set the stage for 11 missions in the late 1990s during the post-Soviet era that linked the space shuttle with the (now-Russian) Mir Space Station.

And when the first space shuttle was launched into orbit on April 12, 1981—the 20th anniversary of the first human spaceflight by Yuri Gagarin—more than 1 million people were there to watch it; two days later, another 300,000 witnessed the landing on the dry lakebed at Edwards Air Force Base in California.

c⊗ɔ

The Apollo 11 equipment, flags, descent stage of the lunar module, and mementos taken to the moon remain on the surface just where the Apollo astronauts left them. Photos of landing sites for Apollo 12, 14, and 17 taken from the Lunar Reconnaissance Orbiter in 2009 clearly show the lunar module descent stages, the lunar rovers, and their tracks on the surface of the moon. The dust kicked up by the astronauts is still visible. In spite of a constant barrage of micrometeorites, the footprints from the astronauts are expected to be visible for 100 million years.

Many of the relics from the lunar missions that did return to Earth— including the Apollo 11 command module—are housed for public view at the National Air and Space Museum in Washington, D.C., the nation's most popular museum. Included in the exhibit is a rock from the moon that visitors are encouraged to touch; millions do.

c⊗ɔ

Bill Jeffries, who as a teenager in October 1957 listened in wonder on his ham radio to the sound of Sputnik flying in orbit overhead, remained fascinated with technology and science throughout his life. He became a mechanical engineer and later a college instructor on the history of science.

c⊗ɔ

After Dwight Eisenhower left the presidency in 1961, he took a public stand against excesses in military spending. The man who, during World War II, had been the leader of the largest military offensive in history, in peacetime, became a stalwart opponent of the nation's "military-industrial complex."

Long before he left office, Eisenhower was stating his case in eloquent commentaries that are remembered as some of the most memorable statements from his presidency.

"Every gun that is made, every warship launched, every rocket fired signifies, in the final sense, a theft from those who hunger and are not fed, those who are cold and are not clothed," Eisenhower told the American Society of Newspaper Editors in 1953. "This world in arms is not spending money alone—it is spending the sweat of its laborers, the genius of its scientists, the hopes of its children."

Eisenhower focused on these issues in his farewell address before leaving office, in a warning about the potential misuse of power in military spending that is as relevant today as it was in 1961.

"Only an alert and knowledgeable citizenry," said Eisenhower, "can compel the proper meshing of the huge industrial and military machinery of defense with our peaceful methods and goals so that security and liberty may prosper together."

Eisenhower's message continued to resonate, but the growth of military spending would go on unchecked. In the second decade of the 21st century, the United States spends more on weapons and defense than the next seven countries combined—including Russia and China.

⸎

Former president Lyndon Johnson, who was among the spectators at the launch of Apollo 11, had left the presidency in January 1969 after declining the Democratic nomination to run for a second full term—in part because of his lack of success in extracting the United States from the Vietnam War and also because his doctors had told him that a failing heart left him incapable of withstanding the strain of office; he died less than four years later. Johnson had been one of the first advocates in Congress for an American space program, but it is John Kennedy who is remembered for it.

A month after Johnson's death in January 1973, NASA's massive complex in Houston and the home of human spacecraft training, research, and flight control, was renamed the Lyndon B. Johnson Space Center.

⸎

The photos and film taken of Earth by the Apollo astronauts were major contributors to creating awareness of the fragility of the global environment. Earth Day, first held in 1970 in the United States, is now an annual event to support environmental protection that is celebrated each April 22 in 193 countries. The first unofficial Earth Day flag, created by peace activist John McConnell, featured a photo of Earth shot from space by Apollo astronauts.

Many American astronauts became strong advocates for environmental causes, largely through their awareness of the delicate nature of the planet that became vividly clear when they were launched into space. When astronaut Walter Schirra was asked by a reporter in 1979 why he had become an environmental advocate, he said, "because of how I saw the Earth while in orbit." "As simple as that?" asked that reporter. "Yes," Schirra replied, "as simple as that."

⌒⦚⦚⌒

Mitch Evans, who walked along the shore of the Indian River lagoon in the darkness before every manned flight, retired from NASA in 1996 as a manager of operations at the Kennedy Space Center. He left his office on a Friday; on the following Monday, Evans went to another building to begin work as a volunteer in NASA's education program, where he teaches a new generation of young Americans about the wonders of exploring space.

COUNTERCULTURE

One issue that continues to fascinate is the question of when did "The Sixties"—not the decade, but as an era of social change and flowering of counterculture values—actually begin and end. By some measures, the 1960s began with the death of John Kennedy in November 1963 and ended with the resignation of Richard Nixon in the wake of the Watergate scandal in August 1974.

Regardless of the actual dates, it was clear that by the mid-1970s, much of the energy of the 1960s had changed, in part because some of the major goals of the 1960s, such as expanding national social programs, the environment, and civil rights, had been at least partially achieved—or perhaps more important, had moved into the ongoing mainstream discussion of America's political and social concerns. Counterculture of the 1960s in its endlessly evolving forms continues today, now as a broad influential force in a spectrum of social movements and cultural expression.

⌒⦚⦚⌒

In the late 1960s, support for the war in Vietnam declined sharply, in part because of the constant and growing social protest. By the autumn of

1969, for the first time more than a majority of Americans thought it was a mistake to send American troops to Vietnam. Three years later, only 29 percent agreed with the American policy.

The Vietnam War ended—at least for American military involvement—in January 1973, with the signing of the Paris Peace Accords that stopped the direct participation of U.S. troops. By then, the United States had been withdrawing personnel from Vietnam for four years; from a peak of more than a half-million military personnel in the country in 1968, the troop numbers declined by more than 100,000 per year. In 1972, the United States had 24,000 troops in Vietnam; a year later, the count was 50.

But the peace accords never stopped the conflict; North Vietnamese incursions in the South continued, and later in 1973 Nixon threatened renewed American military involvement. But Congress and the American people were finished with the war; in June 1973, Congress passed the Case-Church Amendment, which prohibited continued funding for military involvement in Vietnam, Laos, and Cambodia without approval in advance by Congress. The amendment passed overwhelmingly.

Then early in 1975, the North Vietnamese launched a broad military offensive; President Gerald Ford asked Congress for more military assistance for South Vietnam and Cambodia; Congress refused. A full-scale assault led to complete evacuation of Vietnam by Americans and the fall of Saigon in April. By June 1975, North and South Vietnam were joined under communist rule.

The financial cost to America for its 20 years of involvement in Vietnam was more than $168 billion for military operations and aid— enough to fund the nine years of the entire Apollo program six times over. The price of the war for the American people was tragic: 58,220 dead and another 23,214 with permanent disabilities.

MANSON

Charles Manson died on November 19, 2017, a week after his 83rd birthday. The day following his death, the cover of the *New York Daily News* ran his photo, emblazoned with the huge headline "Burn in Hell." Manson had spent 61 of his 83 years in confinement.

Impossible to rehabilitate, antisocial even within the prison structure, he was the ultimate creature of caged, self-made hatred. Through 12 parole hearings—he no longer attended them after 1997—Manson never showed remorse for his crimes, only voicing the endless repetition of his blaming society. Nothing had changed from his first hearing in 1978, when the parole board chair told him, "You are not suitable for parole."

"I agree," replied Manson. "I'm totally unsuitable for that world out there. I don't fit in at all."

⚬∞⚬

Suzanne Cosgrove, whose life path closely resembled Leslie Van Houten's until Cosgrove found love and support with family and friends, also spent part of her life in a prison, but in a much different role than the Tate-LaBianca killers.

After many life experiences, such as living in India, Cosgrove became a nurse, working in hospitals in Los Angeles, including home care at the beginning of the AIDS epidemic. She reconciled with her father and returned from a trip to India to care for him when he was terminally ill with cancer; three months later, he died in her arms.

Cosgrove moved to northern California to work in a tiny rural hospital with 14 beds. Then she took a major step: she became a nurse at Pelican Bay State Prison, the supermax facility in Crescent City that is considered one of the toughest penal institutions in the country.

Cosgrove worked at Pelican Bay for seven years, dealing daily with the "worst of the worst" offenders.

"It's a completely different world," Cosgrove said of Pelican Bay, "and there isn't a lot of humanity there. All I could do was treat my patients with respect. And I wouldn't lie to them—if I said I was going to do something, I did it. Simple humanity."

⚬∞⚬

Although most members of the Family eventually renounced Manson, some were loyal to "Charlie" until the end.

Tragically, the disturbed, the confused, and the misguided of new generations continued to follow Manson for the rest of his life; over the years he received thousands of letters from would-be followers who not only thought he should be released but also fervently believed he was, and always had been, innocent.

However, several of the most prominent of the convicted killers from the Manson Family found new lives in prison. Tex Watson—who had been convicted in a trial separate from Manson and the other defendants—Leslie Van Houten, Patricia Krenwinkel, and Susan Atkins became model prisoners

(Atkins died in 2009). All became active in prison programs, teaching classes and counseling other inmates. Krenwinkel, Van Houten, and Watson earned college degrees, and Watson became an ordained minister.

⚮

Even when Manson did not deliberately attempt to stay in the public consciousness, the work of others was a perennial reminder of his role in the American experience. In 1974, prosecuting attorney Vincent Bugliosi and coauthor Curt Gentry published *Helter Skelter*, a detailed account (502 pages) of the story of the Tate-LaBianca murders and the trial that followed. Released to broad critical acclaim, *Helter Skelter* was, at Bugliosi's death in 2015, the most popular true-crime book ever written.

Manson's role in popular culture has been solidified in a number of ways, including mentions in lyrics (by hip-hop group N.W.A.), performance of his music (Guns N' Roses), and appearances on satirical animated series, including *South Park* and *Family Guy*.

⚮

The photo of a seemingly crazed Charles Manson that appeared on the cover of *Life* magazine in December 1969, which many at the time assumed was a candid photograph, was actually a mug shot taken in 1968 by the Ventura County Sheriff's Department when he was arrested on a minor charge (see plate 11). The photo has since become one of the iconic images of the 1960s—as much a part of the decade's imagery as photos of John Kennedy, Martin Luther King Jr., the Beatles, or astronauts on the moon.

Today that image of Manson can be found on merchandise as diverse as books, posters, fabric (see page 119), urban artwork, and even baby clothes.

WOODSTOCK

After all the concerns, protests, and generational divisions among residents in the two towns in rural New York that declined to host the Woodstock Festival, as well as the initial opposition in the one that finally did, the "three days of peace and music" turned out to be precisely that: there were no riots, no vandalism, and no confrontations between police and spectators.

In fact, given that the population of the Woodstock Festival at its peak would have made it the third-largest city in the state of New York, the concert weekend was remarkably free of the types of local incidents that occur on a daily basis in most metropolitan areas. Two deaths were reported, neither on the concert grounds: a camper sleeping in a grassy field was killed by a tractor, and the other died from an overdose (probably insulin). Two births were also reported: one woman gave birth in a car stuck in traffic and the other at a local hospital after being airlifted. Only a few arrests were reported for minor offenses.

❦

Michael Wadleigh's acclaimed documentary *Woodstock* not only received critical acclaim and an Oscar but was also an overwhelming financial success. Produced with a budget of about $600,000, the film earned more than $50 million worldwide, making it one of the top-grossing documentaries of all time. The three-record soundtrack album went gold ($1 million-plus sales) in two weeks.

The film would also become noteworthy for inspiring thousands of imaginative wannabes who said they were at the event.

"The movie version of the concert led an entire generation to claim they had been to Woodstock," said former editor Ken Paulson, "when in fact they just attended the movie a number of times."

The concert, reinforced by the movie, would be cited as a factor in the increased awareness of young Americans as a marketing force and a contributor to the dominance of the young as primary catalysts for all things social, cultural, and commercial.

"After the movie came out, it seemed like youth and counterculture burst into the mainstream," said Patricia Tempel, who had left Woodstock earlier than planned to travel to graduate school and who would go on to a career in college teaching, advertising, and journalism. "In many respects, Woodstock was a beginning of seeing youth and counterculture values as this incredible market."

❦

When production manager John Morris announced from the stage that the concert was going to be a free event from then on and predicted that the promoters were going to take a "bit of a bath—a big bath," he was

right: the losses from Woodstock were extensive. The festival weekend produced a $1.4 million deficit; soon the Woodstock Ventures partnership split
up bitterly, with Rosenman and Roberts retaining all rights to the company
and Lang and Kornfeld out.

But the loss was only temporary: the deficit was initially covered by
Roberts's family and then later paid off by royalties from the *Woodstock* film
and album sales. The four promoters separately would be involved in many
other projects in music, investment, and film. (Roberts died in 2001.) When
the postfestival emotional heat had dissipated, they occasionally stayed in
touch, such as planning the 25th anniversary reunion concert in 1994 and
an amicable get-together to celebrate the 40th anniversary of the concert.

For all four, the connection to Woodstock would be the defining moment of their lives—the first thing mentioned in any description of them.

"I had moved on," said Lang, "but Woodstock would be with me
wherever I went."

⌀

With so much talk during and after the concert about the rampant
drug use, what may have gone unacknowledged is that the abuse may not
have been as widespread as news coverage reported at the time. It is quite
likely that the reports of hundreds of drug overdoses that were treated by
doctors at Woodstock were exaggerated because many cases were actually
innocent victims. The medical staff reported that a large number of their
patients had drunk from cups or bottles passed to them without knowing
they had been laced with LSD.

"Outside the tent, they were giving out Kool-Aid laced with whatever," said one of the nurses. "A lot of kids hurt by this stuff were just thirsty.
They didn't have any choice."

Michael Lang took no chances during the concert weekend.

"I didn't drink anything that didn't come from a bottle I didn't wash
or open myself," he said.

⌀

Woodstock has assumed such a hallowed place of its own in the
American experience that it is often forgotten that the concert had a tangible impact on many events that have occurred since.

The enduring impact of Woodstock can be said to have inspired a wide
variety of large-scale youth-focused events that were unheard of before the

summer of 1969; today's events are not only large in size but also broad in their scope. Programs as diverse as the Coachella Valley Music and Arts Festival, Burning Man, Comic-Con, and South by Southwest—events that cater to today's interests, lifestyles, and viewpoints are as relevant in the 21st century as Woodstock was in its era—owe much to the "three days of peace and music."

Since Woodstock, other rock festivals have been held with larger attendance than Woodstock, such as Summerfest, an annual 11-day festival held in Maier Park on the shore of Lake Michigan in Milwaukee, which annually attracts upward of 900,000 over 11 days and has earned the well-deserved title of "World's Largest Music Festival." And while many of these events are praised for their music and for the (usually) good conduct of those who attend, none has the milestone cultural status or historical impact that Woodstock earned in August 1969.

⌒◇◇⌒

Today, at the junction of West Shore and Hurd roads stands a monument to the Woodstock Music and Arts Fair. Built in 1984 by local artist Wayne Saward, the five-and-a-half-ton concrete-and-steel shrine commemorates the concert weekend and many of the artists who performed.

The monument is visited every day of the year, in all weather. Often a site interpreter is on hand to describe the grounds—locals such as Duke Devlin, who served there for years, after coming to Bethel for the concert and never leaving.

"You meet everyone here from jail to Yale," said Devlin.

For years, the monument was the only physical memorial to mark Woodstock, and many were concerned about the ultimate fate of the 37 acres where the concert was held. Then in 1996, the concert site and surrounding acreage were bought by local cable executive Alan Gerry, who had built a television sales and repair business he started in 1951 in Liberty (15 miles north of Bethel) into Cablevision Industries, the eighth-largest cable company in the United States when Cablevision was sold to Time Warner for $2.7 billion. Gerry used the proceeds to create a foundation that would support and revitalize the economy of his home county.

Gerry transformed the grounds south of the concert site into the Bethel Woods Center for the Arts, which includes a performance center and the Museum at Bethel Woods. The museum opened in 2008 with displays, interactive exhibits, and events to celebrate the 1969 festival and the entire experience of the 1960s. (Among the many features of the museum's website is an archive of photographs and video shot by those who attended Woodstock, including several of the images that are featured in this book.)

However, a primary mandate of the center is that the concert site itself will always remain untouched. The site was added to the National Register of Historic Places in June 2017. Today it is the same grass-covered slope it was before Woodstock Ventures leased it from Max Yasgur in July 1969.

After the internal struggle at the *New York Times* over the tone of the coverage of Woodstock that nearly resulted in the resignation of several writers—a debate that produced both a blistering attack on the festival followed by a rare semiapologetic editorial the next day—the *Times* would, like all mainstream media, revise its view of Woodstock and recognize the concert as a milestone moment in American culture.

By the 40th anniversary in 2009, the *Times* called Woodstock "a weekend of muddy grace."

"Baby boomers won't let go of the Woodstock Festival," wrote the *Times* chief music editor Jon Pareles, who as a "sheltered teenager" had attended the concert. "Why should we? It's one of the few defining events of the late 1960s that had a clear happy ending."

Richie Havens, who opened Woodstock with a set on acoustic guitar that culminated with his spontaneous creation and performance of the song "Freedom," was prominently featured in the documentary film and became known to a worldwide audience through more than 40 years of touring.

Havens died on April 22, 2013. On August 18—the 44th anniversary of the last day of the festival—Havens's ashes were scattered in a flight over the concert site.

A statement released by Havens's family read, "Though Richie traveled throughout the world for decades visiting and returning to countless locations, Max Yasgur's field always remained the location where Richie felt his deepest connection."

On August 7, 2018, a guest arrived at the Museum of Bethel Woods who turned out to be quite special: he had been one of thousands walking along

Route 17B on the Saturday morning of the event when he heard the concert had been canceled. A mile from Bethel, he turned back and went home.

Forty-nine years later, he finally made it back to Woodstock, and he brought his original ticket with him. The staff admitted him to the museum with their compliments and let him keep his ticket.

INTERNET

By 2019, 50 years after the first tentative steps to connect computers at UCLA and SRI, the Internet had been used by more than 90 percent of the U.S. population for almost five years. The average Internet user in the United States is online about 23 hours a week—almost one full day out of every seven.

The Internet is used in the United States by people in all age ranges, and like most technology, the young have been the fastest adopters: by 2019, Internet use had been near-universal (at least 98 percent) among those under 25 for more than a dozen years.

The rapid acceptance of new technology has resulted in Americans who are increasingly technologically sophisticated with each new generation. The connections between the youth culture and the growth of the Internet are not only intertwined but are also driving forces for each other, as new developments in digital technology—games, apps, and new services for social media connection—lead young users to diverse interests and the emergence of new needs.

And, in an era where it is clearer than ever that "knowledge is power," the digital tools that are embraced, or even created, by young users have resulted in changes in communication and information exchange that continue to evolve with astonishing speed.

❦

There remain high levels of concern about personal security and financial information while online—several national studies show that more than 90 percent of Americans have some level of concern about their privacy while making Internet purchases—but those concerns seem to have no impact on the enthusiasm for e-commerce: more than 80 percent of Internet users buy online.

However, the value of information in a digital age—data gathered about each Internet user, whether shopping, communicating, or simply seeking information online—looms as an increasingly important and controversial issue. Data gathered online about what we buy, do, and think is the "currency" of the information age, raising ever-more-pointed questions about personal privacy or the lack of it.

Describing users' relationships with online companies like Google and Facebook, reporter Manoush Zomorodi said, "On the internet, we let companies get away with more bad behavior than we would ever let our real-life friends get away with."

Data is a driving force behind everything from the ads we see to the products we buy to the multibillion-dollar business deals—some morally questionable—that swap cash for bytes of information. Issues of privacy and the use of digital technology are becoming more entwined and more complex every day.

⌁∞⌁

The ongoing study of those who use the Internet often overlooks those who do not: somewhere between 5 and 9 percent of Americans are nonusers. The single-digit number of those who do not go online represents at least 26 million Americans—a group about the size of the combined populations of New York and Maryland—who are not using the primary communications tool of our age.

Why are millions of Americans still not online? Studies have found surprising characteristics of nonusers. The conventional explanations—the expense, "too busy," or old age—have been discounted by years of national surveys that found only small percentages of nonusers who cited these explanations.

So if age, money, and limited time fail to explain the full story of nonuse, what does? A handful of overlapping reasons coalesce around a lack of will: nonusers simply do not have a computer or say they do not understand the technology—a questionable explanation decades after Internet access became common in school and the workplace—or say they have "no interest."

A bigger question lingers: Will the needs of the nonusers create burdens for users, because nonuse requires more tangible resources, such as increased staff for in-person services and paper documents? If millions remain nonusers, the costs to the rest of the country may be high.

⌁∞⌁

The ongoing issue of foreign manipulation of the U.S. political process—especially by Russian infiltrators—is being compounded by a growing problem of widening divisions within the American experience: discussion of political issues in the United States has deteriorated to the point that some Americans of both political persuasions will swallow anything.

"We are making it easier on the Russians because of the lack of quality in our own political dialogue," said General Michael Hayden, former director of the CIA and the National Security Agency, to Wolf Blitzer on CNN in October 2018.

Hayden's comments followed the discovery of special instructions given to Russian "trolls"—planted Internet users who intrude in the online dialogue to disrupt the American political process—that targeted both Democratic and Republican ideas and leadership.

The instructions were a virtual how-to kit for political interference, including guidance such as, "Say that special prosecutor [Robert] Mueller is a puppet of the establishment," and "accuse CNN of yet another lie," and "expose [Republican Florida senator] Marco Rubio as a fake conservative."

"These themes are already in the American vernacular," said Hayden. "All the Russians have to do is take that, and transplant it, inflame it, reinforce it, and amplify it to increase the divisions that already exist."

"We make this easy," Hayden said, "by creating these divisions ourselves."

⧂⧃

A key to the efforts by Vint Cerf, Robert Kahn, and many others committed to building the Internet was the fundamental idea that online communication should be free to all. In fact, two of the most important developments that opened the Internet to broad use—the work by Cerf and Kahn on TCP/IP and Tim Berners-Lee and Robert Cailliau on the World Wide Web—could have been for-profit projects, sold by those with their bank accounts and not the long-term greater good as their priority.

"It wasn't licensed," Lawrence Roberts said of the work by Cerf and Kahn. "They proved to the world that making something free would make a huge difference in making it a standard."

Maintaining the Internet as a free service was a lofty goal in the 1970s and has continued in the decades since. Today, while users may pay for an Internet service provider to bring online access into their homes or mobile phones, no one pays to use the Internet itself. The most powerful communication tool of its age has remained open to all, without a fee.

Developing software for the greater good began as soon as the personal computer became generally available. Work to develop software distributed without charge continues, with nonprofit organizations working with donations and volunteers worldwide to create open-source tools such as Ubuntu (operating system), Gimp (photo editing), and LibreOffice (word processing, spreadsheets, presentations), among many others.

Today, a PC can be operated using open-source software that includes most of the features of commercial versions such as Windows, Photoshop, Office, and many other products—all for free.

ACKNOWLEDGMENTS

This book is the sum of many moving parts—interviews, websites, books, videos, and articles on four vastly different subjects—in all some 800,000 words of research material and related media. The glue that binds it all together came from everyone who so generously gave their time.

In particular, I wanted to express special thanks to the following people:

- Layne Karafantis, Roger Launius, and Peter Westwick—these three historians not only provided enlightening commentary about the history of aviation and the American space program but also gently guided my impetuous ideas for this project in its earliest stages.
- The retired engineers from NASA, the Ames Research Center, and their contractors shared with me their experiences of the early days of the space program and the Apollo project; their enthusiasm about humanity's adventures in aviation and space is just as strong today as it was during the missions. Tom Snyder of the Owl Feathers Society at the Ames Research Center did much to bring me together with his colleagues. April Gage and Abby Tabor at NASA Ames pointed me toward all the right paths at the start.
- Suzanne Cosgrove graciously recalled the details of her childhood and teen years—many of them painful and all of them most appreciated. The Elkind family kindly allowed me to describe their role in Suzanne's life.
- Richard Pfeiffer, attorney to Leslie Van Houten, directed me to the best information about his client as well as sources about Charles Manson.
- Wade Lawrence, Emily Casey, and Robin Green at the Bethel Woods Center for the Arts did everything I could have hoped for.

My thanks to them especially for connecting me with six eyewitnesses of Woodstock—Elizabeth Alexander, Beth Henry, Charlie Maloney, Jim Shelley, Patricia Tempel, and Glenn Wooddell—who shared their life stories with me and helped me appreciate the magic of the Woodstock experience.

- My colleagues Jeff Cole and Brad Berens, whose own thoughts are included in several chapters, guided me toward others with extraordinary perspectives on the current issues in digital technology and the fascinating future.
- My agent, Felicia Eth, was tenacious in her support of the idea for this book, as she has been about my projects for more than 30 years. My endless gratitude goes to her.
- My editors at Rowman & Littlefield, Jon Sisk and Kate Powers, were willing to take a chance with this approach to historical writing.
- My family and friends have been enthusiastic and supportive right from the beginning—a sustaining influence every step of the way.
- And finally—my wife, Monica Dunahee, has worked on this project since its inception, and has been the primary source of the best of the research, identifying interview subjects, and contributing to the tone and direction. This book exists because her involvement made it possible.

With so many thanks to all,
H. L.
Los Angeles, California

RESOURCES

100 DAYS: RESOURCES

There are, of course, thousands of books, videos, and (especially) websites about the four events described in this book. The resources I have included here are particularly compelling and can serve as starting points for learning more.

For live links to these sources and many others, go to my website for this project: www.100daysbook.com/resources.

PUBLICATIONS ABOUT 1969

Books and websites cover many of the key events of the year 1969, from the January upset win by the New York Jets in the Super Bowl to the first draft lottery in December. For an overview of the year in a single volume, try *1969: The Year Everything Changed*, by Rob Kirkpatrick.

To view a time-capsule exploration of 1969, every issue of *Life* magazine ever published can be explored online—including the December 19, 1969, issue that featured Charles Manson and the cover story "The Love and Terror Cult"—at books.google.com/books/about/LIFE .html?id=N0EEAAAAMBAJ.

MOON

An exploration of the Apollo program can begin with history.nasa.gov, a site of incredible scope and content about America in space. The website features literally years of reading about every U.S. mission as well as background, photographs, documents, and links to other sources.

As one example, see "Apollo by the Numbers: A Statistical Reference," which includes text about each lunar mission as well as background about the creation of the program. If you want to know anything about the lunar missions, from the amount of propellant used on Apollo 11 to the nicknames used for each flight, this is the place (history.nasa.gov/SP-4029/Apollo_00a_Cover.htm). Or an ultra-detailed illustrated chronology of the Saturn V can be found at history.nasa.gov/MHR-5/part-1.htm.

In addition to many fine video series about the moon missions and the people who flew them, a particularly interesting perspective on the Apollo program can be found in "Moon Machines," a six-part series that describes the creation of the main equipment needed for the missions: the command module, lunar module, space suits, guidance computer, lunar rover, and Saturn V rocket. The series is often available on YouTube or for sale on DVD.

"Science: The Endless Frontier," the landmark report by Vannevar Bush that changed the course of America's policy on research and education, can be found on the website of the National Science Foundation (www.nsf.gov/od/lpa/nsf50/vbush1945.htm). Bush's article "As We May Think," which inspired generations of scientists and digital pioneers, can be read on the website of *The Atlantic* magazine. Search by the title on www.theatlantic.com.

Because the internal workings of the millions of parts in a Saturn V rocket cannot be viewed, the next best thing are the slow-motion videos of launches on YouTube, which show the incredible precision required to move the 363-foot rocket off the launch pad.

You can hear the "beep beep beep" of Sputnik I on www.nasa.gov/connect/sounds.

The full text of President John Kennedy's meeting with NASA administrator James Webb and other administrators, during which Kennedy expresses his reservations about the space programs, can be viewed at history.nasa.gov/JFK-Webbconv/pages/transcript.pdf. Highlights of the discussion can be heard at www.youtube.com/watch?v=xZFnTBSRKcg or on the Kennedy Library website.

The text of Kennedy's "Special Message to the Congress on Urgent National Needs," which outlined the challenges of landing on the moon, can be read or heard at https://www.jfklibrary.org/archives/other-resources/john-f-kennedy-speeches/united-states-congress-special-message-19610525. The full text of his 1962 speech at Rice University on the challenges of the moon mission is available at https://er.jsc.nasa.gov/seh/ricetalk.htm.

The history of the space program extends well beyond the Kennedy Space Center—the National Register of Historic Landmarks includes listings for historic space-related buildings, facilities, and objects in Alabama, Arizona, California, Florida, Maryland, Mississippi, New Mexico, Ohio, Texas, and Virginia at www.nps.gov/subjects/nationalregister/index.htm.

The development of the Apollo Guidance Computer, including demonstrations of the incredibly complex core rope memory used on the mission, can be seen in "Computer for Apollo," a mid-1960s video production by MIT. The video is available from several sources on YouTube; search for it by the title. Details about the workings of the computer, including simulations and downloads of the actual code used on the Apollo missions, can be found on several websites, including http://www.ibiblio.org/apollo. A real-time simulation of the computer can be found at https://svtsim.com/moonjs/agc.html.

MANSON

A study of Charles Manson and the Tate-LaBianca murders can start with *Helter Skelter*, the superb book written by attorney Vincent Bugliosi (the prosecutor in the trial against Manson and his co-defendants) with writer Curt Gentry. *Helter Skelter* is the world's best-selling true-crime book, and with good reason; comprehensive and exhaustively detailed, the book is an insider's account of the background of the crimes, the investigation leading to the arrests, and the trials that followed. Particularly interesting is Bugliosi's reporting on the many missteps and errors during the investigation.

The 1976 miniseries based on the book, which stars Stephen Railsback in a chilling portrayal of Manson, is the definitive video about the murders.

For a book specifically about Manson himself, try *Manson: The Life and Times of Charles Manson*, by Jeff Guinn, which dives deep into Manson's background and obsessions.

There are dozens—hundreds—of websites about Manson, the murders, and the Family, with credibility ranging from superb to lunacy. Two of the best are cielodrive.com, which includes much factual material, regular updates, and a large number of links to other responsibly managed sites, and charlesmanson.com, which features a particularly useful menu for reaching specific information about the crimes, victims, and participants.

The full transcripts of the murder trials, as well as the parole hearings for the killers, are public record and are available online and off. For a briefer starting point, the closing argument by Bugliosi can be read at www.charlesmanson.com/closing-argument.html.

WOODSTOCK

To appreciate the impact that Woodstock had on the American experiences, look at the website for the Bethel Woods Center for the Arts (www.bethelwoodscenter.org), the organization that maintains the concert's site and serves as a hub of information and exhibitions about the culture of the 1960s. Among the many features of the center's website are a fully verified schedule of the performers (which for more than 40 years had been subject to considerable debate), facts about the concert weekend, and an archive of hundreds of photographs shot by spectators and professional photographers.

The concert wrap-up stories by the three television networks that appeared on August 18 and helped set the tone for how Woodstock would be remembered; they can be viewed on YouTube.

INTERNET

The original Interface Message Processor, which served as node number one of the network that led to the Internet as we know it, is on display at UCLA with other period-correct equipment in the same room where the work originally occurred in 1969. The room can be visited on tours of the university's engineering school (www.seasoasa.ucla.edu/tours).

The groundbreaking presentation by Doug Engelbart that demonstrated the potential for personal computing and collaborative technology, an event that came to be known as "The Mother of all Demos," can be viewed at www.dougengelbart.org.

The seemingly endless expansion of the Internet is vividly illustrated in several websites that display the growth of Internet use in real time. Particularly illuminating examples of the growth are shown at www.betfy.co.uk/internet-realtime or www.webpagefx.com/internet-real-time.

Several digital "antiques" can be downloaded or accessed online, including the original Mosaic program (www.ncsa.illinois.edu/enabling/mosaic), the Archie search engine (http://archie.icm.edu.pl/archie-adv_eng.html), and a copy of the world's first website (http://info.cern.ch/hypertext/WWW/TheProject.html).

To build a desk using a solid-core door just as Jeff Bezos and his team created them when Amazon was a struggling dot-com, instructions can be found at https://blog.aboutamazon.com/working-at-amazon/how-to-build-your-own-amazon-door-desk.

NOTES

MOON

Chapter 1: Challenging the Impossible

3 "No nation which . . . " Kennedy, Rice University speech.
"Between the lagoon . . . " Evans interview.
5 "'The schedule to come . . . " "Apollo by the Numbers."
"As a single undertaking . . . " Ibid.

Chapter 2: More than Bold Predictions

7 "We shall have rapid . . . " Bush, *Endless Frontier*.
"The vital scientists . . . " *Time*, "Yankee Scientist."
8 "No American . . . " Wiesner, "Bush."
"Can play around . . . " Baxter.
"Long time to come . . . " Herschberg.
"One step ahead . . . " Westwick interview.
9 "The President is first . . . " Pascal, *Endless*.
"The betterment of . . . " Roosevelt, letter to Bush.
"Can an effective . . . " Ibid.
"Closed his letter . . . " Ibid.
10 "Fairly recent development . . . " Westwick interview.
11 "Even Benjamin Franklin . . . " Atkinson.
"The early 19th century . . . " Ibid.
"The federal government had . . . " Hersch.
12 "Without a broad political . . . " Ibid.
"The limited funding . . . " Atkinson.
13 "National priorities intervened . . . " U.S. Congress, Public Law 271.
14 "Outdated airplanes . . . " Hennessy, USAF.
"Bush argued for federal . . . " Westwick interview.

15 "Called a memex . . . " Bush, "As We May Think."

"Sets of buttons . . . " Ibid.

"Consists of a desk . . . " Ibid.

"New forms of encyclopedia . . . " Ibid.

"The lawyer has . . . " Ibid.

"A scientist' war . . . " Ibid.

16 "Would be delivered . . . " Bush, *Endless Frontier.*

"Scientific progress is . . . " Ibid.

"Scientific capital . . . " Ibid.

"We cannot any longer . . . " Ibid.

"First, we must have . . . " Ibid.

17 "Bush argued for . . . " Leslie interview.

"Prior to World War II . . . " Atkinson, "Research Universities."

"Legislation is necessary . . . " Bush, *Endless Frontier.*

"We cannot again rely . . . " Ibid.

18 "Bush is responsible . . . " Ceruzzi.

Chapter 3: That Irresistible Charisma

19 "For von Braun . . . " Neufeld.

20 "The article . . . " Lang, "Romantic."

"Cash-strapped . . . " Neufeld.

"The V-2 was the most . . . "V2rocket.com.

"This day would be . . . " "Von Braun Story."

22 "To avoid allied . . . " Neufeld.

"Eventually some 10,000 . . . " Jacobsen.

"And in August . . . " Neufeld.

"*Paris Match* . . . " Neufeld.

23 "It naturally left on me . . . " Ruland.

"The implicit bargain . . . " Neufeld.

"Stoking . . . " Ibid.

"We despise the . . . " Ordway and Sharpe.

24 "Working closely on . . . " Jacobsen.

"On April 11 . . . " Ibid.

25 "Von Braun posed . . . " Neufeld.

"There is recognition . . . " Ibid.

26 "The thinking of . . . " Jacobsen.

"The Germans worked . . . " Ibid.

27 "Gifted enemy specialists . . . " Lang, "Romantic."

"Destruction . . . " Jacobsen.

"And at its core . . . " Ibid.

"At Fort Bliss . . . " Neufeld.

"Certainly not wishing . . . " Jacobsen.

"I have never thought . . . " Dickson.

28 "Ultra-liberals like . . . " Jacobsen.

28 "President Truman had . . . " Ibid.

"Truman had previously . . . " Lasby.

"This had to be done . . . " Ibid.

29 "Not just a ridiculous . . . " Neufeld.

Chapter 4: The Sight of Whizzing Flashes

31 "Background on Kraus and Ames . . . " Kraus interview.

"The Langley Flight Center . . . " Karafantis interview.

32 "Ames is actually . . . " Ibid.

"For example, across . . . " Kraft, *Flight*.

33 "By the time . . . " Launius interview.

"In February, Secretary . . . " Wallops.

"For example, the . . . " Corliss.

"New Mexicans who life . . . " Lang, "White Sands."

"What we did was specialize . . . " James, "Von Braun Story."

34 "It was interesting . . . " Kraus interview.

"Our concern had . . . " Boyd interview.

"Our mission at . . . " Peterson interview.

"Ames' giant wind . . . " Ibid.

"We were working . . . " Snyder interview.

35 "A crucial major . . . " Peterson interview.

"It turned out . . . " Ibid.

"Without Harvey's work . . . " Ibid.

"White Sands . . . " NASA, "History Home."

36 "Other service branches . . . " Ibid.

Chapter 5: Beep

37 Bill Jeffries background . . . Jeffries interview.

38 "The first few days . . . " *New York Times*, October 1–5, 1957.

39 "International Geophysical Year . . . " National Academies.

40 "The Russians had taken . . . " Dallek interview.

"Recalled General James . . . " Dr. Space.

"Ellender had just . . . " Ibid.

"In June, the Soviets . . . " Dickson.

41 "I am convinced . . . " Newton.

42 "They were informed by . . . " NASA, "Sputnik Night."

"It is small . . . " *Sputnik Mania*.

"We did not speak . . . " Fernlund.

"Soviet fires . . . " *New York Times*, October 5, 1957.

"Russ Satellite . . . " *Los Angeles Times*, front page.

"Russians launch . . . " *Arizona Daily* 10-5-57.

"NBC Radio . . . " *Sputnik Mania*.

"Life Magazine . . . " *Life,* "Sputnik's Significance."
43 "Two weeks after . . . " Erickson.
"The Eisenhower administration . . . " Hollings.
"I was almost . . . " Cloudynights.com.
"On a crisp . . . " Ibid.
44 "In Oklahoma . . . " Ibid.
"Johnson aide George . . . " Mieczkowski.
"Von Braun, in his . . . " Dickson.
"However, at the time . . . " Cohen.
"But another poll . . . " Ibid.
45 "Anthropologist Margaret . . . " Library of Congress.
"Charles Wilson . . . " Rothman, "Sputnik."
"When asked how . . . " Ibid.
"Years later, Eisenhower . . . " Foyle.
"Adams would recall . . . " Ibid.
"Sputnik reinforced . . . " Launius interview.
"The United States . . . " Karafantis interview.
46 "We believe . . . " NASA, "Sputnik Night."
"An American reporter . . . " Mieczkowski.
"In the eyes . . . " Launius, *Origins.*
"Senator Henry Jackson . . . " Dickson.
"Clare Booth Luce . . . " Spacedaily.com.
"Johnson called Sputnick . . . " Dickson.
47 "Said Senator Alexander . . . " *Sputnik Mania.*
"It is unpleasant . . . " Walker.
"If properly handled . . . " Ibid.
"Johnson certainly used . . . " Dallek interview.
48 "On October 9 . . . " UC Santa Barbara.
50 "It was simply . . . " "Von Braun Story."
"When Sputnik . . . " Ibid.

Chapter 6: A Dull Thud

53 "I am not . . . " Eisenhower, 1958 State of the Union Address.
"On December 6 . . . " Vanguard TV3.
54 "Satellite flops . . . " *LA Daily Mirror.*
"A dull thud . . . " *CBS Radio.*
"Forward March . . . " *Sputnik Mania.*
"Oh, What a Flopnick . . . " *London Daily Herald.*
"It is our judgment . . . " Killian memo.
"Although it is . . . " Ibid.
"It was all . . . " Ibid.
55 "I promised . . . " "Von Braun Story."
"Kennedy appreciated . . . " Dallek interview.

56 "A three-way collaboration . . . " *Sputnik Mania.*
"The Explorer satellite . . . " Explorer 1, NASA History.
"With the success . . . " *Sputnik Mania.*
57 "America would soon . . . " Ibid.
"More and more teenagers . . . " Ibid.
"But in spite . . . " Dickson.
"We have firmly . . . " Granath.
"Khrushchev could not resist . . . " Ibid.
"Van Allen's . . . " Vanguard 1, NASA History.
58 "On October 1 . . . " NASA History, Chronology.
59 "We would keep . . . " Peterson interview.
"The public demanded . . . " Dow.
"The education issue . . . " Saegesser.
60 "Of course, part . . . " Dow.
"The act served . . . " Schwegler.
61 "Institutions across the . . . " Maher.
"Introduction to Outer Space . . . " NASA, "Introduction."
62 "On December 20 . . . " Mieczkowski.
63 "There are too many . . . " Ibid.
"As a tactical error . . . " Dallek interview.
"Before the election . . . " Lapp, et al.

Chapter 7: Three Steps Ahead of a Pack of Hounds

65 "We are neither . . . " NASA, "Project Apollo."
"It was a difficult . . . " Sorensen.
66 "The impression began . . . " Kennedy, "Remarks at Municipal Auditorium, Canton, Ohio."
"I was deeply . . . " Sorensen.
"That project . . . " Ibid.
"That ray . . . " Ibid.
"The very notion . . . " Ibid.
67 "Young whippersnapper . . . " Ibid.
"A son of a bitch . . . " Ibid.
"Johnson was a . . . " Dallek interview.
"Johnson helped Kennedy . . . " Ibid.
68 "In a one-page memo . . . " NASA, "Project Apollo."
"Are we making maximum . . . " Ibid.
"The Space Council . . . " Ibid.
"This country should be . . . " Ibid.
"An achievement with . . . " Ibid.
"We are neither . . . " Ibid.
69 "We have a sporting . . . " Logsdon.
"Kennedy was focused . . . " Dallek interview.

"The American public . . . " NASA, "Project Apollo."
"The idea was . . . " Dallek interview.
70 "The president fired . . . " Sorensen.
"Now is the time . . . " Kennedy, National Needs Speech.
"I believe we possess . . . " Ibid.
"Recognizing the head . . . " Ibid.
"We take an additional . . . " Ibid.
71 "I believe that . . . " Ibid.
"If we are to go . . . " Ibid.
"Kennedy's speech shocked . . . " Moon Machines.
72 "An accelerated program . . . " Moon Machines.
"Paralyzed with shock . . . " Kraft, *Flight*.
"It wasn't just a case . . . " Westwick interview.
"We were confident . . . " Boyd interview.
"I was so excited . . . " Moon Machines.
"I didn't realize . . . " Ibid.
73 "We were all young . . . " Ibid.
"This generation does not . . . " Kennedy, Rice University.
"We have vowed . . . " Ibid.
"In short, our leadership . . . " Ibid.
"But why some say . . . " Ibid.
"We choose to go . . . " Ibid.
74 "Will be enriched . . . " Ibid.
"The great British explorer . . . " Ibid.
"Well, space is . . . " Ibid.
"Why don't we do it together . . . " Dallek, *Unfinished Life*.
75 "Why should man's . . . " Ibid.
"The idealistic Kennedy . . . " Logsdon.
"The meeting . . . " Kennedy transcript.
77 "Ultimately, Kennedy agreed . . . " Day, "Historic."
"Kennedy's reasons . . . " Dallek interview.
"The one who saw it . . . " Ibid.
78 "I partly agree . . . " Sorensen.
"I do not believe . . . " Ibid.
79 "In 10 short . . . " Bilstein.

Chapter 8: No Choice but to Be Pioneers
81 "There was just so much . . . " Moon Machines.
"We shall send . . . " Kennedy, Rice speech.
Saturn V background . . . Marshall Space Flight Center History Office.
82 "We all recognized . . . " Blackburn interview.
83 "At the start . . . " Westwick interview.

"There was just so much . . . " Moon Machines.

"As a result . . . " Marshall Space Flight Center History Office.

84 "The level of personal . . . " Westwick interview.

85 "They were going to . . . " Hansen.

"His figures lie . . . " Ibid.

"He doesn't know . . . " Ibid.

"Houbolt didn't say . . . " Moon Machines.

86 "The only thing . . . " Hansen.

"Somewhat as a voice . . . " Moon Machines.

"I had to meet . . . " Ibid.

"Had the Lunar Orbit . . . " Hansen.

"But NASA's usual . . . " Moon Machines.

87 "The supervisors responsible . . . " Brock.

"From my own perspective . . . " Weinstock.

"The result of . . . " Brock.

"The full code . . . " Collins.

88 "It's difficult . . . " Shillito.

89 "At North American . . . " Moon Machines.

"They did a great . . . " Binns.

Morea background. Marshall.

"The answer was   " Moon Machines; Space Suit, NASA headquarters

90 "For Alan Shepard . . . " Pomeroy.

"The unglamorous . . . " Moon Machines.

"Large worked . . . " Ibid.

"The bag system . . . " National Air and Space Museum.

"The system of . . . " Moon Machines.

91 "For example, in testing . . . " IAC Acoustics.

"The first time . . . " Moon Machines.

92 "Years later, Armstrong . . . " Neil Armstrong, YouTube.

92–93 "Consider one example . . . antispark properties" NASA, "Vehicle Assembly Building"; NASA, "Crawler-Transporter"; NASA, "Design of the Crawlerway."

Chapter 9: Go

95 "If we die . . . " White.

"The previous year . . . " NASA, "Gemini."

"The unyielding pressure . . . " NASA, "Apollo 1."

96 "At a meeting . . . " Murray, Cox.

"If we die . . . " White.

"Shea became dependent . . . " Kraft, *Flight*.

97 "We had taken . . . " When We Left Earth.

"The reviews produced . . . " Apollo 1.

Apollo 4 commentary. *CBS News*, "Apollo 4."

98 "Everyone who had made . . . " Blackburn interview.

"I think this is OK . . . " Moon Machines.

"What's wrong . . . " Ibid.

"It's working . . . " Ibid.

99 "We were all just transfixed . . . " Ibid.

"In the CBS . . . " *CBS News*, "Apollo 4."

"My golly . . . " Ibid.

"The sound was so crushing . . . " Blackburn interview.

100 "The crew of . . . " Apollo 8.

"My father and other ministers . . . " Wilford.

101 "It was ironic . . . " When We Left Earth.

"The most influential . . . " Australian Broadcasting Corporation.

"It is possible . . . " Poole.

"To see the Earth . . . " MacLeish.

Chapter 10: A Magnificent Sight

103 "This has been . . . " Courtright.

Apollo 11 flight information and mission details in this chapter. "Apollo by the Numbers," history.nasa.gov.

104 "Roger, Tranquility . . . " "Apollo 11 landing."

"All hell broke . . . " Kraft, *Flight*.

"For a moment . . . " Ibid.

"In the Bronx . . . " Ibid.

"Eagle . . . " Ibid.

"For millions . . . " Ibid.

105 Viewing of moon walk . . . *New York Times*.

106 "Moon or no moon . . . " Ibid.

"The poor . . . " Ibid.

"Mementos for eternity . . . " Smith, K., history.nasa.gov.

107 "The Saturn V rocket . . . " Blake.

Chapter 11: A Sense of Possibilities

109 "Somewhere, something . . . " Quote Investigator.

"On a warm . . . " Sorensen.

"Was it really possible . . . " Ibid.

"I partly agree . . . " Ibid.

"The most important test . . . " Ibid.

110 "As a civilian . . . " Hersch interview.

111 "Many people point . . . " Launius interview.

112 "Equally important . . . " Ibid.

113 "When we all think . . . " Boyd.

Counterculture

115 "The story of . . . " Paulson interview.

"In late December . . . " *Time*, Person of the Year.

"In the closing third . . . " Ibid.

116 "Some of the counterculture . . . " Marx interview.

"The story of . . . " Paulson interview.

117 "There were at least . . . " Turner interview.

118 "CBS News tried . . . " *CBS News*, "Generations Apart."

"It is a time . . . " Ibid.

"The survey showed . . . " Ibid.

"Will they find . . . " Ibid.

MANSON

Chapter 12: Like Moths to a Flame

121 "How the hell . . . " Rivera.

"The first two . . . " Torgerson.

"Manson was born . . . " Sawyer.

123 "The only thing . . . " Ibid.

"At six years . . . " Guinn Sawyer.

"My father is . . . " BrainyQuote.

"Before he was . . . " Sawyer.

"Aggressively antisocial . . . " Ibid.

"After more time . . . " Newell.

124 "A dead-end kid . . . " Ibid.

"Manson's crimes became . . . " Criminal Record.

"Marriage—first at 20 . . . " Ibid.

125 "Always attracted . . . " Guinn; Sawyer.

"What we saw . . . " Ibid.

"It was a scene . . . " Sawyer.

"Psychopaths are incredibly . . . " BBC, "Mass Murderer."

"He met Mary Brunner . . . " Bugliosi.

126 "Manson, said Roger . . . " Sawyer.

"Mad Rasputin eyes . . . " *Rolling Stone*.

"While living in . . . " Biography.com, Charles Manson.

"I really felt loved . . . " Sawyer.

"How the hell . . . " Rivera.

Chapter 13: Mesmerized

127 "Your children would . . . " Sawyer, Manson Part 2.

Van Houten background and quotes throughout . . . Leslie Van Houten parole hearings, Cielodrive.com.

"Born in 1949 . . . " Cielodrive.com. Charles Manson page.

128–29 "As a child, Suzanne Cosgrove . . . actively looking for a way out." Cosgrove interview with the author.

130 "Main reason . . . "Walters.

131 "Intrigued . . . " Sawyer.

"Mesmerized . . . " King.

"Empty shell . . . " Sawyer.

"Very normal . . . " Ibid.

"Tough question . . . " Cosgrove interview.

132 "This is fate . . . " Sawyer.

"Piece of work . . . "Waters.

"The more you take acid . . . "Walters.

133 "Said actor Peter . . . " Coyote.

196 "In the evenings . . . " Sawyer.

"Every day . . . " Ibid.

"Family followers were . . . " Ranker.com.

"He had a way with . . . "Van Houten parole hearing.

"For Manson, I . . . " Sawyer.

"I felt humiliated . . . " Ibid.

"I tried to think . . . " Ibid.

134 "And, remembered Krenwinkel . . . " Sawyer.

"I would see . . . "Van Houten parole hearing.

"To leave was to die . . . " Van Houten parole hearing.

"I am Jesus . . . " Sawyer.

Chapter 14: A Carnival Ride to the Apocalypse

135 "The idea that . . . " Maslin.

"Karen . . . " Daniels interview.

136 "Women were used . . . " *Rolling Stone.*

137 "In the article . . . " Rxstr.com.

"Manson had nothing . . . " Guinn.

138 "He said that he was going . . . " King.

"When we were . . . " Walters.

"It was like war . . . " Ibid.

139 "It was sad and tragic . . . " King.

140 LaBianca murder descriptions,Van Houten parole hearing.

"Had to be a good soldier . . . " King.

141 "I acted like . . . "Van Houten parole hearing.

"Posted a $25,000 reward . . . " Cielodrive.com., News Archive.

Acquiring guard dogs . . . McFadden.

"One agency in Los Angeles . . . " Ibid.

142 "At his booking . . . " *Rolling Stone.*

"Howard told the prison . . . " Ibid.

"Al Springer . . . " Springer.

"Titled 'The Love and Terror Cult' . . . " *Life*, December 19, 1969.

"Long-haired, bearded . . . " Ibid.

143 "I have X'd myself . . . " Deutsch.

"In court, Manson . . . " Ibid.

144 "The idea that those . . . " Maslin.

"Here is a man . . . " Nixon.

"I have ate . . . " Manson trial transcript.

145 "Had Manson's death sentence . . . " Levin interview.

"It took me a good . . . " *Barbara Walters.*

"I knew I was . . . " Van Houten, parole hearing.

"Part of my responsibility . . . " Sawyer.

"He is an opportunist . . . " King.

146 "I didn't produce . . . " *Sarasota Herald.*

"I ask you back . . . " 1992 parole hearing.

"I am only what lives . . . " BrainyQuote.com.

"I am only . . . " Famous Trials.

"Years ago . . . " *Forbes.*

147 "Before Manson . . . " Toobin.

"Manson just played . . . " Williams interview.

"We've certainly known . . . " Levin interview.

148 "Had Manson been . . . " Ibid.

"The electronic . . . " Ibid.

"Even though viewers . . . " Ibid.

"Manson was not Jesus . . . " Sawyer.

WOODSTOCK

Chapter 15: Grasshoppers in the Grain Fields

151 "The Woodstock Music . . . " WNEW commercial.

152 "The often-told story . . . " Lang interview.

153 "In rural New York . . . " Woodstockwhisperer, Chronology page.

"Even good news . . . " Collier, "Pop Festival."

154 "Woodstock, reporter Jim Miller . . . " Miller.

"This thing could . . . " *Poughkeepsie Journal.*

"Nothing against those . . . " Ibid.

"Forty miles to the north . . . " Lang, *Road to Woodstock.*

"About a quarter . . . " Ibid.

155 "You're the people . . . " Ibid.

"When Yasgur learned . . . " Mud2museum.com.

"I hear you are . . . " Woodstockwhisperer, Chronology page.

156 "The Yasgurs were . . . " Mud2museum.com.

"I never expected . . . " Evans.

"The new site . . . " Concertposterart.com.

"Certain people of Walkill . . . " Ibid.

157 "Bill Hanley, the incomparable . . . " Woodstockwhisperer, Chronology page.

Chapter 16: Overtaken by the Feeling

159–62 "Halfway up the sloping concert grounds . . . Woodstock has succeeded in its purpose." Maloney interview with the author.

162–65 "Behind the stage and across West Shore Road . . . and still act so civilly." Alexander interview with the author.

165–67 "At the top of the hill . . . So we closed up." Wooddell interview with the author.

167 "Emergency food . . ." Bramen.

167–69 "The Hog Farm seemed . . . to sleep for a few hours." Wooddell interview with the author.

169 "Beth Henry described her life . . . to believe in people." Henry interview with the author.

170–71 "At the top edge of the bowl . . . I was shocked and horrified." Tempel interview with the author.

171 "Yasgur noticed . . ." *New York Times*, "Max Yasgar [sic]."

171–73 "Tempel's group turned up . . . what actually happened there." Tempel interview with the author.

173–75 "On Saturday, in the center . . . the Sunday sun came up" Shelley interview with the author.

175 "The vision . . ." Woodstockwhisperer.info, "My Story" page.

175–76 "For Shelley and Tufano . . . their turn to be involved" Shelley interview with the author.

Chapter 17: Coming from a Dream

177 "When the cars . . . " Woodstockwhisperer.info, Ibid.

"When rides were needed . . . " Nightflight.

178 "When the town . . . " Lang interview.

"I was completely overwhelmed . . . " Bloom.

"I was very . . . " *Woodstock*, directed by Michael Wadleigh.

"Now, let's face . . . " "John Morris," YouTube.

"But, the one major . . . " Ibid.

"You might take it . . . " Ibid.

179 "That would have been . . . " Lang interview.

"The guitarist performed . . . " O'Brien.

180 "I looked out . . . " Wadleigh; Ventre.

"Anything you can do . . . " *Woodstock*, directed by Michael Wadleigh.

"My most vivid . . . "Woodstock documentary.

"More than 300,000 . . . " *United Press International.*

181 "To me, it looked like . . . " Collier, YouTube.

"Every major *Times* editor . . . " Fornatale.

"Despite massive traffic . . . " Collier, "300,000 at Folk-Rock Fair."

182 "To Collier, that was . . . " Inside Media, YouTube.

"Widely recognized . . . " Fornatale.

"The dreams of . . . " *New York Times*, "Nightmare."

"Now that Bethel . . . " *New York Times*, "Morning after."

183 "The news media . . . " Paulson interview.

"Media slowly began . . . " Ibid.

"I think the gap . . . " Ibid.

"But I think . . . " Ibid.

"Suddenly we began . . . " Collier, YouTube.

184 "This weekend says . . . " Poynter.

"Unfortunately, because much . . . " Ibid.

"It's true one . . . " Ibid.

185 "What happened this weekend . . . " Ibid.

"So what was learned . . . " Ibid.

"Over the last few . . . " Ibid.

"It was incredible . . . " Cavett.

186 "Anything you always . . . " Ibid.

"I got one . . . " Ibid.

"The remarkable thing . . . " Ebert.

"The notoriety of . . . " Tempel interview.

187 "The movie began . . . " Paulson interview.

"The first night . . . " *CBS News*, "CBS News Woodstock."

"This concert was contracted . . . " Ibid.

"On Max Yasgur's . . . " Lang, *Road.*

188 "For me, Woodstock . . . " *An Untold Woodstock Story.*

"That's what the . . . " Ibid.

"No longer can . . . " Sander.

189 "The power to the people . . . " *Woodstock*, directed by Michael Wadleigh.

"Woodstock declared that . . . " Lang interview.

"Woodstock showed that . . . " Ibid.

"What Woodstock represented . . . " Nikkhah.

"Woodstock showed that . . . " Ibid.

INTERNET

Chapter 18: Color and Flash

193 "Did you ever . . . " Kleinrock interview, September 24, 1999.

"If you live in . . . " Tedrow interview.
194 "Did you ever . . . " Kleinrock interview, September 24, 1999.

Chapter 19: "LO"

195 "Here is a question . . . " Kleinrock, Daily Bruin video.
196 "I was a tech guy . . . " Kline interview.
"I was interested . . . " Ibid.
197 "Klemrock gave his graduate students . . . " Cerf.
"As of now . . . " UCLA press release.
"In simplest terms . . . " Kleinrock interview, July 21, 2018.
198 Background on early networking . . . " Ibid.
199 "SRI was involved . . . " SRI website.
"Duvall, at 25 . . . " Duvall interview.
"Our goal was . . . " Kline interview.
"At 9:30 p.m. . . . " Kline and Duvall interviews.
"We couldn't . . . " Kleinrock interview, July 21, 2018.
200 "It was no . . . " Duvall.

Chapter 20: How to Move the World from the Right Place

203 "The obvious idea . . . " Mayo.
"Could hear a faint melody . . . " Berlin.
204 "Time-sharing was really . . . " Kleinrock interview.
"In my office . . . " Mayo.
"To get something . . . " Mayo.
Project SCORE background . . . Appel.
205 "He pretty much . . . " Mayo.
"Licklider was a strong . . . " Kleinrock interview.
"Consider the situation . . . " Licklider.
"Proposed to investigate . . . " Kleinrock interview, July 21, 2018.
206 "These problems appear . . . " Ibid.
"Packet switching is . . . " Ibid.
"In the 1960s . . . " Ibid.
207 "I would type . . . " Kline interview.
"None of the . . . " Kline, NPR.
"I remember thinking . . . " Cerf, *Nature*.
"And the ARPANET . . . " Zacon.
"Between 1969 . . . " Kline interview.
208 Tomlinson background . . . Grimes.
"The @ sign . . . " Tomlinson, Openmap.
"A few years . . . " Templeton.
"This was a flagrant . . . " Ibid.
209 "Spam, spam . . . " Monty Python.

"Irrelevant or . . . " Oxford English Dictionary, 2003.

"Almost half . . . " Infoplease.com.

"We were . . . " Kline interview.

"In 1973 . . . " Reardon.

"Kahn foresaw . . . " Cerf, *Nature*.

"At the time . . . " Reardon.

210 "After we built . . . " Mayo.

211 "Englebart background . . . " History–computer.com.

"A proposal from Doug . . . " Collective IQ.

"Mother of all Demos background . . . " Dougenglebart.org.

212 "It's hard to believe . . . " Metz.

"The first Apple . . . " Knight.

Email use . . . " Pew Research Center, "The Internet News."

Chapter 21: Four Steps in Gaining Momentum

215 Background on Requests for Comments . . . RFC–editor.org.

216 "A friend of mine . . . " NPR.

"I found it . . . " Berners–Lee FAQ.

217 "I actually wrote . . . " Ibid.

"Can't we convert . . . " Ibid.

"Most of the technology . . . " Ibid.

"Tim and I . . . " Gromov.

"At one point . . . " Mayo.

218 "Recalled Berners–Lee . . . " CDS Videos

219 "Alan Emtage . . . " Internet Society.

"While training for . . . " Deutsch, "Archie."

"I'm not a billionaire . . . " Internet Society.

"The great great grandfather . . . " Grandoni.

"I don't feel . . . " Ibid.

220 "I remember learning . . . " Thompson interview.

Andreessen background . . . NCSA.

"We targeted . . . " Andreessen, Smithsonian.

221 "When it comes to . . . " Wolfe.

"In the 18 months . . . " Ibid.

"More than 50,000 . . . " Vaughan-Nichols.

Chapter 22: On Hold

223 "One of my . . . " Buchanan interview.

"A study . . . " Pew Research Center, "Americans Going Online."

"The number of Americans . . . " Ibid.

"The survey title . . . " Ibid.

"The World Wide Web . . . " Ibid.

224 "Only 18 percent . . . " Newburger.

"By 2000, that number . . . " Center for the Digital Future, 2000.

"By then, almost half . . . " Madrigal.

"In those days . . . " Cole interview.

225 "We always believed . . . " Mayo.

"Jan Brandt came . . . " Hatch.

"The reason I started . . . " Ibid.

"One of my earliest . . . " Buchanan interview.

"But AOL faced . . . " McCullough.

226 "The marketing campaign . . . " Internet Archive.

"By then . . . " Cole interview. "In 2000, AOL merged . . . " Ingram.

Chapter 23: Pumpkins and Mice

229 "When will the . . . " Willoughby.

230 "Investors desperately . . . " Cole interview.

"For many . . . " *Vanity Fair.*

"An indisputable . . . " Willoughby.

"Barron's followed . . . " Crain Communications Inc.

231 "Even with such . . . " Tarsala.

"In light of . . . " Ibid.

"Pets.com stopped taking . . . " Ibid.

232 "Possibly the worst of all . . . " Richtel.

232 "With huge expenses . . . " Goldman, Webvan.com.

"The next morning . . . " Aboujaoude.

"After the bubble . . . " BBC, "Warren Buffett."

"After a heady . . . " Ibid.

"Buffet—whose purchases . . . " Ibid.

233 "When the dot-com . . . " Rouse.

"And thousands of . . . " Bureau of Labor Statistics.

"Perhaps worse . . . " Gray.

"Of the 14 dot-com . . . " *E-trade,* YouTube.

"After the bubble burst . . . " Cole interview.

"Those who watched . . . " Center for the Digital Future, 2001.

234 "Once you used . . . " Hamilton.

235 "For the first time . . . " Brooks, Marsh.

236 "But after noting . . . " Kyncl.

"In 2013, when Netflix . . . " West.

"In 2015, Collins . . . " BBC, "Binge-Watch."

"*House of Cards* . . . " Emmys.com.

"Netflix still delivers . . . " Sheetz.

237 "But even worse . . . " Tschmuck.

"The recorded music . . . " Ibid.

"By the early . . . " Jarvey.

"Just as the arrival . . . " Center for the Digital Future, 2004.

Chapter 24: All the Heavy Lifting

239 "In either 1971 . . . " Markoff.

"Many other private . . . " Aldrich.

240 "At about the same time . . . " Bezos, YouTube.

"I decided I would . . . " Bezos, YouTube.

"This crazy thing . . . " Clifford.

241 "In the earliest . . . " *South China Morning Post.*

242 "For Amazon, the early . . . " Karlinsky.

"If you think . . . " Boyle.

"From the start . . . " Döpfner.

243 "But the company expanded . . . " Funding Universe.

"When you have . . . " Bezos, YouTube.

"Like other dot-coms . . . " Hall.

"Bezos prefers to meet . . . " Griffith.

"We don't meet . . . " Joseph.

244 "I believe we are . . . " Hayes.

"Prominently featured . . . " Amazon, "Annual Reports."

"For patient . . . " Ibid.

"Amazon focuses . . . " Ibid.

245 "Their expectations . . . " Ibid.

"First offered . . . " Amazon, About Amazon Prime

"Once you become . . . " McCorvey.

246 "For Amazon, Prime . . . " Berens interview.

"And for Amazon . . . " Stone.

247 "Computer scientist Pierre Omidyar . . . " Welles.

"Craig Newmark was distributing . . . " Internet Archive, Craigslist.

"Walmart, for example . . . " Lauchlan.

"However, as late as 2018 . . . " Lauchlan.

"For the last . . . " Ibid.

"First and foremost . . . " Ibid.

248 "These days . . . " Berens interview.

"For many . . . " Ibid.

249 "As it . . . " Ibid.

Chapter 25: Dissolving Containers

251 "We will be able . . . " Weldon interview.

"Facebook, for instance . . . " Carlson.

252 "Facebook had more . . . " Facebook, Investor Relations.

"YouTube was produced . . . " Graham.

"The first posted video . . . " "Me at the Zoo."

"Seventeen months . . . " La Monica.

"Uploaded . . . " BusinessofApps.com.

"With the exception . . . " Alexa.

"Twitter took the . . . " Sano.

"With Twitter, it . . . " Lapowsky

"Twitter became . . . " *Omnicore.*

253 "Twitter debuted with . . . " Rosen.

"YouTube reportedly . . . " Nicas.

"Twitter has been . . . " *CBS News*, "Twitter."

"The even broader issue of . . . " Scola.

254 "In 2019, an estimated . . . " *Statista*, "Number of smartphone users."

"The vinyl record . . . " Berens interview.

255 "The desktop computer . . . " Ibid.

"For example, we've . . . " Ibid.

"Why do we . . . " Weldon interview.

"Biological sensors . . . " Ibid.

"Computing and digital . . . " Kleinrock interview.

256 "It won't be . . . " Weldon interview.

"It's easy to . . . " Berens interview.

"But some . . . " Astor.

"However, not everyone . . . " Surveying the Digital Future.

257 "The internet is changing . . . " Bell interview.

"Social media has . . . " Berens interview.

"How people view . . . " Morin.

"On Facebook . . . " Cole interview.

258 "We need to be . . . " Tobaccowala interview.

"Nobody saw . . . " Kleinrock interview.

Epilogue

260 "Every state . . . " Digest of Education Statistics.

"By the first . . . " *Times Higher Education.*

"However, the . . . " Skylab, history.nasa.gov.

262 "Every gun . . . " Eisenhower, "Chance for Peace."

"Only an alert . . . " UC Santa Barbara.

263 "As simple . . . " Schirra.

264 "The Vietnam War . . . " 25th Aviation Battalion.

"Impossible to rehabilitate . . . " Manson parole hearing, 1978.

265 "Suzanne Cosgrove, whose . . . " Cosgrove interview.

266 "The photo . . . " *Life*, "The Love and Terror Cult."

267 "Woodstock data . . . " Woodstockwhisperer.info.

"The movie version . . . " Paulson interview.

"After the movie . . . " Tempel interview.

270 "By the 40th anniversary . . . " Pareles.

"A statement released . . . " Coulehan.

"On August 7 . . . " Tempel interview.

271 "By 2019 . . . " Surveying the Digital Future.

"There remain . . . " Ibid.

272 "Describing user's relationships . . . " Zomorodi.

"The ongoing . . . " Blitzer.

274 "It wasn't . . . " Mayo.

BIBLIOGRAPHY

INTERVIEWS

Alexander, Elizabeth (Woodstock attendee) in discussion with the author, August 14, 2018.

Anderson, Terry (professor, Texas A&M), October 3, 2018.

Arnold, Jim (engineer, NASA Ames), August 3, 2018.

Bell, Genevieve (professor, Australian National University), September 27, 2018.

Berens, Brad (principal, Big Digital Ideas), September 4 and November 5, 2018.

Blackburn, Jerry (engineer, North American Aviation), August 18, 2018.

Boyd, Jack (senior adviser, NASA Ames), July 31, 2018.

Braudy, Leo (professor, USC), November 7, 2018.

Buchanan, Andy (historian), August 22, 2018.

Cole, Jeff (director, Center for the Digital Future), August 15, 2018.

Cosgrove, Suzanne (nurse), July 27–28, 2018.

Dallek, Robert (presidential historian), July 27 and October 19, 2018.

Daniels, Karen* (crime victim), August 22, 2018.

Deverell, William (historian, USC), August 9, 2018.

Doyle, Michael William (historian), August 14, 2018.

Evans, Mitch* (administrator, Kennedy Space Center), August 15, 2018.

Henry, Beth (Woodstock attendee), August 15, 2018.

Hersch, Matthew (Harvard science historian), September 13, 2018.

Jeffries, Bill* (Sputnik witness), March 14, 1999.

Karafantis, Layne (historian, USC), July 30, 2018.

Kleinrock, Leonard (Internet pioneer), September 24, 1999, and July 21, 2018.

Kline, Charley (Internet pioneer), July 27, 2018.

Kraus, Sam (engineer, NASA), November 17, 2017.

Lang, Michael (promoter, Woodstock), July 21, 2018.

Launius, Roger (historian, NASA), August 4, 2018.

Leslie, Stewart W. (historian, Johns Hopkins University), August 23, 2018.

Levin, Brian, (director, Center for the Study of Hate and Extremism), October 18, 2018.

Maloney, Charlie (Woodstock attendee), July 31, 2018.

Marx, Gary (historian, MIT), August 15, 2018.

Paulson, Ken (columnist, dean, Middle Tennessee University), August 8, 2018.

Shelley, Jim (Woodstock attendee), July 30, 2018.

Skey, Samantha (technology executive), August 28, 2018.

Snyder, Tom (engineer, NASA Ames), August 8, 2018.

Tedrow, Leslie (Silicon Valley resident), August 11, 2018.

Tempel, Patricia (Woodstock attendee), August 8 and 9, 2018.

Thompson, Cynthia (artist), August 24, 2018.

Tobaccowala, Rishad (futurist), August 28, 2018.

Turner, Fred (professor, Stanford), August 15, 2018.

Weldon, Marcus (president, Bell Labs), October 8, 2018.

Westwick, Peter (historian, USC), August 16, 2018.

Williams, David (social scientist, George Mason), October 7, 2018.

Wooddell, Glenn (Woodstock attendee), August 6, 2018.

(★ real name withheld at the request of the interview subject)

PUBLICATIONS AND WEBSITES

Aboujaoude, Elias, *Virtually You: The Dangerous Powers of the E-Personality*, New York: W. W. Norton, 2011.

Academy of Television Arts and Sciences, "Complete Listing of 70th Emmy Awards Winners," http://www.emmys.com/news/press-releases/70th-emmy-winners -announced, accessed November 3, 2018.

Aldrich, Michael, "Online Shopping in the 1980s," https://stirlingretail.files.word press.com/2018/06/anhc-33-4-anec-aldrich.pdf.

Alexa, "The Top 500 Sites on the Web," https://www.alexa.com/topsites.

Amazon, About Amazon Prime, https://www.amazon.com/gp/help/customer/ display.html?nodeId=201910360.

Amazon, "Annual Reports, Proxies and Shareholder Letters," https://ir.aboutamazon .com/annual-reports.

Andreessen, Marc, "Excerpts from an Oral History Interview with Marc Andrees-sen." In *Smithsonian Institution*, David K. Allison, June 1995, http://americanhistory .si.edu/comphist/ma1.html.

"Apollo by the Numbers: A Statistical Reference," history.nasa.gov/SP-4029/ Apollo_00a_Cover.htm.

Appel Knowledge Services, NASA, https://appel.nasa.gov/.

Arizona Daily Star, "Russians Launch Baby Moon," October 5, 1957.

Astor, Maggie, "Microchip Implants for Employees? One Company Says Yes," *New York Times*, July 25, 2017, https://www.nytimes.com/2017/07/25/technology/ microchips-wisconsin-company-employees.html.

Atkinson, Richard and Blanpied, William, "Research Universities: Core of the U.S. Science and Technology System," *Technology in Society*, 2008. http://www.rca.ucsd.edu/docs/TIS_Research%20Universities%20Core%20of%20the%20US%20science%20and%20technology%20system.pdf.

Australian Broadcasting Corporation, "That Photograph," http://www.abc.net.au/science/moon/earthrise.htm.

Barnstorff, Kate, "The Rendezvous That Almost Wasn't," NASA, July 19, 2004, https://www.nasa.gov/vision/space/features/apollo_lor.html.

Baxter, James Phinney, *Scientists Against Time*, Little, Brown, 1946.

BBC, "Warren Buffett: 'I Told You So,'" March 13, 2001, http://news.bbc.co.uk/2/hi/business/1217716.stm.

BBC, "Mass Murderer Charles Manson Granted Marriage Licence," November 18, 2014, https://www.bbc.com/news/world-us-canada-30089036.

BBC, "Binge-Watch Is Collins' Dictionary's Word of the Year," November 5, 2015, https://www.bbc.com/news/entertainment-arts-34723515.

Berlin, Leslie, *Troublemakers: Silicon Valley's Coming of Age*, Simon & Schuster, 2017.

Berners-Lee, Tim, FAQ, https://www.w3.org/People/Berners-Lee/FAQ.html.

Bilstein, Roger, *Stages to Saturn: A Technological History of the Apollo/Saturn Launch Vehicles*, Diane Publishing Inc., 1996.

Biography.com, "Patricia Krenwinkel Biography," last updated April 14, 2016, https://www.biography.com/people/patricia-krenwinkel-20902495.

Biography.com, "Charles Manson Biography," last updated January 9, 2019, https://www.biography.com/people/charles-manson-9397912, accessed October 17, 2018.

Bloom, Julie, "Weekly Popcast: Woodstock at 40," ArtsBeat, *New York Times*, August 6, 2009, https://artsbeat.blogs.nytimes.com/2009/08/06/weekly-popcast-woodstock-at-40/.

Bort, Julie, "Marc Andreessen Gets All the Credit for Inventing the Browser but This Is the Guy Who Did 'All the Hard Programming,'" *Business Insider*, May 12, 2014. https://www.businessinsider.com/eric-bina-is-the-unsung-hero-of-the-web-2014-5.

Boyd, Jack, Astrogram, October 2003, https://history.arc.nasa.gov/hist_pdfs/45nasa.pdf.

Boyle, Alan, "Interview: Jeff Bezos lays out Blue Origin's space vision, from tourism to off-planet heavy industry," *Geekwire*, April 13, 2016, https://www.geekwire.com/2016/interview-jeff-bezos/.

BrainyQuote.com, Charles Manson quotations, https://www.brainyquote.com/authors/charles_manson, accessed October 30, 2018.

Bramen, Lisa, "Woodstock—How to Feed 400,000 Hungry Hippies," *Smithsonian.com*, August 14, 2009, https://www.smithsonianmag.com/arts-culture/woodstock-how-to-feed-400000-hungry-hippies-65740098/#px3DPO3e2XJbE772.99.

Brock, David, "*Software as Hardware: Apollo's Rope Memory*," IEEE Spectrum, September 29, 2017, https://spectrum.ieee.org/tech-history/space-age/software-as-hardware-apollos-rope-memory.

Brooks, Tim and March, Earle, *The Complete Directory to Prime Time Network and Cable TV Shows 1946–Present* (Ninth Edition), Ballantine Books, 2007.

Bugliosi, Vincent, *Helter Skelter*, W.W. Norton & Company, 1974.

Bush, Vannevar, "As We May Think," *Atlantic*, July 1945, https://www.theatlantic.com/magazine/archive/1945/07/as-we-may-think/303881/.

Bush, Vannevar, "Science: The Endless Frontier," A Report to the President July 1945, *United States Government Printing Office*, https://www.nsf.gov/od/lpa/nsf50/vbush1945.htm.

BusinessofApps.com, YouTube Revenue and Usage Statistics, http://www.businessofapps.com/data/youtube-statistics/#1, June 1, 2018.

Carlson, Nicholas, "At Last—The Full Story of How Facebook Was Founded," *Business Insider*, March 5, 2010, https://www.businessinsider.com/how-facebook-was-founded-2010-3.

CBS Evening News, October 7, 1957, played in *Sputnik Mania*.

CBS News, "Twitter to add labels to U.S. political candidates," May 23, 2018, https://www.cbsnews.com/news/twitter-to-add-labels-to-u-s-political-candidates/.

CBS Radio News, December 6, 1957, played in *Sputnik Mania*.

Center for the Digital Future at USC Annenberg, "Surveying the Digital Future," The UCLA Internet Report, 2000, https://www.digitalcenter.org/wp-content/uploads/2012/12/2000_digital_future_report_year1.pdf.

Center for the Digital Future at USC Annenberg, "Surveying the Digital Future," The UCLA Internet Report (Year Two), 2001, https://www.digitalcenter.org/wp-content/uploads/2013/02/2001_digital_future_report_year2.pdf.

Center for the Digital Future at USC Annenberg, "Surveying the Digital Future: Ten Years, Ten Trends," The Digital Future Report (Year Four), 2004, https://www.digitalcenter.org/wp-content/uploads/2013/02/2004_digital_future_report-year4.pdf.

Cerf, Vinton G., "Opinion: The Day the Internet Began," *Nature*, October 29, 2009.

Cielodrive.com, (website for Manson and Tate-LaBianca murders), the Family web page, http://www.cielodrive.com/thefamily.php, accessed October 27, 2018.

Cielodrive.com, Charles Manson web page, http://www.cielodrive.com/charles-manson.php, accessed October 15, 2018.

Cielodrive.com, News Archive, http://www.cielodrive.com/1969.php, accessed November 5, 2018.

Cielodrive.com, "Audio Archives: Al Springer LAPD Parker Center Interviews, November, 1969—Tape One," http://www.cielodrive.com/updates/the-alan-springer-interviews/.

Cielodrive.com, Leslie Van Houten biography and parole hearings, http://cielodrive.com/leslie-van-houten.php.

Coulehan, Erin, "Richie Havens' Ashes Scattered at Woodstock," *Rolling Stone*, August 19, 2013, https://www.rollingstone.com/music/music-news/richie-havens-ashes-scattered-at-woodstock-180886/#ixzz2cQaGC7BA.

Crain Communications Inc., "'Barron's' Offers Follow-up to 'Burning Up,'" *Ad Age*, June 20, 2000, https://adage.com/article/news/barron-s-offers-follow-burning/9658/.

Criminal Record of Charles Manson through arrest in 1969, *Cielodrive.com*, http://www.cielodrive.com/charles-manson%27s-record.php.

Clifford, Catherine, "How Amazon founder Jeff Bezos went from the son of a teen mom to the world's richest person," *CNBC Make It*, October 27, 2017, https://www.cnbc.com/2017/10/27/how-amazon-founder-jeff-bezos-went-from-the-son-of-a-teen-mom-to-the-worlds-richest-person.html.

Cloudynights.com, "Was Sputnik Visible Naked Eye?" https://www.cloudynights.com/topic/125805-was-sputnik-visible-naked-eye.

Cohen, Jeffrey, *Presidential Responsiveness and Public Policy-Making: The Publics and the Policies that Presidents Choose*, Ann Arbor: University of Michigan Press, 1999.

Collier, Barney, "Pop Festival Lures Youths and Underground Dealers," *New York Times*, July 7, 1969.

Collier, Barney, "300,000 at Folk-Rock Fair Camp Out in a Sea of Mud," *New York Times*, August 17, 1969.

Corliss, William, *NASA Sounding Rockets, 1958–1968: A Historical Summary*, NASA, 1971.

Courtright, Edward, "Apollo: Expeditions to the Moon," *NASA*, https://www.hq.nasa.gov/pao/History/SP-350/cover.html.

Dallek, Robert, *An Unfinished Life: John F. Kennedy, 1917–1963*, 2003, Kindle.

Day, Dwayne, "A Historic Meeting on Spaceflight," https://history.nasa.gov/JFK-Webbconv/pages/backgnd.html.

Deutsch, Linda, "'This is crazy': Former AP reporter remembers Manson trial," *The Associated Press*, November 20, 2017, https://www.apnews.com/241c4ea7873e4e8ab3284250faf6533a.

Deutsch, Peter, "Archie—An Electronic Directory Service for the Internet," 1992, http://www1.chapman.edu/gopher-data/archives/Internet%20Information/whatis.archie.

Dickson, Paul, *Sputnik: The Shock of the Century*, Berkley, 2001.

Digest of Education Statistics, "Earned degrees conferred by degree-granting institutions, by level of degree and sex of student: 1869–70 to 2009–10," https://nces.ed.gov/programs/digest/d00/dt248.asp.

Döpfner, Mathias, "Jeff Bezos reveals what it's like to build an empire and become the richest man in the world—and why he's willing to spend $1 billion a year to fund the most important mission of his life," *Business Insider*, April 28, 2018, https://www.businessinsider.com/jeff-bezos-interview-axel-springer-ceo-amazon-trump-blue-origin-family-regulation-washington-post-2018-4.

Doug Englebart Institute, www.dougengelbart.org.

Doughty, Roger, "Rock Rumbles into Rip Van Winkle Country," *The Daily Times News*, July 16, 1969, https://www.newspapers.com/clip/20922953/woodstocks_aquarian_exposition_rumbles.

"Douglas Englebart biography," *History-computer.com*, http://history-computer.com/People/EngelbartBio.html.

Dow, Peter, *Schoolhouse Politics: Lessons from the Sputnik Era*, Harvard, 1991.

Ebert, Roger, *Review of Woodstock Film, directed by Michael Wadleigh*, https://www
.rogerebert.com/reviews/woodstock-1970.

Eisenhower, Dwight, "The Chance for Peace," speech delivered April 16, 1953,
http://www.edchange.org/multicultural/speeches/ike_chance_for_peace.html.

Eisenhower, Dwight, Presidential Press Conference, October 9, 1957.

Eisenhower, Dwight, 1958 State of the Union Address, January 9, 1958.

Engelbart, Christina, "RIP Robert Taylor Who Shaped Modern Computing," Collective IQ Review, April 16, 2017, https://collectiveiq.wordpress
.com/2017/04/16/rip-robert-taylor-who-shaped-modern-computing/.

Erickson, Mark, *Into the Unknown Together*, CreateSpace, 2012.

Esquire, "Steve McQueen's Womanizing Ways Stopped Him from Being Murdered
by Charles Manson," March 21, 2017, https://www.esquire.com/uk/culture/
film/news/a13833/steve-mcqueen-infidelity-charles-manson-murder.

Evans, Mike and Kingsbury, Paul, *Woodstock: Three Days that Rocked the World* (Museum at Bethel Woods, Sterling Publishing, 2009).

Facebook, Investor Relations, https://investor.fb.com/home/default.aspx.

Famous Trials, *Testimony of Charles Manson in the Tate-LaBianca Murder Trial*, November 20, 1970, http://www.famous-trials.com/manson/258-mansontestimony.

Felton, David and Dalton, David, "Charles Manson: The Incredible Story of the Most
Dangerous Man Alive," *Rolling Stone*, June 25, 1970, https://www.rollingstone
.com/culture/culture-news/charles-manson-the-incredible-story-of-the-most
-dangerous-man-alive-85235/.

Fernlund, Kevin, *Lyndon Johnson and Modern America*, Norman: University of Oklahoma Press, 2012.

Fornatale, Pete, *Back to the Garden: The Story of Woodstock and How It Changed a Generation* (Touchstone, 2010).

Foyle, Douglas, *Counting the Public In: Presidents, Public Opinion, and Foreign Policy*,
New York: Columbia University Press, 1999.

Funding Universe, "Amazon.com, Inc. History," updated 2004, http://www.funding
universe.com/company-histories/amazon-com-inc-history/.

Fuster, Jeremy, "Manson Girl Leslie Van Houten and John Waters: An Unlikely
Friendship," *The Wrap*, September 6, 2017.

Gilbert, Sophie, "The Real Cult of Charles Manson," *The Atlantic*, November 20,
2017, https://www.theatlantic.com/entertainment/archive/2017/11/the-real
-cult-of-charles-manson/546206/.

Goldman, David, "10 big dot.com flops: Pets.com," *CNN Money*, March 10, 2010,
https://money.cnn.com/galleries/2010/technology/1003/gallery.dot_com
_busts/.

Goldman, David, "10 big dot.com flops: Webvan.com," *CNN Money*, March
10, 2010, https://money.cnn.com/galleries/2010/technology/1003/gallery.dot
_com_busts/2.html.

Graham, Jefferson, "Video websites pop up, invite postings," *USA Today, Gannett
Company, November 21, 2005.*

Granath, Bob, America's First Satellite Established 'Foothold in Space,' *NASA*, https://www.nasa.gov/feature/americas-first-satellite-established-foothold-in -space.

Grandoni, Dino, "Alan Emtage: The Man Who Invented the World's First Search Engine (But Didn't Patent It)," *Huffington Post*, April 1, 2013, https://www .huffingtonpost.com/2013/04/01/alan-emtage-search-engine_n_2994090.html.

Gray, Jules, "The history of the dotcom bubble—and how it could happen again," *The New Economy*, October 5, 2015, https://www.theneweconomy.com/technology /dotbomb-are-tech-investments-about-to-destabilise-the-economy.

Griffith, Erin, "Why Amazon CEO Jeff Bezos only Spends Six Hours a Year Talking to Investors," *Fortune*, December 2, 2014, http://fortune.com/2014/12/02/ amazon-jeff-bezos-investors/.

Griffiths, David, "Dennis Wilson: 'I Live With 17 Girls'," *Record Mirror*, December 21, 1968, https://rxstr.com/2013/11/26/charles-manson-made-the-news-even -before-the/.

Grimes, William, "Raymond Tomlinson, Who Put the @ Sign in Email, Is Dead at 74," *New York Times*, March 8, 2016, https://www.nytimes.com/2016/03/08/ technology/raymond-tomlinson-email-obituary.html.

Gromov, Gregory, "Roads and Crossroads of the Internet History," Chapter 3, *NetValley.com*, updated 2012, http://history-of-internet.com/history_of_internet .pdf.

Guinn, Jeff, *Manson: The Life and Times of Charles Manson*, Simon & Schuster, 2013.

Haldeman, Peter, "A Dream Reimagined," *Architectural Digest*, January 31, 2010, https://www.architecturaldigest.com/story/dream-reimagined-article.

Hall, Mark, "Amazon.com," *Encyclopedia Britannica*, updated November 1, 2018, https://www.britannica.com/topic/Amazoncom.

Hamilton, Ian, "Two Henrys chip in to change the world," *Orange County Register*, August 13, 2011, https://www.ocregister.com/2011/08/13/two-henrys-chip-in-to-change -the-world/.

Hansen, James, *Enchanted Rendezvous: John Houbolt and the Genesis of the Lunar-Orbit Rendezvous Concept*, NASA Monograph, 1999, https://history.nasa.gov/monograph 4.pdf.

Hatch, Denny, "2001 Direct Marketer of the Year," *Target Marketing*, October 1, 2001, https://www.targetmarketingmag.com/article/2001-direct-marketer-year -28374/all/.

Hayes II, Julian, "What 20 Years of Jeff Bezos's Shareholder Letters Can Teach You about Becoming a Top Performer," *Inc.com*, May 30, 2018, https://www.inc .com/julian-hayes-ii/what-20-years-of-jeff-bezoss-shareholder-letters-can-teach -you-about-becoming-a-top-performer.html.

Hedegaard, Erik, "Charles Manson Today: The Final Confessions of a Psychopath," *Rolling Stone*, November 21, 2013. https://www.rollingstone.com/culture/culture -news/charles-manson-today-the-final-confessions-of-a-psychopath-58782/.

Hennessy, Juliette, "USAF Historical Study No. 98: The United States Army Air Arm, April 1861 to April 1917," *USAF Historical Division*, 1958.

"Hermann Oberth: Short Biography," *The Hermann Oberth Raumfahrt Museum*, http://www.oberth-museum.org/index_e.html.

Hershberg, James G. *James B. Conant: Harvard to Hiroshima and the Making of the Nuclear Age*, New York: Knopf, 1993.

Hollings, Ken, http://topfamousquotes.com/quotes-about-sputnik/.

IAC Acoustics, *Comparative Examples of Noise Levels*, http://www.industrialnoisecontrol.com/comparative-noise-examples.htm.

Ingram, Mathew, "AOL-Time Warner deal," *Fortune,* http://fortune.com/2016/10/24/att-time-warner-aol/.

Internet Archive, "Craigslist Online Community: Fact Sheet," updated March 12, 2012, https://web.archive.org/web/20120805110958/http://www.craigslist.org/about/factsheet.

Internet Archive, "Thank you, it's over. AOL has stopped sending out CDs. Thank you for all your assistance!," updated August 10, 2007, https://web.archive.org/web/20070820184342/http:/www.nomoreaolcds.com/.

Internet Society, "Internet Hall of Fame Inductee—Alan Emtage," Internet Hall of Fame, https://www.internethalloffame.org/inductees/alan-emtage.

"Internet Timeline," *Infoplease.com*, November 25, 2018 https://www.infoplease.com/science-health/internet-statistics-and-resources/internet-timeline.

Jacobsen, Annie, *Operation Paperclip: The Secret Intelligence Program that Brought Nazi Scientists to America*, Kindle, 2014.

Jarvey, Natalie, "Apple's iTunes Division Touts Record $8.5B Revenue," *Billboard*, November 3, 2017, https://www.billboard.com/articles/business/8023006/apples-itunes-division-touts-record-85b-revenue.

Joseph, Devan and Angelova, Kamelia, "Jeff Bezos Reveals Why He Spends So Little Time Talking to Traders," *Business Insider*, December 22, 2014, https://www.businessinsider.com/jeff-bezos-amazon-investor-relations-2014-12.

Karlinsky, Neal and Stead, Jordan, "How a door became a desk, and a symbol of Amazon," *The Amazon Blog*, January 17, 2018, https://blog.aboutamazon.com/working-at-amazon/how-a-door-became-a-desk-and-a-symbol-of-amazon.

Kennedy, John F., "Remarks at Municipal Auditorium, Canton, Ohio", September 27, 1960, https://www.jfklibrary.org/archives/other-resources/john-f-kennedy-speeches/canton-oh-19600927.

Kennedy, John F., "Special Message to the Congress on Urgent National Needs," May 25, 1961, https://www.jfklibrary.org/archives/other-resources/john-f-kennedy-speeches/united-states-congress-special-message-19610525.

Kennedy, John F., "Speech at Rice University," September 12, 1962, https://er.jsc.nasa.gov/seh/ricetalk.htm.

Kennedy, John F., "Transcript of Presidential Meeting, Supplemental appropriations for NASA," November 21, 1962, https://history.nasa.gov/JFK-Webbconv/pages/transcript.pdf.

Killian, James, memo to Dwight Eisenhower, December 28, 1977, Eisenhower Presidential Library, https://www.eisenhower.archives.gov.

Kleinrock, Leonard "UCLA Home Page," *UCLA*, updated September 18, 2014, https://www.lk.cs.ucla.edu/ucla_and_the_Internet.vhtml/.

Kline, Charlie, "40 Years Later, Looking Back at the Internet's Birth," interview by Guy Raz, *All Things Considered*, NPR, November 1, 2009, https://www.npr.org/templates/story/story.php?storyId=114376728.

Knight, Daniel, "Personal Computer History: 1985–1994," *lowendmac.com*, March 5, 2018, http://lowendmac.com/2018/personal-computer-history-1985-1994/.

Koch, Lucy, "More Than Half of US Households Will Be Amazon Prime Members in 2019," e-Marketer, https://www.emarketer.com/content/more-than-half-of -us-households-will-be-amazon-prime-members-in-2019, February 26, 2019.

Kraft, Chris, *Flight: My Life in Mission Control*, New York: Dutton, 2001.

Kyncl, Robert, "The inside story of how Netflix transitioned to digital video after seeing the power of YouTube," recode.net, https://www.recode.net /2017/9/13/16288364/streampunks-book-excerpt-youtube-netflix-pivot -video.

La Monica, Paul R., "Google to buy YouTube for $1.65 billion," *CNNMoney*, CNN, October 9, 2006.

Lang, Daniel, "White Sands," *New Yorker*, July 24, 1948.

Lang, Daniel, "A Romantic Urge," *New Yorker*, April 21, 1951.

Lang, Michael, *The Road to Woodstock*, New York: Harper Collins, 2009.

Lapowsky, Issie, "Ev Williams on Twitter's Early Years," *Inc.*, October 4, 2013.

Lasby, Clarence, *Project Paperclip: German Scientists and the Cold War*, New York: Atheneum, 1971.

Lauchlan, Stuart, "Walmart boss—'frictionless' shopping within 5 years," *Diginomica*, March 15, 2018, https://diginomica.com/2018/03/15/770186/.

Launius, Roger, *Sputnik and the Origins of the Space Age*, https://history.nasa.gov/sputnik/sputorig.html.

Lebo, Harlan, "Are non-users a voluntary underclass?" Center for the Digital Future, https://www.digitalcenter.org/columns/internet-nonusers/.

Library of Congress, "Margaret Mead: Human Nature of the Power of Culture," http://www.loc.gov/exhibits/mead/oneworld-learn.html.

Licklider, J. C. R., "Memorandum For Members and Affiliates of the Intergalactic Computer Network," December 11, 2001, http://www.kurzweilai.net/memo randum-for-members-and-affiliates-of-the-intergalactic-computer-network.

Life, "Sputnik's Significance," Google Books, *Life* Magazine Collection, October 21, 1957, https://books.google.com/books/about/LIFE.html?id=N0EEAA AAMBAJ.

Life, "The Love and Terror Cult," Google Books, *Life* Magazine Collection, December 19, 1969, https://books.google.com/books/about/LIFE.html?id =N0EEAAAAMBAJ.

Logsdon, John, "John F. Kennedy and NASA," *NASA*, www.nasa.gov/feature/john-f-kennedy-and-nasa.

London Daily Herald, "Oh, What a Flopnick!" December 7, 1957.

Los Angeles Daily Mirror, front page, December 7, 1957.

Los Angeles Times, front page, October 5, 1957.

MacLeish, Archibald, "A Reflection: Riders on Earth Together," *New York Times*, December 25, 1968.

Madrigal, Alexis, "The Fall of Facebook," *The Atlantic*, December 2014, https://www.theatlantic.com/magazine/archive/2014/12/the-fall-of-facebook/382247/.

Maher, Brent, "Divided by Loyalty: The Debate Regarding Loyalty Provisions in the National Defense Education Act of 1958," *History of Education Quarterly*, 2016 https://www.cambridge.org/core/journals/history-of-education-quarterly/article/divided-by-loyalty-the-debate-regarding-loyalty-provisions-in-the-national-defense-education-act-of-1958/93C3ABD4A01D81A41F10677B579CA6DA.

Mann, Amar and Nunes, Tony, "After the Dot-Com Bubble: Silicon Valley High-Tech Employment and Wages in 2001 and 2008," *U.S. Bureau of Labor Statistics Regional Reports*, August 2009, https://www.bls.gov/opub/btn/archive/after-the-dot-com-bubble-silicon-valley-high-tech-employment-and-wages-in-2001-and-2008.pdf.

Manson, Charles, quotes at https://en.wikiquote.org/wiki/Talk:Charles_Manson

Manson, Charles, quotes at https://www.mansondirect.com/quotes-cm.html.

Manson, Charles, trial transcript, bio, and parole hearings, *Cielodrive.com*, http://www.cielodrive.com/charles-manson.php.

Markoff, John, *What the Dormouse Said: How the Sixties Counterculture Shaped the Personal Computer Industry*, New York: Penguin, 2006.

Marshall Space Flight Center History Office, https://history.msfc.nasa.gov/.

Maslin, Janet, "Video: The Manson Mythology and Pop Culture," *The New York Times*, November 20, 2017, https://www.facebook.com/nytopinion/videos/the-manson-mythology-and-pop-culture/1943573622526817/.

Mayo, Keenan and Newcomb, Peter, "How the Web was Won," *Vanity Fair*, January 7, 2009, https://www.vanityfair.com/news/2008/07/internet200807.

McCorvey, J. J., "Amazon Fresh Is Jeff Bezos' Last Mile Quest for Total Retail Domination," *Fast Company*, August 5, 2013, https://www.fastcompany.com/3014817/amazon-jeff-bezos.

McCullough, Brian, "She Gave the World a Billion AOL CDs—An Interview with Marketing Legend Jan Brandt," *Internet History Podcast*, August 12, 2014, http://www.internethistorypodcast.com/2014/08/she-gave-the-world-a-billion-aol-cds-an-interview-with-marketing-legend-jan-brandt/.

McFadden, Robert, "A Reply to Rising Crime: Guard Dogs," *New York Times*, November 23, 1969.

Metz, Cade, "The Mother of All Demos—150 years ahead of its time," *The Register*, December 11, 2008, https://www.theregister.co.uk/2008/12/11/engelbart_celebration/.

Mieczkowski, Yanek, *Eisenhower's Sputnik Moment*, Cornell University Press, 2001.

Miller, Jim, "Did Woodstock Change America?," interview by Ben Wattenberg, *Think Tank*, PBS, 2009.

Mockapetris, Paul, "Interview on NPR," NPR, December 12, 2009, https://www.npr.org/templates/story/story.php?storyId=121378703.

Monty Python, "Spam" sketch, *Monty Python's Flying Circus*, season 2, episode 12, December 1970.

Morin, Amy, "Science Explains How Facebook Makes You Sad," *Psychology Today*, March 7, 2016, https://www.psychologytoday.com/us/blog/what-mentally-strong-people-dont-do/201603/science-explains-how-facebook-makes-you-sad.

Mud2Museum.com, "Tabletop Protest sign," http://www.mud2museum.com/Protest-Sign.html.

Murray, Charles, and Cox, Catherine, *Apollo: Race to the Moon* (Touchstone, 1990).

NASA, "Apollo 1, the Fire," https://history.nasa.gov/SP-4029/Apollo_01a_Summary.htm.

NASA, "A Chronology of Defining Events in NASA History, 1958–1998," https://history.nasa.gov/40thann/define.htm, accessed October 20, 2018.

NASA, "Crawler-Transporter," NASAfacts, https://www.nasa.gov/centers/kennedy/pdf/638823main_crawler-transporter.pdf, accessed September 29, 2018.

NASA, "Design of the Crawlerway," https://www.hq.nasa.gov/office/pao/History/SP-4204/ch11-6.html, accessed September 29, 2018.

NASA, "Explorer 1," https://www.nasa.gov/mission_pages/explorer/explorer.html, accessed October 1, 2018.

NASA, "Gemini," https://www.nasa.gov/mission_pages/gemini/index.html, accessed September 30, 2018

NASA, "History Home," NASA History Program Office, Office of Communications, https://history.nasa.gov.

NASA, "Introduction to Outer Space," NASA Historical Reference Collection, https://history.nasa.gov/sputnik/16.html.

NASA, "Project Apollo: A Retrospective Analysis," https://history.nasa.gov/Apollomon/Apollo.html.

NASA, "Skylab: Our First Space Station," https://www.nasa.gov/mission_pages/skylab, accessed October 23, 2018.

NASA, "SP-4103 Model Research," history.nasa.gov/SP-4103/ch2.htm.

NASA, "Space Suit," https://www.hq.nasa.gov/alsj/CSM21_Spacesuits_pp223-228.pdf, accessed September 22, 2018.

NASA, "Sputnik Night: October 4–5, 1957," NASA Monographs, https://history.nasa.gov/monograph10/sputnite.html.

NASA, "Vanguard 1," https://www.nasa.gov/content/vanguard-satellite-1958, accessed October 17, 2018.

NASA, "Vehicle Assembly Building at Kennedy Space Center," accessed September 28, 2018, https://www.nasa.gov/content/vehicle-assembly-building-at-kennedy-space-center.

NASA, Wallops Flight Facility, https://www.nasa.gov/centers/wallops/home.

National Academies, International Geophysical Year, http://www.nas.edu/history/igy/.

National Air and Space Museum, Collection System, Fecal, https://airandspace.si.edu/collection-objects/collection-assembly-fecal-apollo-6.

NCSA Mosaic, http://www.ncsa.illinois.edu/enabling/mosaic.

Neufeld, Michael, *Von Braun: Dreamer of Space, Engineer of War*, New York: Vintage Books, 2008.

New York Times, front pages, October 1–5, 1957.

New York Times, "In New York, Fatigue—but Some Work was Done," July 22, 1969.

New York Times, "Nightmare in the Catskills," editorial, August 18, 1969, http://woodstockpreservation.org/Gallery/NYT-PDF/17_NightmareInTheCatskills.pdf.

New York Times, "Morning after at Bethel," editorial, August 19, 1969, http://woodstockpreservation.org/Gallery/NYT-PDF/19_MorningAfterAtBethel.pdf.

New York Times, "Max Yasgar [sic] Dies; Woodstock Festival Was on His Farm," February 10, 1973, https://www.nytimes.com/1973/02/10/archives/max-yasgur-dies-woodstock-festival-was-on-his-farm-undaunted-by.html.

Newell, Robert, "Dream Comes True for Lad; He's Going to Boy's Town," *Indianapolis News*, March 7, 1949.

Newsweek, cover, March 4, 1957.

Newburger, Eric, "Home Computers and Internet Use in the United States: August 2000," *U.S. Census Bureau Current Population Reports*, September 2001, https://www.census.gov/prod/2001pubs/p23-207.pdf.

Newton, Jim, *Eisenhower: The White House Years*, New York: Anchor, 2011.

Nicas, Jack, "How YouTube Drives People to the Internet's Darkest Corners," *Wall Street Journal*, February 7, 2018, https://www.wsj.com/articles/how-youtube-drives-viewers-to-the-internets-darkest-corners-1518020478.

Nightflight.com, "By the Time We Got to Woodstock, We Were Half a Million Strong: August 15, 1969," (photo on web page), accessed September 14, 2018.

Nikkhah, Roya, "Woodstock 40 years on: The legend, the legacy," The Telegraph, August 8, 2009, https://www.telegraph.co.uk/culture/music/5995703/Woodstock-40-years-on-The-legend-the-legacy.html.

Oberg, James, "Satellite Turns 50 Years Old ... in Orbit!" NBC, March 17, 2008, http://www.nbcnews.com/id/23639980/ns/technology_and_science-space/t/satellite-turns-years-old-orbit/#.W4y9XcInZQI.

O'Brien, Andrew, "Jimi Hendrix's National Anthem Channels the Beauty and Chaos of the 60's at Woodstock, on This Day in 1969," *Live for Live Music*, August 18, 2017, https://liveforlivemusic.com/features/jimi-hendrix-national-anthem-woodstock-thisday-1969/.

Omnicore, "Twitter by the Numbers: Stats, Demographics and Fun Facts," updated October 26, 2018, https://www.omnicoreagency.com/twitter-statistics/.

Ordway, Frederick, and Sharpe, Mitchell, *Rocket Team*, Ty Crowell Co., 1979.

Oxford Dictionary of English, 2003, Spam definition.

Pareles, Jon, "Woodstock: A Moment of Muddy Grace," *New York Times*, August 5, 2009, https://www.nytimes.com/2009/08/09/arts/music/09pare.html?pagewanted=all&_r=0.

Pew Research Center for The People & The Press, "Americans Going Online . . . Explosive Growth, Uncertain Destinations," October 16, 1995, http://www.pewresearch.org/wp-content/uploads/sites/4/legacy-pdf/136.pdf.

Pew Research Center for The People & The Press, "The Internet News Audience Goes Ordinary," January 14, 1999, http://www.pewresearch.org/wp-content/uploads/sites/4/legacy-pdf/72.pdf.

Poole, Robert, *Earthrise: How Man First Saw the Earth*, New Haven: Yale, 2010.

Purcell, Carey, "Why Charles Manson and Helter Skelter Still Fascinate America after Almost 50 Years," *Forbes*, January 22, 2018, https://www.forbes.com/sites/careypurcell/2018/01/22/why-charles-manson-and-helter-skelter-still-fascinate-america-after-almost-50-years/.

Quote Investigator, "Somewhere, Something Incredible Is Waiting to Be Known," https://quoteinvestigator.com/2013/03/18/incredible.

Ranker.com, "Members of the Manson Family," https://www.ranker.com/list/members-of-the-manson-family/reference?page=2.

Raz, Guy, "40 Years Later, Looking Back at the Internet's Birth," *NPR*, November 1, 2009. https://www.npr.org/templates/story/story.php?storyId=114376728.

Reardon, Marguerite, "Internet Fathers Get Presidential Medal," *CNET Magazine*, November 7, 2005, https://www.cnet.com/news/internet-fathers-get-presidential-medal/.

RFC Editor, https://www.rfc-editor.org/.

Richtel, Matt, "Webvan Stock Price Closes 65% Above Initial Offering," *New York Times*, November 6, 1999, https://www.nytimes.com/1999/11/06/business/webvan-stock-price-closes-65-above-initial-offering.html.

Rivera, Geraldo, interview with Charles Manson, 1988, posted September 17, 2008 https://www.youtube.com/watch?v=Q4Xw5Dc_vWs.

Rolling Stone, "Obituary: Max Yasgur, Woodstock Patron," March 15, 1973, http://www.experiencewoodstock.com/Max-Yasgur.html.

Roosevelt, Franklin D., "Letter to Vannevar Bush," November 17, 1944. http://scarc.library.oregonstate.edu/coll/pauling/war/corr/sci13.006.4-roosevelt-bush-19441117.html.

Rosen, Aliza, "Tweeting Made Easier," Twitter Blog, November 7, 2017. https://blog.twitter.com/official/en_us/topics/product/2017/tweetingmadeeasier.html, accessed October 17, 2018.

Rothman, Lily, "Fifty Years Ago This Week—How Young People Changed the World," *Time*, January 2, 2017, http://time.com/4607270/1967-january-6-anniversary/.

Rothman, Lily, "Sputnik," *Time*, October 3, 2017, http://time.com/4958422/sputnik-1957-report/

Rouse, Margaret, "Definition: Dot-com bubble," *TechTarget*, last updated August 2014, https://searchcio.techtarget.com/definition/dot-com-bubble.

Ruland, Bernd, *Wernher von Braun*, Munich: Burda Verlag, 1970.

Sander, Ellen, "Woodstock Music and Art Fair: The Ultimate Pop Experience," *Saturday Review* September 27, 1969, http://www.unz.com/print/SaturdayRev-1969sep27-00059/.

Sano, David, "Twitter Creator Jack Dorsey Illuminates the Site's Founding Document," *Los Angeles Times*, February 18, 2009.

Sarasota Herald, Charles Manson comment, 1980, listed at https://www.mansondirect.com/quotes-cm.html, accessed October 6, 2018.

Schwegler, Stephan, *Academic Freedom and the Disclaimer Affidavit of the National Defense Education Act*, Dissertation (Columbia University, 1982).

"Science: Yankee Scientist," *Time*, April 3, 1944.

Scola, Nancy, "Twitter to verify election candidates in the midterms," Politico.com, May 23, 2018, https://www.politico.com/story/2018/05/23/twitter-verify-candidates-midterms-2018-1282802.

Shedden, David, "Today in media history: The 1969 Woodstock music festival," *Poynter.org*, August 18, 2014, https://www.poynter.org/news/today-media-history-1969-woodstock-music-festival.

Sheetz, Michael, "Netflix is adding almost as many subscribers in one year as HBO did in 40 years," *CNBC*, October 17, 2018, https://www.cnbc.com/2018/10/17/netflix-added-subscribers-in-1-year-nearly-as-fast-as-hbo-in-40-years.html.

Smith, J. Y., "Dr. Wernher von Braun, 65, Dies," *Washington Post*, June 18, 1977.

Smith, Kiona N., "The Apollo 11 Astronauts Left a Lot of Junk on the Moon," July 20, 2017, https://www.forbes.com/sites/kionasmith/2017/07/20/the-apollo-11-astronauts-left-a-lot-of-junk-on-the-moon/#5f757c2f4ca0.

Sorenson, Theodore, *Counselor: A Life at the Edge of History*, New York: HarperCollins, 2008.

South China Morning Post (International Edition), "Jeff Bezos convinced 22 investors to back his new company Amazon in 1994. Their returns? Mind-boggling," April 26, 2018, https://www.scmp.com/news/world/united-states-canada/article/2143375/1994-he-convinced-22-family-and-friends-each-pay.

"Sputnik 1," *Spacedaily.com*, October 4, 2007, www.spacedaily.com/2006/071004110741.pfxxkk4b.html.

Sputnik Mania, directed by David Hoffman, Varied Directions, 2007.

SRI Homepage, https://www.sri.com/.

Statista, "Number of households in the U.S. from 1960 to 2017 (in millions)," 2018, https://www.statista.com/statistics/183635/number-of-households-in-the-us/.

Statista, "Number of smartphone users worldwide from 2014 to 2020 (in billions)," 2018, https://www.statista.com/statistics/330695/number-of-smartphone-users-worldwide/.

Stearns, Richard, "Wallkill Aroused by Folk Festival," *Poughkeepsie Journal*, June 17, 1969, https://www.newspapers.com/clip/20922664/wallkill_worried_about_woodstock/.

Stone, Brad, "Amazon Erases Orwell Books from Kindle," *New York Times*, July 17, 2009.

Tarsala, Mike, "Pets.com killed by sock puppet," *Market Watch*, November 8, 2000, https://www.marketwatch.com/story/sock-puppet-kills-petscom.

Templeton, Brad, "Reaction to the DEC Spam of 1978," *Templetons.com*, https://www.templetons.com/brad/spamreact.html#msg.

Time, cover, January 6, 1958.

Time, "Person of the Year: Photo History," Time Inc., accessed October 21, 2018, http://content.time.com/time/specials/packages/completelist/0,29569,2019712,00.html.

Times Higher Education, "World University Rankings 2018," 2018. https://www.timeshighereducation.com/world-university-rankings/2018/world-ranking#!/page/1/length/25/sort_by/rank/sort_order/asc/cols/stats.

Tomlinson, Ray, website, https://openmap.bbn.com/~tomlinso/ray/firstemailframe.html.

Toobin, Jeffrey, "The Sinister Influence of Charles Manson," *New Yorker*, November 20, 2017, https://www.newyorker.com/news/daily-comment/the-sinister-influence-of-charles-manson.

Torgerson, Dial, "Sharon Tate, Four Others Murdered," *Los Angeles Times*, August 10, 1969.

Tschmuck, Peter, "The recorded music market in the US, 2000-2013," *Music Business Research Blog*, March 21, 2014, https://musicbusinessresearch.wordpress.com/2014/03/21/the-recorded-music-market-in-the-us-2000-2013/.

UCLA, "Computer Network," press release, July 3, 1969.

UC Santa Barbara, American Presidency Project, http://presidency.proxied.lsit.ucsb.edu.

United Press International, "Drugs and Mud Plague 300,000 at N.Y. Music Fair," August 16, 1969.

U.S. Congress, Public Law 271, 63rd Congress, 3rd session, passed March 3, 1915 (38 Stat. 930), https://history.nasa.gov/SP-4103/app-a.htm#1.

V2Rocket.com, A-4/V-2 Makeup—Tech Data and Markings, http://www.v2rocket.com/start/makeup/design.html.

Van Gelder, Lawrence, "For Most in U.S., a Day of Joy and Reverence," *New York Times*, July 22, 1969.

Van Houten, Leslie, "Leslie Van Houten," Cielodrive.com, parole hearing transcripts, http://www.cielodrive.com/leslie-van-houten.php.

Vaughan-Nichols, Steven, "Mosaic turns 25: The beginning of the modern web," *ZDnet U.S. Edition*, April 25, 2018, https://www.zdnet.com/article/mosaics-birthday-25-years-of-the-modern-web/.

Ventre, Michael, "Hendrix created banner moment at Woodstock," Today.com, October 14, 2016, https://www.today.com/popculture/hendrix-created-banner-moment-woodstock-2D80555766.

"Vietnam War Statistics and Facts 1: Church Committee Report On Diem Coup-1963," 25th Aviation Battalion website, http://25thaviation.org/facts/id430.htm#allied_troop_levels___vietnam_1960_to.

Walker, Martin, *The Cold War: A History*, New York: Macmillan, 1995.

Ward, Bob, *Dr. Space: The Life of Wernher von Braun*, Annapolis, MD: Naval Institute Press, 2009.

Weinstock, Maia, "Scene at MIT: Margaret Hamilton's Apollo code," *MIT News*, August 17, 2016.

Welles, Suzanne, "The Beginnings of Ebay," *The Balance*, July 20, 2018, https://www.thebalancesmb.com/how-did-ebay-start-1140007.

West, Kelly, "Unsurprising: Netflix Survey Indicates People Like to Binge-Watch TV," *Cinemablend*, 2013 https://www.cinemablend.com/television/Unsurprising-Netflix-Survey-Indicates-People-Like-Binge-Watch-TV-61045.html.

When We Left Earth: The NASA Missions, Discovery Channel, 2008.

White, Mary, Gus Grissom biography, https://history.nasa.gov/Apollo204/zorn/grissom.htm.

Wiesner, Jerome, "Vannevar Bush: 1890–1974. A Biographical Memoir" *National Academy of Sciences Biographical Memoir*, http://www.nasonline.org/publications/biographical-memoirs/memoir-pdfs/bush-vannevar.pdf.

Willoughby, Jack, "Burning Up," *Barrons*, March 20, 2000, https://www.barrons.com/articles/SB953335580704470544.

Wolfe, Gary, "The (Second Phase of the) Revolution Has Begun: Don't look now, but Prodigy, AOL, and CompuServe are all suddenly obsolete—and Mosaic is well on its way to becoming the world's standard interface," *Wired*, October 1, 1994, https://www.wired.com/1994/10/mosaic/.

Woodstock, directed by Michael Wadleigh, DVD (Warner Bros., 1970).

Woodstock, Internet Movie Database (IMDB), https://www.imdb.com/title/tt0066580/reference.

Woodstock Diary 1969, directed by D. A. Pennebaker and Chris Hegedus, DVD (Warner Bros., 1994).

Woodstock radio commercial, *WNEW*, July 1969. Woodstockwhisperer, chronology page, accessed September 20, 2019, https://woodstockwhisperer.info.

"We've Left Wallkill" ad, *WoodstockWhisperer.info*, https://woodstockwhisperer.info/2016/07/26/bethel-becomes-woodstock/.

Woodstockwhisper.info, "Chronology Woodstock Music Art Fair," accessed August 29, 2018, https://woodstockwhisperer.info/2018/06/04/chronology-woodstock-music-art-fair/.

Woodstockwhisperer.info, "My Woodstock Story," accessed August 30, 2018, https://woodstockwhisperer.info/why-woodstock-whisperer/my-woodstock-story/.

Zachary, G. Pascal, *Endless Frontier: Vannevar Bush, Engineer of the American Century*, New York: The Free Press, 1997.

Zachary, G. Pascal, "The Godfather," *Wired*, November 1997, https://www.wired.com/1997/11/es-bush/.

Zacon, Robert H., "Hobbes' Internet Timeline 25," *Zacon Group*, updated January 1, 2018, https://www.zakon.org/robert/internet/timeline.

Zephoria Digital Marketing, "The Top 20 Valuable Facebook Statistics—Updated January 2019," updated November 2018, https://zephoria.com/top-15-valuable-facebook-statistics/.

Zomorodi, Manoush, "The Surveillance Economy," season 4, episode 5, *IRL*, produced by Mozilla, podcast, accessed February 4, 2019, https://irlpodcast.org/season4/episode5/.

VIDEOS

Apollo 8: Christmas Eve Message, YouTube video, https://www.youtube.com/watch?v=ToHhQUhdyBY.

"Apollo 11 landing from PDI to Touchdown," posted October 10, 2014, https://www.youtube.com/watch?v=RONIax0_1ec.

Barbara Walters Special, "Leslie Van Houten 1977 Interview Part 1," ABC, https://www.youtube.com/watch?v=DZPuksTVZh0&t=2s.

Bezos, Jeff, 1997 Interview, YouTube video, 5:39, posted by Chuck Severance, December 22, 2013, https://www.youtube.com/watch?v=rWRbTnE1PEM.

Blitzer, Wolf, "Interview with General Michael Hayden, former director of CIA and NSA," *The Situation Room with Wolf Blitzer*, CNN, October 19, 2018, https://archive.org/details/CNNW_20181019_210000_Situation_Room_With_Wolf_Blitzer.

CBS News, "Apollo 4 launch," https://www.youtube.com/watch?v=1uoVfZpx5dY.

CBS News, "CBS News Woodstock followups 8-25 and 8-29 1969," YouTube video, August 25 and 29, 1969, https://www.youtube.com/watch?v=Md7dock MKQ.

CBS News, "Generations Apart (A Profile in Dissent)," May 27, 1969, https://www.c-span.org/video/?444554-2/generations-apart-profile-dissent.

CDS Videos, *Ten Years Public Domain for the original Web Software: message from Tim Berners-Lee*, April 3, 2003, https://videos.cern.ch/record/615845.

CNN, "Leslie Van Houten Interview / Larry King 1994," https://www.youtube.com/watch?v=xZVXtTXYtM4.

Coyote, Peter, interview in *Inside the Manson Cult: The Lost Tapes*, Naked Entertainment, Randy Murray Productions, 2018.

E-Trade Chimp on a Horse TV Commercial, YouTube video, posted by Nikos Kapsomenakis, November 24, 2016, https://www.youtube.com/watch?v=ONZFkqzuMjI.

Inside Media: Live from Woodstock (Part 1), YouTube video, 1:34, posted by Newseum, https://www.youtube.com/watch?v=Ai7q8ZZCo7I.

"John Morris—Announcements—Woodstock," YouTube video, 5:45, posted by Gintaras Kovaitis, January 26, 2011, https://www.youtube.com/watch?v=ov-m3iBaMNA.

Joni Mitchell, Jefferson Airplane, Crosby Stills & Nash on Dick Cavett—1969, ABC, August 18, 1969, available in segments of various lengths on YouTube.

Kleinrock, Leonard, *UCLA Daily Bruin*, http://dailybruin.com/2016/08/21/film
-lo-and-behold-documents-the-internets-beginning-at-ucla/.

"Me at the Zoo," YouTube, https://www.youtube.com/watch?v=jNQXAC9IVRw.

"Moon Machines," Science Channel, 2008.

Shillito, Paul, "How did the Apollo flight computers get men to the moon and
back?" https://www.youtube.com/watch?v=ULGi3UkgW30.

20/20, Diane Sawyer, "Truth and Lies: The Family of Manson (Full Documentary)
Updated," ABC, https://www.youtube.com/watch?v=v4qZB2ytq10&t=674s.

20/20, Diane Sawyer, "Truth and Lies: The Family of Manson: Part 2," ABC,
https://www.youtube.com/watch?v=RA7Kh6cgwks.

An Untold Woodstock Story, YouTube Video, 12:28, posted by Montana Brock, January
24, 2016, https://www.youtube.com/watch?v=M_TGFMedruM.

Vanguard TV3 Failed Rocket Launch, YouTube video, 0:53, posted by NASA Langley
CRGIS, August 11, 2009, https://www.youtube.com/watch?v=zVeFkakURXM.

The Wernher Von Braun Story—Space Documentary, YouTube video, 1:01:20,
posted by "Lunar Docu," August 10, 2017, https://www.youtube.com/watch
?v=wPse3oNHBt0.

White House Press Conference, "Synd04/08/70 President Nixon Speaks about
the Manson Trial," AP Archives, April 8, 1970, https://www.youtube.com/
watch?v=p-E-0DJvg7I.

Woodstock—Duke Devlin, YouTube video, 3:09, posted by Margaritaville, May 24,
2017, https://www.youtube.com/watch?v=84HKzPbP-tg.

INDEX

ABOUT THE AUTHOR

Harlan Lebo is a senior fellow at the Center for the Digital Future at USC Annenberg. He writes about history, science, the humanities, society, and digital technology.

Lebo is the author of four books about the making of a trio of America's finest films: *The Godfather Legacy*, *Casablanca: Behind the Scenes*, and two books on *Citizen Kane*: a coffee-table project for the film's 50th anniversary in 1991 and a comprehensive book for the 75th anniversary titled *Citizen Kane: A Filmmaker's Journey*, published in 2016.

Lebo is the 16-time author of "Surveying the Digital Future," the annual study by the Center for the Digital Future that explores the impact of the Internet and digital technology on users and nonusers.

Lebo is also a communications consultant for organizations involved in core research, health care, higher education, technology start-ups, and social communication. He served as the historical consultant to Paramount Pictures during the 50th-anniversary release of *Citizen Kane*.

Lebo is a lifelong resident of Los Angeles.